FALKLANDS WAR - GET STUFT

(Ships Taken Up From Trade)

A Diary from the Falklands War with the RMS ST HELENA,
Royal Navy Party 2100, HMS BRECON and HMS LEDBURY

by

Ivan H. Milburn

BEWARE

This book is DIFFERENT

First published by IH Milburn March 2012

ISBN 978-1-4716-3999-9

Printed in Great Britain by Lulu

R.M.S. St. HELENA

A copy of the letterhead, used on the RMS St. Helena official paperwork, as issued by the Curnow Shipping Company, for her days of cruising from Bristol to Cape Town and back, before the war.

A copy of a luggage label used by passengers on cruises on the RMS St. Helena, and also used by the taxi drivers on St. Helena island to show they are doing taxi service!

A copy of the badge used on sweaters for the next cruise - must have been psychic!

INDEX

<u>DEDICATION</u>

To my wife Carol, thanking her wholeheartedly for the love and support she gave me during my time with the "Big C" and for her continuing support - a truly lovely lady!

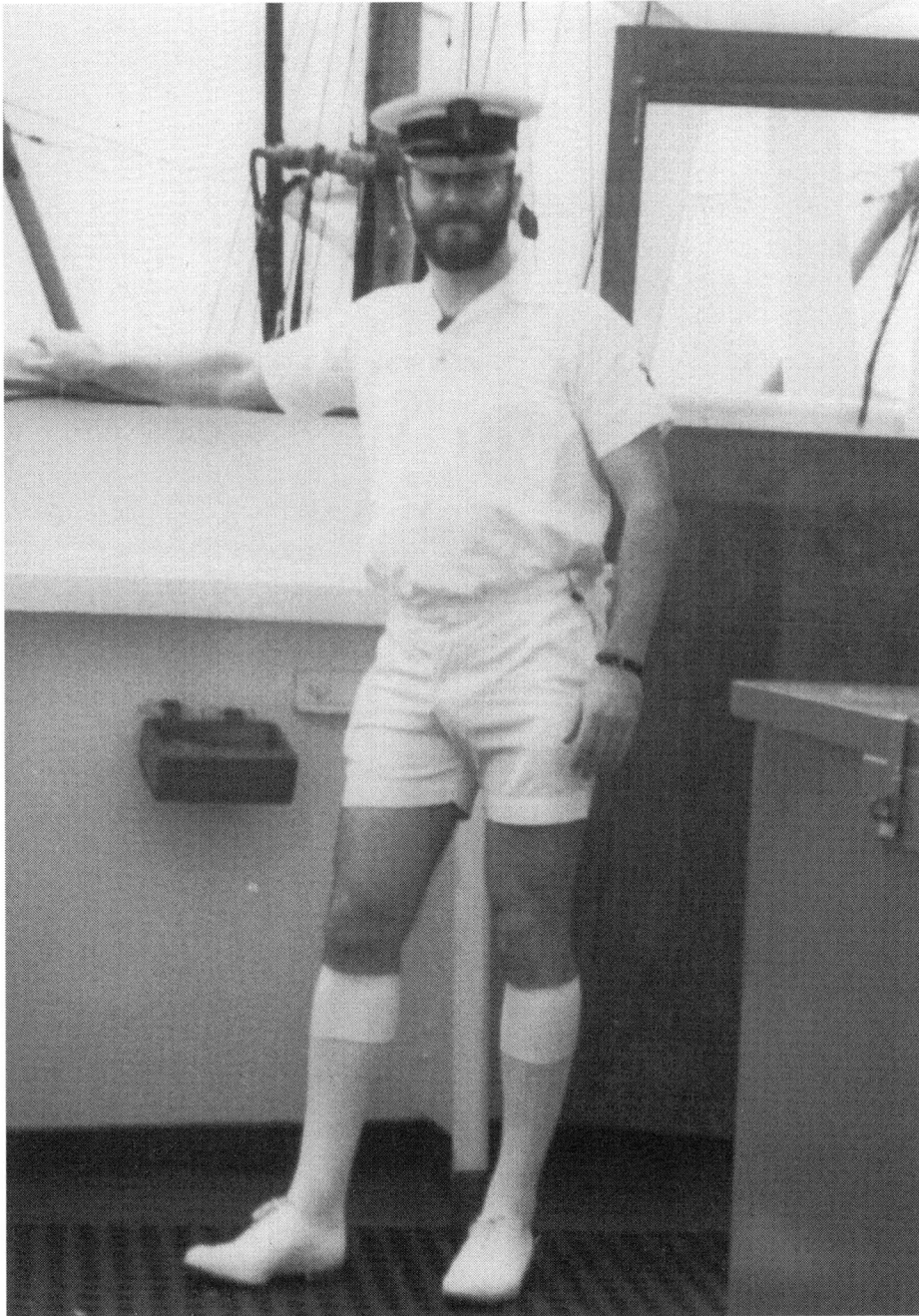

Author on the Bridge Wing of RMS St. Helena looking very happy, having survived, and now on the way home.

PREFACE

I was born after World War II, at the Cottage Hospital in Penrith, in what was then called Cumberland. This hospital was later 'binned' in the re-shaping and updating of the National Health Service. They also 'binned' Cumberland, re-shaped it, gave bits away, added bits to it and then called it Cumbria!

I spent my childhood in various hamlets in the wonderful countryside of what was then called Westmorland, (without an 'e'!). Westmorland was later 'binned' in the same re-shaping and updating of Cumbria Local Government. (Funnily enough, some of the counties that disappeared at that time have re-appeared because this re-shaping didn't work too well!).

From 4 years of age to 11 years of age, I lived in the Station House at Smardale, a glorious place for a child of that age to grow up in. Miles of countryside with woods and fells to roam, steam trains, lanes where motor vehicles were rarely seen, becks with fords and lots of snow in winter! The railway station and line were later 'binned' by Doctor Beeching in the re-shaping and updating of British Railways. (Funnily enough, a lot of time and money has been spent putting back a lot of the railway lines that the good doctor got rid of, as they might help to clear the congestion we now have on the roads!).

When I was 11 years old, we moved to a hamlet near Garstang in Lancashire. We lived in a house facing a Creamery yard. The main Creamery buildings were behind us and alongside us was the main London to Glasgow railway line. The smell from the Creamery was nearly as horrendous as the view! What a culture shock! However, they later 'binned' the Creamery in the re-shaping and updating of the company. We lived approximately 200 yards from the Garstang and Catterall railway station, which, at that time, regularly won 'prettiest station' awards. They 'binned' it in the further modernisation of British Rail. Luckily, we only stayed there for 12 months and then we moved to north Lancashire, to Heysham, where I was to spend my teenage years.

At this time I was attending the Royal Grammar School at Lancaster. They later 'binned' a lot of other grammar schools in the re-shaping and updating of the Education System. (Funnily enough, I read recently that they are thinking of re-shaping and updating the Education System yet again!).

At school I used to get caned for being a naughty boy! They later 'binned' caning in another re-shaping and updating of the Education System. (Funnily enough, there are those who think it should be brought back in an attempt to sort out the increasing problems in our schools!).

Whilst at school I obtained a few GCE 'O' Level passes without putting too much effort into it - homework came a distant second to soccer - but I don't know why I bothered as, yes you've guessed it, they later 'binned' the bloody things in yet another re-shaping and updating of the Education System! (Funnily enough, this didn't solve any problems either!).

I then left school due to a massive cash flow problem! It was the so called "Swinging Sixties", I didn't have any money and all my friends did. So there was only one answer – work! I joined the Lancashire Constabulary! (No they haven't 'binned' that yet but there are a lot of people attempting to make a mess of it!).

One of my first jobs was working at the Lancaster Assizes where I saw one of the last hanging verdicts given. Quite an experience! They later 'binned' hanging and Assize Courts in the re-shaping and updating of the Legal System. (Funnily enough, there are some who think that a few 'deterrents' might be useful in the fight against crime!).

My choice of the police in the late 1960s, as a solution to my cash flow problem, was a great mistake. It was a good career but the pay at that time was abysmal. So I left and went to work for a leading national brewery as a Relief Manager. They haven't 'binned' all the pubs yet but they've made a real mess of some really lovely old ones and created a lot of rubbish with their modern 'fun' pubs. As I was single, they refused to let me have a pub of my own, even though they had promised that the rules would change. So I decided to move on again! (Funnily enough, they later 'binned' these rules due to Women's Liberation, in order that single women could run pubs - when their husbands left them to run away with the barmaid!).

So I ran away to sea and joined the Royal Navy, where they'd just 'binned' the Rum Ration and were planning the 'binning' of the monthly duty free cigarette allowance, the infamous 'Blue-Liners'! Anyway, I still joined and went round the world with Prince Charles! There are some who are trying to 'bin' his family and have actually succeeded in 'binning' their yacht! (Funnily enough, there are a lot of us about who totally disagree with this!).

I then went to war three times - the Cod War, the Lebanon and the Falklands. The first two were very boring 'dits', so here's the story of Leopoldo Galtieri and my part in his downfall! 2100 and all that! What a bloody "Pot Mess"!

By the way, the Royal Navy has not been 'binned' yet, but between them, their lordships are trying very hard! (When I joined up we had a joke about more admirals then ships – guess what, we have now!)

I wonder if wars will ever be 'binned', they've had a go at nearly everything else?

INTRODUCTION

Strange stuff so far, eh? My sincere apologies to the Land Forces in this War, you were in a completely different conflict to those of us who were sailing around in TARGETS! – as submariners call surface ships! (In our case, STUFT ships, pretending to be warships!). We had to spend a lot of time relieving the stress and boredom, whilst we sat around waiting to be blown to smithereens! We couldn't fight back and had realistically no chance of defending ourselves! All we had to do was survive after being sunk! (Some of you may recall your trip down south onboard and how you enjoyed it!) Has anybody mentioned Falklands War Stress Syndrome yet? Read on it gets stranger!

In 1982 I saw 3 winters one after another. I saw horizontal snow trying to fall in the Falklands Islands in August. I saw the results, at first hand, of modern warfare! I saw friends and colleagues killed and injured. I saw British Servicemen being ignored and made unwelcome by the very people they thought they'd come to save. I saw stupidity from people who were supposed to be intelligent. I saw idiocy from people being paid a lot of money to be sensible. I saw fear in the faces of young men as they completed Will Registration Forms after they realised it wasn't just a game any more. I saw millions of pounds worth of war machinery and equipment brought out of hiding. I saw British 'Jingoism' re-invented. I saw people with 'Pay Queries' when the ship was at war. I saw senseless decisions from trained leaders of men. I saw how the Civil Service actually rules this country. I saw one hand not knowing what the other hand was doing. I saw boys turn into men very quickly. I saw the squalour and smelled the smell that is left after a battle. I saw the barren empty islands that this conflict had all been about. I saw the lists of men who died in this war. I saw 6 months of my life disappear. I saw all this and more - for what purpose, in the end? AND NOW IT MIGHT HAPPEN AGAIN!!

At the end of it all, I was left on my own in a strange dock on the South Coast of England with boxes full of paperwork in the back of a hire car! What to do with this paperwork? Nobody wanted to know!

Since then I have read the odd account of this madness in magazines and books written by sensationalist journalists or RN Officers, most of which were pretty boring factual, statistical accounts of the proceedings (like this diary is probably!) and jingoistic crap. I, personally, left this epic and spent 6 months on shore and then joined an RN ship, which eventually went to the Lebanon for another load of idiocy and another war!

I then got cancer in my nasal cavity and after my chemotherapy and radiation treatment, I was thrown out of the RN because of my health! I then found it rather difficult to get a job due to my medical record! So when I found boxes of paperwork whilst moving house, I decided to have a read. I had a full set of copies of Daily Orders, so I thought why not tell the 'Falklands story' from a different point of view?

So this book contains a tarted-up version of the Daily Orders for the whole trip. They are used as the foundation of the book, so as life at sea can be, they get very boring! However, to miss any of it out would ruin the whole effect, in my view, so you get the lot, warts and all, with my comments on the end of each day, where I have any!

AUTHOR'S NOTE

Let's first explain "STUFT" to our readers (Ships Taken Up From Trade).

In the 1960s, the Government 'saved money' by 'blitzing' the railway system. It was a disaster for the whole country. So in the 1980s, their policy of "let's do what the USA does" continued with the mass introduction of 'budgeteering' in all government services. The Armed Forces were slashed because "the Cold War had ended"! The Royal Navy had lost many ships, and come the Falklands War was unable to put together an Assault Force using its own ships. So it had to sub-contract! (STUFT). Then they had to turn these ships into WARSHIPS!

ALL THIS WAS DONE TO SAVE THE GOVERNMENT MONEY!

This is an AUTHENTIC history of the Royal Mail Ship St Helena's (RMS ST HELENA) role in the Falklands War (Voyage 26 - RN Charter). The book is based on the ship's Daily Orders, with added comments from my fading memories of the events. You don't get any more authentic than a ship's Daily Orders!! You also don't get any more boring! This may be because, a lot of the time, life at sea on a 'warship' is boring! However, to retain the authenticity, the Daily Orders have been reproduced virtually in their entirety. This may appear repetitive and unnecessary, at first glance. But that's the way it was, so that's the way it is! Also, read carefully, because as their lordships will ever remind you - "Things might change"!

Individuals will not be named in this chronicle. However, some individuals may be recognised by their jobs, ranks, titles, etc. I can only apologise for this and for any glory or embarrassment which may therefore occur. Also, a ship's nominal list is at the end, so that all those involved in this charade are remembered for their efforts. (Because nobody else has bothered!)

As I collated and embroidered this catalogue of duteousness and absurdity, I toyed with various titles for the finished article, please see Annex C" In the end, however, I couldn't resist it, it fitted it all so well - "GET STUFT" - said with feeling!

Many apologies for the poor quality of some of the illustrations/pictures. This was 1982 for goodness sake!

A fair amount of bad language will also be found, because this is a normal thing with sailors at sea! You'd swear too if you had to do the work they do for the wages they get paid! I can only apologise to members of my family, friends and any others who may be upset or offended by this.

"LIFE IN A BLUE SUIT"!

GLOSSARY

The Royal Navy has a language all of its own called "Jackspeak". Where this rears its ugly head, the following glossary should hopefully help to translate!

AB(M)	Able Seaman (Missile)
AB(MW)	Able Seaman (Mine Warfare)
ADRIFT	Late back from leave or late in general
AEA/APP(M)	Air Engineering Artificer/Apprentice (Mechanical)
AEM(L)1	Air Engineering Mechanic (Electrical) 1st Class
AEM(M)1	Air Engineering Mechanic (Mechanical) 1st Class
AEMN(L)1	Air Engineering Mechanician (Electrical) 1st Class
AEMN(M)1	Air Engineering Mechanician (Mechanical) 1st Class
AGR	Anti-Gas Respirator (Gas Mask)
ALMEM(L)	Acting Leading Marine Engineering Mechanic (Electrical)
ALWEM(O)	Acting Leading Weapons Engineering Mechanic (Ordnance)
ALWEM(R)	Acting Leading Weapons Engineering Mechanic (Radio)
ANDREW	Old name for the Royal Navy
ARPO	Acting Regulating Petty Officer
AS12	Air-to-surface missile carried by Wasp
AVCAT	Kerosene-based aviation fuel
AVDATES	Availability for draft dates
AWD	Action Working Dress
BADGES	Good Conduct Badges awarded every 4 years to Ratings
BANYAN	Outdoor picnic-style meal with beer
BFBS	British Forces Broadcasting Service
BINNED	Discarded (a modern-day 'budgetary' term for saving money!)
BLUE LINERS	Duty free RN cigarettes
BOSUN'S MATE	The JR in charge of the gangway and entry on and off it
BUDGETEERS	Civil Service Administrators and anybody taken away from his proper job to play with imaginary figures and forecasts to save money!
BUFFER	Chief Boatswain's Mate (Bosun) (CBM)
BUZZ	A messdeck rumour
BZ	Bravo Zulu - Well done, congratulations

CALL THE HANDS	Another pipe – waking up the ship's company – just like Butlin's!
CASEVAC	Casualty Evacuation
CBM	Chief Boatswain's Mate (Buffer)
CDO	Commando (RM)
CHACON	Cargo container
CINCFLEET	Commander-in-Chief Fleet
CLEAR LOWER DECK	All ship's company to muster as directed
CLUBSWINGER	Physical Training Instructor (PTI)
CMEM(M)	Chief Marine Engineering Mechanic (Mechanical)
COMEX	Communications Exercise
CRABS	RAF Personnel
CROSSING THE LINE	Crossing the Equator
CTG	Commander of Task Group
CTP	Cocktail Party (Officers only)
CWEM(O)	Chief Weapons Electrical Mechanic (Ordnance)
C126	Order to pay for lost or damaged stores
DAILY ORDERS	Extension of Standing Orders covering planned everyday occurrences/activities
DC	Damage Control
DCI	Defence Council Instruction
DCX	Damage Control Exercise
DEFAULTERS	RN court system for offenders
DEFENCE WATCHES	A 24 hour shift system for ship defence
DHOBYING	Washing of clothes, laundering
DIT	A story or tale
DIT SPINNER	Story teller
DMS BOOTS	Non-slip, steaming boots with reinforced toe caps
DO	Divisional Officer
DOG WATCH (DOGS)	4 – 6 pm/6 – 8 pm, a time for R & R
DRIPPING	Complaining, moaning, groaning, etc
ELWE	Extended Long Weekend
ETA	Estimated Time of Arrival
EXOCET	Surface/Air to surface homing missile
FCPO	Fleet Chief Petty Officer (later renamed Warrant Officers as in the other services)
FCMEA(P)	Fleet Chief Marine Engineering Artificer (Propulsion)
FCPO(EW)	Fleet Chief Petty Officer (Electrical Warfare)
FI	Falkland Islands
FLATS	Empty spaces outside offices/cabins etc
FLYEX	Flying Exercise
FOP	Flag Officer Portsmouth

GASH	Rubbish, waste etc
GCBs	Good Conduct Badges presented every 4 years, as long as you've been a good boy, culminating after 22 years with a medal
GDP	Gun Direction Platform
GESTETNER	Old style duplicating machine
GI	Gunnery Instructor (now a PO(M))
GOFFERS	Soft non-alcoholic drinks
GPMG	General Purpose Machine Gun (belt-fed)
GREENIE	Electrical Branch rating
GREY JOB	RN Warship
GUNNEX	Gunnery Exercise
GUZZ	Plymouth
HARD LYING MONEY	Extra pay for ship in extreme conditions eg very cold/very hot areas
HDS	Helicopter Delivery Service
HEADS	Toilets
HODs	Heads of Departments
HQ	Headquarters
HQLFFI	Headquarters Land Forces Falkland Islands
HUNTS	Minehunters/Minesweepers
JACK	A nickname for RN sailors
JOLLY	A 'fun' trip, picnic, etc.
JRs	RN Junior Rates
LACPO(MW)	Local Acting Chief Petty Officer (Mine Warfare)
LACWEA	Local Acting Chief Weapons Engineering Artificer
LCK	Leading Cook
LCU	Landing Craft Utility
LCVP	Landing Craft Vehicles and Personnel
LMEM(M)	Leading Marine Engineering Mechanic (Mechanical)
LOAFING	Lying about where it shouldn't be as in clothing etc/not being at your place of work when you should be
LORDSHIPS (THEIR)	The Government, Civil Service etc
LRO	Leading Radio Operator
LSA	Leading Stores Accountant
LSP	Long Service Pay
LSTD	Leading Steward
LS(MW)	Leading Seaman (Mine Warfare)
LT	Lieutenant
LT CDR	Lieutenant Commander
LWEM(O)	Leading Weapons Electrical Mechanic (Ordnance)

MA	Medical Assistant
MAILIES	Letters, parcels etc to & from home
MAKE & MEND	Afternoon off work. (In olden days it was the chance to make and mend your kit!)
MARISAT	Maritime Satellite Communications System
MCM	Mine Counter Measures
MEA1(L)	Marine Engineering Artificer 1st Class (Electrical)
MEA1(M)	Marine Engineering Artificer 1st Class (Mechanical)
MEA1(P)	Marine Engineering Artificer 1st Class (Propulsion)
MEM(L)1	Marine Engineering Mechanic (Electrical) 1st Class
MEM(M)1	Marine Engineering Mechanic (Mechanical) 1st Class
MEMN1(P)	Marine Engineering Mechanician 1st Class (Propulsion)
MHSCs	Mine Hunters/Sweepers Coastal
MN	Merchant Navy
MO	Medical Officer
MOD PLOD	Ministry of Defence Police
NAAFI	Navy, Army & Air Force Institute (Shops, bars, canteens, etc.)
NAVCOMEX	Navigation & Communications Exercise
NBCDEX	Nuclear Biological & Chemical Defence Exercise
NIGHT CLOTHING	Clean dark blue trousers and white shirt
No1s	RN Uniform - best suit with gold badges
No2s	RN Uniform - with red badges
No8s	RN Uniform - blue working rig
No10s	RN Uniform - tropical rig, white, best
No10As	RN Uniform - tropical rig, blue, working
NUTTY	Chocolate, sweets, confectionery
O/C	On completion
OERLIKON	Upper deck gun
OOD	Officer of the Day
OOW	Officer of the Watch
OUT PIPES	Get back to work. (Old days –'put out your pipe')
PAY OFFICE RANGER	Constant complainer about pay
PENNANT NUMBERS	Ships' numbers taken off on going to war
PIPE DOWN	Go to bed. (Old days-'put out your pipe')
PIPES	The ship's tannoy system. Each message was preceded by a whistle – all orders

	before tannoys were given by whistle due to the noise of the sea etc.
PLR	Permanent Loan Record - List of expensive stores held by crew members
POACMN	Petty Officer Air Crewman
POAEM(L)	Petty Officer Air Engineering Mechanic (Electrical)
POAEM(R)	Petty Officer Air Engineering Mechanic (Radio)
PO(AH)	Petty Officer (Air Handler)
PO(M)	Petty Officer (Missile)
POMA	Petty Officer Medical Assistant
POMPEY	Portsmouth
PONGOS	Army personnel
PO(R)	Petty Officer Radar
POSA	Petty Officer Stores Accountant
POT MESS	RN stew cooked in emergencies, etc. (Broth made in a panic with little choice of ingredients in a chaotic environment). Also RN name for chaotic situations where things are in a mess and getting slowly worse!
POWEM(R)	Petty Officer Weapons Engineering Mechanic (Radio)
POWTR	Petty Officer Writer
PTI	Physical Training Instructor (Clubswinger)
PUSSERS	Appertaining to or belonging to the RN
QHM	Queen's Harbour Master
QM	Quartermaster (On-shore sentry on gangway)
QR(RN)	Queen's Regulations (Royal Navy)
RAS	Replenishment at Sea
RATCATCHER	Nickname for RPOs and Regulators (Ships' policemen)
R & R	Rest and Recreation
REQUESTMEN	A formal ceremony where the Captain presents GCBs, advancements, etc
REQUESTS	RN paperwork system for addressing complaints/requests of ratings re. pay, advancement etc
RFA	Royal Fleet Auxiliary - supply ships
RM	Royal Marines
RMS	Royal Mail Ship
RN	Royal Navy
RNAS	Royal Naval Air Station
RNDQs	Royal Navy Detention Quarters (Prison!)
RNP	Royal Navy Party

ROUNDS	Officers' checks on accommodation, workplaces, offices etc
ROUTINES	RN systems for all aspects of running a ship. There are routines for all events!
RO1(G)	Radio Operator 1st Class (General)
RPO	Regulating Petty Officer (Policeman)
RS	Radio Supervisor
RV	Rendezvous
SA	Stores Accountant
SAS	Special Air Squadron - Elite Forces
SBS	RM Special Boat Squadron - Elite Forces
SCRANBAG	Sack containing clothing etc left loafing
SCRIBES	Nickname for RN Writers (Clerks)
SECURE	Stop work for the day, and tidy/lock up your workplace
SG	South Georgia
SLOPS CHIT	Nickname for PLR
SLOPS WAGON	Naval Stores clothing van
SNIPS	Parsnip wine – found in vast amounts in Portland
SNOFI	Senior Naval Officer Falkland Islands
SODS (OPERA)	Sailors' Operatic & Dramatic Society! A concert provided by members of the ship's company
SPLICE THE MAINBRACE	A celebratory free tot of rum
SRs	RN Senior Rates
SSD	Special Sea Dutymen
STAND EASY	Break from work, eg tea break
STANDING ORDERS	The ship's bible/rules evolved over the years. All types of RN ships had these to suit the ship in its everyday role. Any additions/extras for particular or one-off occasions were put in 'Daily Orders'
STATION CARDS	System for checking JRs on/off the ship
STD	Steward
STUFT	Ships taken up from trade – the government-requisitioned civilian ships!
TENDERS	Small establishments/ships which were administered from the Pay & Records Centre at HMS Centurion Gosport
TEZ	Total Exclusion Zone-started 1/5/82 and covered 200 miles around the Falklands
'THEY'	Bosses, people in power, our masters, their lordships etc!
TN	Technical Note - Only for this book!
TURNING TO	Starting a period of work
TWA	Trans-World Airlines
TX	Transfer

UCKERS	RN-style Ludo with mixey blobs etc. Could turn nasty resulting in 'up boards'.
VERTREP	Vertical Replenishment with a helicopter
VICTUALLING STORES	Food
WAAFUs	Nickname for Fleet Air Arm personnel
WARDROOM	RN Officers' Mess
WE	Weapons Electrical Branch
WEMN1	Weapons Engineering Mechanician 1st Class
WEMN2	Weapons Engineering Mechanician 2nd Class
WEM(O)1	Weapons Engineering Mechanic (Ordnance) 1st Class
WEM(R)2	Weapons Engineering Mechanic (Radio) 2nd Class
WHITE FRONT	JRs' short sleeved shirt
WIDEAWAKE	USAAF Base Ascension Island
WIND UP	Playing a joke/teasing someone
WR	Wardroom
WRITER	RN clerk
WRNS	Womens Royal Naval Service
XO	Executive Officer (Captain's 2 I/C)

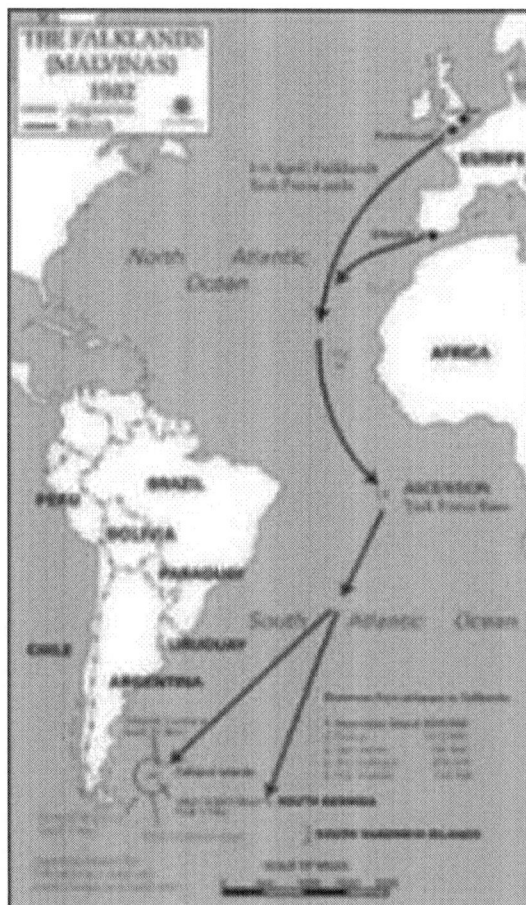

THE BUILD-UP

09 Jan 82	Rumour and rumblings start about South Georgia (SG) and Falkland Islands (FI) invasion by Argentines. Great Britain and Argentina have been arguing about the sovereignty of the FI since the 16th Century.
09 Feb 82	Prime Minister Thatcher confirms retirement of HMS ENDURANCE – the RN South Atlantic Survey ship (the only permanent RN presence in that area).
06 Mch 82	Argentine Hercules military aircraft, containing senior Argentine officers, lands at Port Stanley airport, falsely claiming a 'fuel leak'. It appears to have been a test for the capabilities of the airport and a recce of the surrounding area.
08 Mch 82	PM asks for contingency plans in case of Argentine invasion.
19 Mch 82	Argentine 'scrap metal merchants' land at Leith harbour on SG.
20 Mch 82	Trefor Edwards and his team of three, from the British Antarctic Survey camp, inform them that they must leave, on behalf of FI Governor Rex Hunt. PM sends HMS ENDURANCE, plus 24 Royal Marines from Port Stanley to SG.
23 Mch 82	Argentine workmen (NOT troops) on BAHIA BUEN SUCESO sail from Leith.
24 Mch 82	HMS ENDURANCE arrives at Grytviken, SG.
25 Mch 82	Argentine navy ship BAHIA PARAISO lands stores and more marines ashore at Leith.
26 Mch 82	Argentine government says that it will protect its people on SG. British Intelligence in Buenos Aires warns of Argentine invasion of islands. British Government dismisses warning and MOD advises against a military response. Argentine navy sets off on 'manoeuvres'.
27 Mch 82	Argentine naval ships DRUMMOND and GRANVILLE set sail for SG.
28 Mch 82	Argentines restate claim to FI, cancel all leave for political and military personnel, and start moving stores and equipment. Britain begins contingency plans for a 'Task Force' to be sent to the islands.
29 Mch 82	Britain sends submarines south to FI with RFA FORT AUSTIN. New RM detachment arrives in Port Stanley.
31 Mch 82	Argentine Junta takes final decision to invade FI on 02 Apl 82.
01 Apl 82	Governor Rex Hunt is warned of impending invasion.
02 Apl 82	Argentine ships in position off the FI. State of emergency declared on FI. First Argentines land at Mullet Creek and the war has begun! FI surrender. SG surrenders. (The day some spotty little Civil Servant in the MOD in London decreed that this War officially started).
03 Apl 82	RAF arrive on Ascension Island.
04 Apl 82	Argentines take Goose Green and Darwin.

05 Apl 82	HMS HERMES and HMS INVINCIBLE sail from Pompey (Operation Corporate begins).
07 Apl 82	Restricted Maritime Zone announced for 26 Apl 82.
	RFA STROMNESS sails from Pompey.
09 Apl 82	3 Cdo Brigade sail from Southampton on cruise liner CANBERRA (a STUFT ship).
12 Apl 82	Restricted Maritime Zone implemented early.
14 Apl 82	Argentine fleet sails from Puerto Belgrano.
	British ships deployed to re-take SG.
21 Apl 82	SG operation begins – HMS ANTRIM and HMS PLYMOUTH sail for SG with RFA TIDESPRING.
	Two Wessex helicopters crash.
23 Apl 82	Britain warns that any ship/aircraft threatening the Task Force will be destroyed.
25 Apl 82	SG recaptured by Royal Marines.
	Argentine submarine beached on SG after attack by Wessex 3 helicopters from HMS ANTRIM.
26 Apl 82	Argentines occupy Port Howard on West Falkland.
30 Apl 82	USA peace mission eventually fails and President Reagan declares support for Britain.
	Restricted Maritime Zone declared a Total Exclusion Zone (TEZ).
01 May 82	SAS and SBS land on FI.
	Bombing raids on Port Stanley airport and Goose Green by Vulcan and Sea Harrier aircraft.
	3 Argentine planes shot down.
	RN bombard Port Stanley.
	114 inhabitants imprisoned by Argentines at Goose Green (for 4 weeks).
02 May 82	GENERAL BELGRANO sunk by HMS CONQUEROR (because of the threat to HMS HERMES) – 368 Argentines die.
03 May 82	Argentine patrol boat ALFEREZ SIBRAL sunk.
04 May 82	HMS SHEFFIELD sunk by Exocet missile (made in France!) – 20 die.
	Sea Harrier shot down over Goose Green.
	British forces begin bombarding Argentine positions around Port Stanley.
06 May 82	2 British Sea Harriers crash in fog.
09 May 82	Argentine trawler (intelligence ship) NARWAAL sunk by Sea Harriers.
10 May 82	Argentine supply ship ISLAS DE LOS ESTADOS sunk by HMS ALACRITY.
	Argentina declares entire South Atlantic a war zone!
12 May 82	QE2 (a STUFT ship!) sails from Southampton.
13 May 82	Decision made on HMS FEARLESS to attack Argentines on FI.
14 May 82	PM Thatcher warns that a "peaceful settlement "may not be possible!! (Bit late for that!).
	SAS attack Pebble Island and destroy supplies and 11 Pucara aircraft.
	3 Argentine Skyhawk aircraft shot down by Sea Harriers.
19 May 82	British Sea King helicopter crashes.
20 May 82	RMS ST. HELENA requisitioned – 19 locals volunteer to go to war!

21 May 82   San Carlos landings from North Sea ferry NORLAND (another STUFT ship) began, and they were attacked by Argentine Mirage jet aircraft.
HMS ARDENT sunk in San Carlos Water – 22 die.
HMS ARGONAUT and HMS ANTRIM attacked – 2 die.
2 British helicopters and 15 Argentine aircraft shot down.

PLEASE NOTE:-

On sailing, the ship doesn't receive daily newspapers until it visits a port, and doesn't receive TV or Radio signals, only foreign ones sometimes! It only has very restricted radio communications, not available to the crew, only for official ship business. In quiet periods however, sailors are sometimes allowed a few pre-booked and monitored calls home to already reported Next-of-Kin. These are few and far between and cost money – NOT cheap on our wages! So the only news we got was what their lordships told us. On visiting a port, we receive mail and can buy foreign or home newspapers - again not cheap and usually out of date.

What our younger readers need to realise is that modern technology at that time consisted of the video recorder and cassette tapes! End of story! DVDs, CDs, PCs, mobile phones, the internet, eBooks, Twitter, Facebook, iPhones, iPads, X-boxes etc etc etc had not yet been invented!! So, all in all, the news we got was rare and thin. Some of you may know the old dit "mushroom farming" – kept in the dark and fed s**t! What more can I say?! So our main source of information and entertainment was the ship's 'Daily Orders', which takes us into Part One on 'Day minus 2'.

At the end of some days you will see the "Lest we forget" notes; these will continue from the 'Build Up' you have just read. You must remember however, that after we sailed, we DID NOT know of these events until much later in the voyage, and some of it not until we got home! Going back to the "mushroom farming", was this maybe a good thing!

HMS FEARLESS at Ascension Island

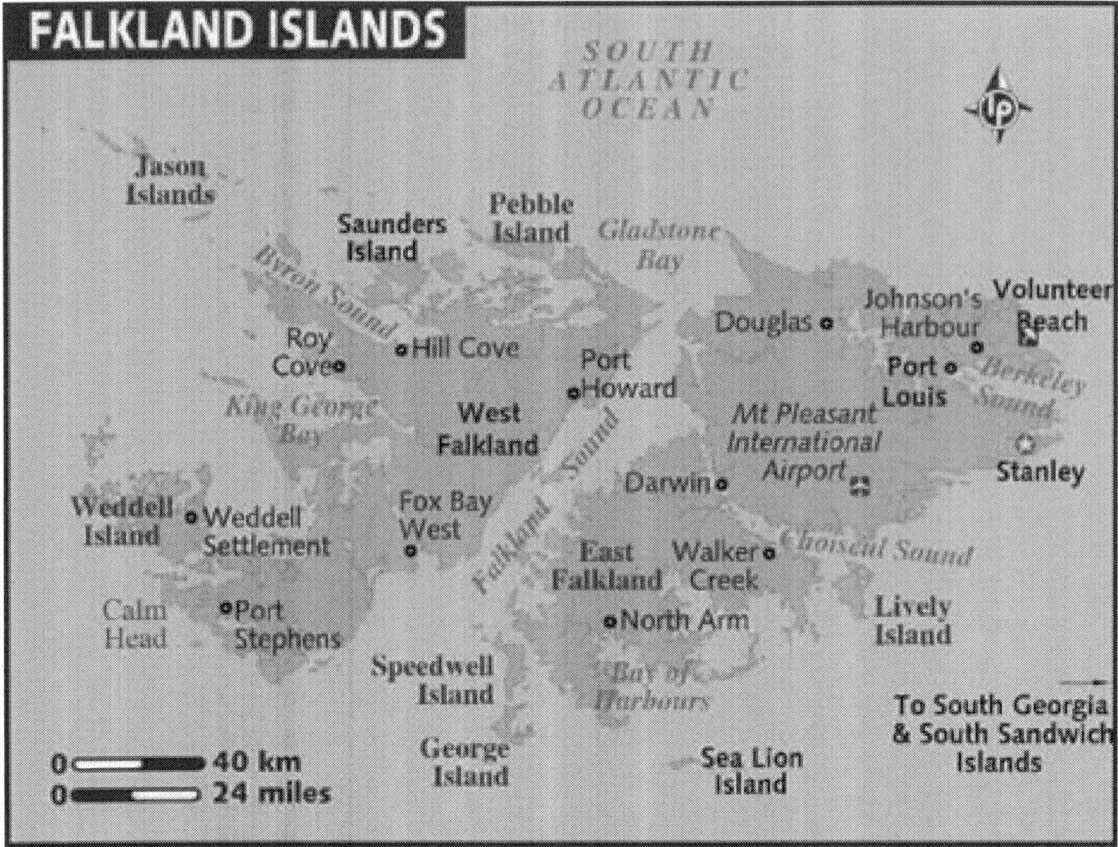

FALKLAND ISLANDS

SOUTH ATLANTIC OCEAN

Jason Islands

Saunders Island

Pebble Island

Gladstone Bay

Byron Sound

Roy Cove

Hill Cove

Douglas

Johnson's Harbour

Volunteer Beach

Port Howard

Port Louis

Berkeley Sound

King George Bay

West Falkland

Mt Pleasant International Airport

Stanley

Fox Bay West

Darwin

Weddell Island

Weddell Settlement

Falkland Sound

East Falkland

Walker Creek

Choiseul Sound

Calm Head

Port Stephens

North Arm

Lively Island

Speedwell Island

Bay of Harbours

George Island

Sea Lion Island

To South Georgia & South Sandwich Islands

0 — 40 km
0 — 24 miles

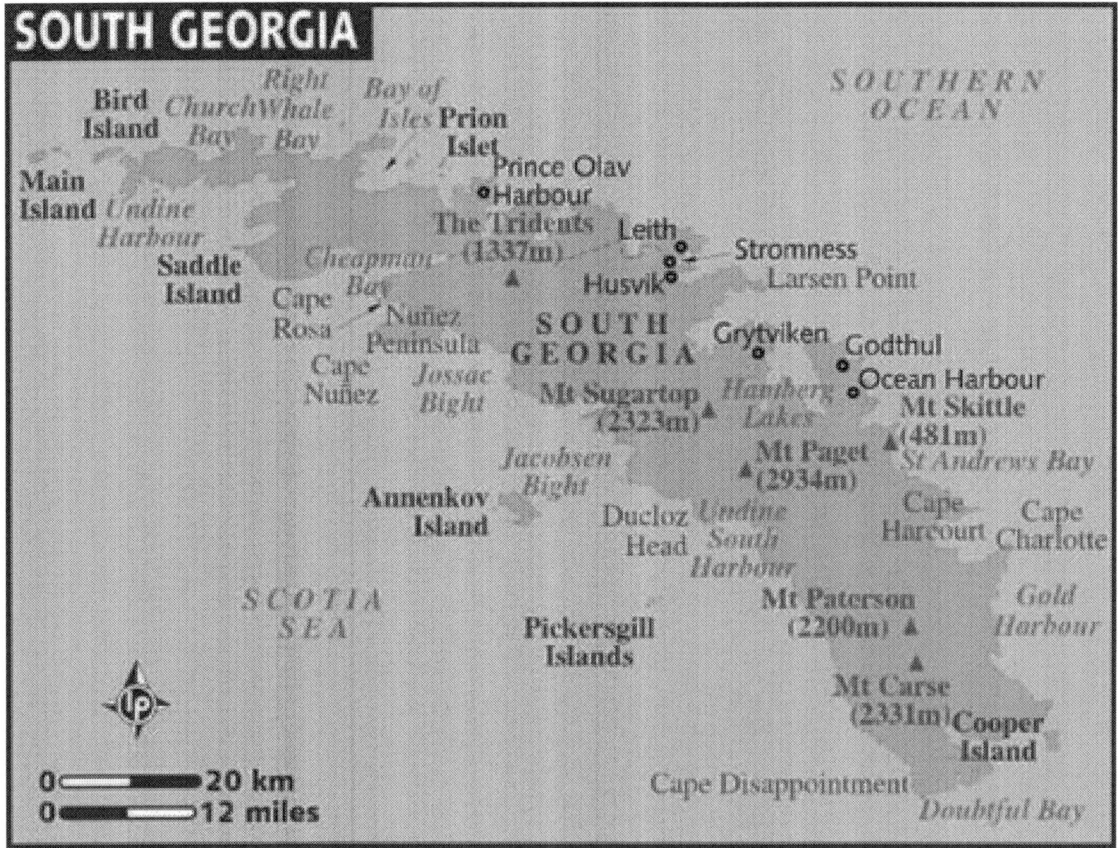

SOUTH GEORGIA

SOUTHERN OCEAN

Bird Island

Right Whale Bay

Church Bay

Bay of Isles

Prion Islet

Main Island

Undine Harbour

Prince Olav Harbour

The Tridents (1337m)

Leith

Stromness

Larsen Point

Saddle Island

Cheapman Bay

Husvik

Cape Rosa

Nuñez Peninsula

SOUTH GEORGIA

Grytviken

Godthul

Ocean Harbour

Cape Nuñez

Jossac Bight

Mt Sugartop (2323m)

Hamberg Lakes

Mt Skittle (481m)

St Andrews Bay

Jacobsen Bight

Mt Paget (2934m)

Annenkov Island

Ducloz Head

Undine South Harbour

Cape Harcourt

Cape Charlotte

SCOTIA SEA

Pickersgill Islands

Mt Paterson (2200m)

Gold Harbour

Mt Carse (2331m)

Cooper Island

Cape Disappointment

Doubtful Bay

0 — 20 km
0 — 12 miles

PART ONE

BIRTH OF A NAVAL PARTY

or

I HATE MONDAYS

SATURDAY, 22 MAY 82 - DAY minus 2

At 1030 hrs the Senior Naval Officer (SNO) joined the RMS ST HELENA at Avonmouth. This was the 'birth' of Royal Naval Party Number 2100 (RNP2100). The RMS ST HELENA was one of many 'ships taken up from trade' (STUFT), to enhance the Royal Navy's depleted forces during the Falklands War.

The RMS ST HELENA had been built by the Burrard Dry Dock Company in Vancouver, Canada, in 1963. She had been employed on the British Columbia to Alaska coastal trade and was 321 feet long, 3,150 gross registered tons, speed 14 knots and originally known as the NORTHLAND PRINCE. In 1977 she was bought by the St Helena Shipping Company, a subsidiary of the Curnow Shipping Company of Porthleven in Cornwall. She was refitted and later renamed "St Helena" by HRH The Princess Margaret. The ship had been chartered by the St Helenian Government to act as their Mail Ship and her job was to run from Avonmouth to Ascension Island, St Helena Island, Capetown and return via the same islands. She was the only link the people of St Helena had with the rest of the world, the island being a volcanic rock rising high out of the Atlantic with only one harbour at Jamestown. The only flat area was the football pitch which had been built years ago by the Royal Engineers, so an airfield would be impossible, the nearest land being Africa several thousand miles away. A very remote and isolated place, stuck in the middle of the Atlantic Ocean!

At 1600 hrs the RMS ST HELENA set sail for Portsmouth Dockyard in order that the Royal Navy could sort her out to go to war!

She was manned by Merchant Navy Officers and St Helenian crew members. She had the cabin capacity to normally carry approximately 76 passengers per cruise. In addition, local traffic of animals and people, housed on the upper decks, was transported between the islands and South Africa.

This passage was therefore spent with the SNO, Ship's Master, Purser and Caterer allocating cabins, recreational spaces and dining areas for Wardroom, Senior Rates and Junior Rates, drawing up a comprehensive list of stores and also turning the Ship's Bureau into an RN style Ship's Office/Regulating Office. The SNO also started work on a temporary set of 'Standing Orders', laying out routines, leave, 'out of bounds' areas within the ship (there would be females on board!) etc, etc.

SUNDAY, 23 MAY 82 - DAY minus 1

Passage to Portsmouth Dockyard, 'C' Lock. SNO working very hard at sorting out himself and his new command.

I have just received a letter from my parents, back home in Morecambe, containing a cutting from a recent daily newspaper. It referred to and contained a picture of an old friend of mine from my childhood days, Trefor Edwards (see below)! (The picture makes him look remarkably like Sean Connery!). He had been my mate since we were kids in the Boy's Brigade together (3rd Morecambe & Heysham). He was a member of the British Antarctic Survey Team. I knew he was down there on the ice and also that he was due home shortly. (I later obtained a copy of Reader's Digest, dated February 1983 which gave a much more detailed account of his activities, in an article called the "The Human Side of the Falklands Conflict" (page 156)). Briefly, he had been leading three other junior members of the Team on a stores check at their various outstations around the island of South Georgia, when they had stumbled upon the Argentine Naval Supply Ship BAHIA BUEN SUCESO at the deserted Whaling Station at Leith. The Argentines claimed they were there to salvage the Whaling Station's equipment and had even run the Argentinian flag up a pole!! He and his party were ordered by the Governor of the Falkland Islands to inform them they were trespassing and to take down their flag and leave the island. The ship had forty Marine Commandos onboard, for some strange reason, so this was a bit of an awesome task to say the least! Anyway they brazened it out and went onboard and through an interpreter passed the message across! They then returned to their base at Grytviken, 20 miles east along the coast. Four days later the Argentines sailed leaving 12 of their 40 scrap metal merchants behind. Politics and politicians then took over and the rest is history, as they say! So it turned out that my old mate actually started the war!!

Lest we forget - HMS ANTELOPE was bombed, sinking the following day – 1 died.
7 Argentine aircraft shot down.

SOUTH GEORGIA

MONDAY, 24 MAY 82 - DAY 1

At 0730 hrs RMS ST HELENA arrived at 'C' Lock in Portsmouth Dockyard. Round the clock dockyard work commenced immediately, estimated time of completion 1400 hrs Sunday 30 May 82. (Dream on!!).

Meanwhile at 0830 hrs in the Computer Division of HMS CENTURION, the Royal Navy's Pay and Records Computer Centre at Gosport, across the harbour from Portsmouth, I was working quietly at my desk. I looked up and saw the Chief Petty Officer Writer, from upstairs in the Drafting Division, walking towards me and smiling! That was a novelty! I suddenly had a feeling that the piece of paper in his hand wasn't going to be good news!! It wasn't, it was a Draft Order telling me I was going to war!

Was this excitement or panic I was feeling? Fear?

I was to join RNP2100 at Southampton Docks at 1000 or as soon after as was possible – classic, it was already 1010! Things had obviously changed since the old 5 months notice for a sea draft, when I was in Drafting Division! To be serious, however, what the devil was RNP2100? So I handed my desk over to my 'less than happy' civvy boss and within seconds was in the Regulating Office, having said my sorrowful goodbyes along the corridor! What a way to go - I never did get a leaving do!! The Master-at-Arms informed me that I was to join the RNP2100 in Portsmouth Dockyard at 1400, through HMS NELSON. The chaos had started already - 2 different stories in only a matter of minutes!

I rushed home to pack my kit and then head for Portsmouth Dockyard. I said a speedy goodbye to my wife and two children, put the car in the garage and away I went. Taxi to the Gosport Ferry with a dopey driver who wished he was going to war, the short trip on the ferry and another taxi to HMS NELSON Main Gate! Not cheap this war business!

HMS NELSON was one of the Royal Navy's Release Depots and also the place where they kept people who were going through investigations, Courts Martial, etc, etc. It was also the accommodation centre for ships in the dockyard, so as usual the Regulating Office was chaos. I did my Joining Routine and headed for the Dockyard, where I would definitely find the RMS ST HELENA, which was where the RNP 2100 was situated according to the brain-dead Regulator I had just talked to! This, however, was the limit of his knowledge - where exactly it was he wasn't sure, what it was he wasn't sure, what it was going to do he wasn't sure, when it was going to do it he wasn't sure! More stress!

As I walked through the Dockyard I picked up more information from faces I knew and from civvy dockyard workers. So after 10 minutes I had heard all sorts of wonderful rumours, dits and bright ideas about my destiny! Talk about the 'Journey into the Unknown'!

So there I was trudging through the Dockyard, with a kit bag that was getting very heavy, without a clue about this RNP 2100 and what the devil this RMS ST HELENA was. What was its part in this war? Where were we going?
What was I, a Petty Officer Writer, actually going to do? When were we going?
Even more important, when were we coming back? Nothing - not a bloody clue - something about life in a blue suit yet again!! It was one of those times in your life when you take a long, hard look around you and think "What the bloody hell am I doing here? Especially for these wages!" It was at times like this when your brain would remember all those wonderful little bank-type people sitting in their cosy little offices refusing you an overdraft! They should definitely bring back conscription for these people!

My philosophising was suddenly rudely interrupted! Was that the RMS ST HELENA or was somebody pulling my leg? There it was in all its glory! This tiny green and white ship surrounded by chaos! I was going to war on that? Still not convinced that this wasn't a wind up, I fought my way through the crates, boxes, chacons, immobile dockyard workers and general debris to the gangway. Nothing! Where was the Bosun's Mate? Where was the Royal Navy in fact? Nothing but civvies milling about!

After a few gentle enquiries I found that there were a couple of RN people about but they could be anywhere! What a way to run a bloody navy! Then a 'set of 8s' (RN ratings' working rig) was spotted in the melee, so I headed for them in the hope of getting a few answers to the odd question that was beginning to prey on my mind! Eureka, an RN Senior Rate! At last some sanity in the world! He took me below towards the SNO's cabin, explaining to me on the way what little he knew. As I waited to see the SNO, I realised that the chaos was not confined to up top, it was just as bad down here. People rushing around everywhere, noisy drills and hammering coming from all directions. We must be going somewhere in a hurry, I decided!

Eventually, I saw 'the man'! The SNO appeared to be the only person in the area who wasn't rushing around like a headless chicken. We had a long chat and I gleaned the following titbits from him.

The RMS ST HELENA was to provide logistic and technical support to the Royal Navy Minehunters HMS BRECON and HMS LEDBURY, who were going south to minesweep, clear unexploded ordnance and dive on RN wrecks for security purposes. She was the only ship, of the appropriate size, that the RN could obtain at short notice to do this job. So she had been sub-contracted or 'taken up from trade' (STUFT), because the RN didn't have a ship for this task as minehunters and minesweepers never normally went this far, certainly not 8000 miles. They stayed near to ports and land. The sailing of the ship would be undertaken by her normal crew of Merchant Navy Officers and St Helenian crewmen. The RNP2100 would consist of a number of mixed RN Officers and ratings from the Portsmouth area along with the Forward Support Unit 01 (FSU01) from Rosyth in Scotland, who were the normal shore technical support for the minehunters, and a Wasp helicopter flight (Flight033) from RNAS Portland in Dorset. The trip down and back was expected to last 90 days. (Famous last words!)

The present noise and turmoil was due to armaments, RAS gear fitments and a Flight Deck being fitted to the ship. (The addition of a Flight Deck required structural re-strengthening between decks. This along with an instability problem and shortage of length on the ship, meant a cantilevered Flight Deck had to be built over the stern! The normal refit time for a STUFT ship had been 2 days, ours took 16 days!) So there I was - mystery solved! Not quite - what was my personal role in all this technical mayhem? I was to set up a Ship's Office, Royal Navy style, in the Purser's Bureau. I was then to be responsible for all the routine RN paperwork, etc, etc, for the RMS ST HELENA. On enquiring about my staff, I was politely informed that HMS CENTURION hadn't got any spare Writers, so I was 'it'! Was this what those Leadership Courses had meant by 'Hands on management'? Well, at least I wouldn't have any staff reports to write!

The ships would be tenders to HMS CENTURION for pay and administration purposes so there would not be much Writer-type work. However, I had to collect some cash from HMS NELSON as I would be running a Cash Account. I was also informed that I would be sharing this office with the Regulating Petty Officer and the Warrant Officer who was to be the Ship's Coordinator. So this tiny office would in fact be the Ship's Office, the Routine Office, the Regulating Office and the Duplicating Machine Office all rolled into one!! We were obviously going to have some fun here, weren't we?!

My first tasks were to sort my accommodation out, sort the office out and help with the storing of the ship, which was about to start and would really add to the chaos! It appeared that the rest of the RNP2100 would be joining the ship over the next 2 days. This meant immediate work had to be done on setting up routines, duties, watches, orders, etc, etc, along with all the other things that make navy life so pleasant!

The SNO gave me a cabin number and informed me that when I had sorted my accommodation I should get on with 'building' the Ship's Office. As far as he was concerned, with the present circumstances, he had to trust me to run my own 'empire' as there would be nobody else of my ilk to watch over me. Marvellous, I thought, nobody from the Wardroom looking over my shoulder, that should get the job done quicker and easier. So away I went to my cabin!

CABIN!!!???? A mere rating with a cabin?? Whatever next? However, when I got there I found 2 other senior rates already in there, the Radio Supervisor (RS) and the Chief Bosun's Mate (Buffer). All the accommodation was of course cabins because this was normally a small cruise ship. The cabins had 2 or 3 bunks with shower/toilet facility - wonderful - pure luxury! I unpacked my gear then headed for the office just up the passage.

The office wasn't very big. It had to house 3 people and an old Gestetner printing machine. There would definitely be problems! The office itself was very 'pretty'! I found that, normally, the Purser was helped on each cruise by a lady assistant. That explained a lot, including, thankfully, the nice smells that wafted from the drawers and cupboards and the curtains. The Purser had cleared his gear out of the office and into his cabin next door from where he was going to work. However, his idea of 'clearing out' and mine were two very different things. He'd obviously never had a lot to do with the Royal Navy in the past. So I set about turning his sacred Bureau into a real RN Ship's Office. He watched me working and was devastated - all his carpet went, all the nice pictures went, all his chinzy office furniture went, plus all the other decorations from past cruises and the pap that had been collected over the years. Blitzed down to bare metal and bare wood! Poor man must have thought I was a barbarian. I did, however, try to explain to him that if the sea got rough we would not be heading for the nearest harbour as they normally did and that things had to be secure therefore. Also if we were going to Action Stations, Emergency Stations, Defence Watches, Air Raid Warning Red, etc, etc, the same would apply with knobs on! He still wasn't fully convinced at the time but did get the picture in later days!

It was then that it hit me! Where was all my gear? No paper, no pens, no typewriter, no pencils, no nothing!

I had heard, however, that most of the STUFT ships leaving from Plymouth were fitted up by HMS DEFIANCE staff. A chacon would appear on the dockside and there was your 'instant office'! So I thought I had better nip along to the boss to ask how I obtained my 'instant office'. His reply to my question was what finally got the message through to me that day. It went something like this - "This is Pompey not Guzz, it's your problem, sort it!"

Nothing changes, life in a blue suit! Where do you start? Organisation nil! The government had been slowly running down the Royal Navy Organisation to save money on various peoples' budgets, so now we had to sub-contract ships to go to war! So stop dripping and "make it so", all those admirals can't be wrong!

So I went back to the office and sat down and started making my list! All I had was the use of a typewriter (ancient) and a Gestetner printing machine (very ancient)! So, it was quite a long list! I decided to stock up for war and peace! You could guarantee if we were going to be away for 3 months (or so their lordships had said), somebody would have a pay problem and we would definitely be away for longer!

I was suddenly interrupted by an "all RN hands on deck" pipe! So away I went. The storing had started and all hands were required to do the loading. What about my office, I thought. Never mind, I'll show willing and give the boys a hand, just to show that not all 'scribes' are wimps! Anyway, I had all week to sort the office out, so it wasn't a problem. (Famous last words again)! We stopped storing about 2100, knackered, we'd shifted some stuff - it was obviously going to be a long war if we needed all those toilet rolls! Night leave was piped. We could go home - or those that lived locally could. As I made my way back to my cabin, to get changed before heading for the Gosport Ferry, a voice beckoned me into one of the other cabins. A few of the boys were in there having a well-earned drink. One of the MN Officers had donated some beer to the stores party for their efforts. I was about to experience my first 'Cabin Party'! However, having quenched my thirst on a couple of cans, I then began to think about home and the kids. I'd better make the most of this night leave as it might be the last time I'd see them for a while! So being the dutiful family man I made my excuses and managed to escape! When I arrived back at home they were quite surprised to see me back so soon! All in all it had been one of those days!

Lest we forget - RFAs SIR LANCELOT, SIR GALAHAD and SIR BEDEVERE
were bombed in San Carlos Water.

PART TWO

PREPARATION FOR WAR

or

ARE WE SAILING OR AREN'T WE?

TUESDAY, 25 MAY 82 - DAY 2

0755 Senior Rates leave expired! So it hadn't all been a bad dream after all! I was back having said farewell to my family again. I looked around me, nothing had changed - chaos still reigned! Today, I was determined to make a start on my office. However, as I was getting changed into my uniform I heard that wonderful pipe again "all RN hands to the upper deck for storing ship". So away I went. After a couple of hours I got a message to go and see the SNO, he was concerned about his new Ship's Office - like where was it? I explained the story so far and was politely informed to get my finger out and sort the office problems - forget the storing ship, he was getting help in to do that! He did too, working parties from HMS NELSON, HMS VERNON, HMS COLLINGWOOD and even from Detention Quarters (RNDQs) - it must have been desperate to let them out!

So I obtained some transport and headed for the stores department in HMS NELSON. In I walked, full of innocence and my own importance as a potential war hero, and produced my list of stationery stores. They laughed! What's so funny I thought, as they proceeded to put a few bits and pieces on the counter? After a few seconds they stopped and stood looking at me ready for the next instruction! I noticed that what was on the counter was a long way short of what was on my list! In fact not even near! So I used my best important-sounding voice and enquired as to the rest of my shopping list. I was informed that was it, they had no more, all the other ships had already been and plundered them on their way down south. They suggested I wait until I got down there and scrounged a few bits from the ships there! I thought about this and had a mental picture of me trying to get pens and pencils off some ship in the middle of a battle! Not a good idea! It was also suggested I visit some of the other local RN establishments and see what I could scrounge but they didn't hold out much hope for me. There wasn't a lot of point in arguing, as obviously nothing was going to change much in the immediate future.

I therefore set off on a tour of the local Portsmouth RN Establishments - HMS VERNON, HMS TEMERAIRE, RM DEPOT EASTNEY, HMS PHOENIX and the Firefighting School at Horsea Island. (If it had been the 1990s, this task would have been much easier, as most of these places no longer exist having been binned or 'budgeted out'!). By the end of the working day, I'd collected a fair amount of gear but still needed a lot more!

I went back onboard to unload as the transport driver was mentioning his tea, overtime and other 9 - 5 items! When I arrived at my office, the door was shut but the light was creeping under the door!? So thinking security, I tried the door and it opened! Inside was an MN Officer squeezing ink from a tube into the Gestetner. Messy! An RN Senior Rate was also 'plonking' away with two fingers on the typewriter. He was typing (I use the term loosely) Daily Orders at the behest of the SNO! The MN Officer was showing him how to operate the Gestetner and could I supply them with some paper? By this time my brain was on overtime! My office, my printer, my typewriter, my paper - surely this could all be done elsewhere, not forgetting it was a daily operation! My office was too small for this circus and me!! Problems were beginning to emerge! So I gave them some paper, unloaded and locked away my gear and quickly got out of the office before they wanted something else!

Having escaped this performance it dawned on me that the RN was definitely here now - DAILY ORDERS! As I wandered down the corridor, with my brain in automatic, I was seconded again to storing ship as night leave wasn't going to be piped until much later. After another long evening of passing hundreds of various boxes along the line (would we really use all those toilet rolls?), night leave was piped. Away I went, changed and off I thought! Wrong, another cabin party that was well under way!   They seemed like a very sociable sort of ship's company to me! They were all engulfed in copies of the new 'Daily Orders', which had been delivered to all the cabins. (What paper shortage?). Tonight there was a good mix, with some St Helenian crewmen and two MN Officers also in attendance. After a couple of cans the light banter was being replaced by some 'lower deck' dripping about how it was getting more like the RN every day, especially now we'd got Daily Orders! Up until then of course Jack thought he was on to a good thing and was actually looking forward to the cruise, as it was referred to by the MN personnel! Why, you might ask?   They were living in 3s and 4s in spacious cabins with their own heads and shower, instead of the usual 20+ on a cramped, smelly messdeck with a five minute walk to the nearest heads or showers! They were working with MN Officers who called them by their first names! They were working to civilian routines on a civilian ship - bliss, totally different to the 'grey funnel line'. They were having cabin parties every night with a lot of free and cheap booze about, no restrictions of 3 cans of beer for Junior Rates and no Mess Bills for the Senior Rates. Another added bonus was the two St Helenian waitresses, who had volunteered to stay onboard to work in the galley/dining room, where everybody ate together - officers and crew! The boys didn't mind the long hours as that was normal at sea in the RN - you could always fall back on the old adage "work hard, play hard"! The only fly in the ointment was this bloody war going on down south! I had a feeling that the best of the dripping was yet to come as the conversion from cruise ship to war ship continued in earnest!

The remainder of the Senior and Junior Rates of the RNP2100 had joined the ship during the day, along with the FSU01 from Rosyth. (Forward Support Unit 01 was based in Rosyth RN Dockyard on the east coast of Scotland, north of Edinburgh. Their job was to attend to the problems experienced afloat and ashore of their squadron of minehunters and minesweepers. So they were used to travelling all over the British Isles to mend their 'babies'. But this was a whole new ball game – they themselves had to go to sea – God forbid!) So now there were a lot of RN uniforms about and life was definitely changing. There were now also more RN Officers about, so life that had been hard work in a relaxed atmosphere, now became even harder with the added pain in the backside of the 'Wardroom'! Yes, the cruise ship theme had definitely had its day! "For the times they were a changing"! Efforts had been made to further turn the 'cruise ship' into a warship! Curtains, paintings, photographs, etc, were removed and carpets covered with heavy duty plastic covering. This helped protect the carpet but left a lot to be desired on the 'Fire Hazard' front!

As I headed for the Gosport Ferry, I noticed that the boys from Scotland were already on their way ashore to sample the delights of Pompey and eventually Jo's the sailors' nightclub in Southsea! Well, they were on their way to war weren't they?! So they had to make the best of what little time ashore they had left! Also they might not be coming back! If the Argies could sink our warships, what were the chances of that rustbucket they had just joined? Jack would not openly discuss this of course but it was always at the back of his mind! Make that a large one barman, was as serious a response as you were likely to get! Eventually, I got home to Rowner yet again!

HMS FEARLESS being attacked in San Carlos Water (Bomb Alley)

Lest we forget - HMS COVENTRY sank – 20 die.
ATLANTIC CONVEYOR (STUFT) ship abandoned after hit by
Exocet missiles – 12 die – sank under tow on 29 May 82.
8 Argentine aircraft shot down.

WEDNESDAY, 26 MAY 82 - DAY 3

0700*	Call the hands
0730*	Hands to breakfast
0800	HMS VERNON working party arrives
0800*	Out pipes
0805	Both watches of the hands muster in the Stern Gallery
	Commence storing ship
0810	Jetty Leading Hand muster at the Ship's Office
1000	NAAFI stores
1000*	Stand easy
1015*	Out pipes, hands carry on with your work
1200*	Hands to dinner
1310*	Out pipes
1315*	Both watches of the hands muster in the Stern Gallery
	Continue storing ship
1700	HMS VERNON working party depart

Well, there it was! The first Daily Orders. Other information on them told us that the Daily Routine was 'Daily Harbour', we now had an Emergency Party and Dining Hall Party and who they were, Dress of the Day was No.8s and leave for Senior Rates (SRs) was 1615 - 0755 (that meant I was going home again that night!), and 1620 - 0745 for Junior Rates (JRs). The RN had also taken over the gangway and the pipe system (ship's broadcast), as you could see from the asterisks next to the times, these had to be piped. We now had the FSU01 personnel sleeping onboard with the few single men already ensconced, which was not easy with dockyard hammering and drilling all night, so we had to have 'Call the hands', etc - that bloody whistle and the stupid little dits to boot! After all this came the 'NOTES'!

Funnily enough, the very first note was about the waitresses! Their cabins were out of bounds to RNP2100 personnel! They had also been re-titled 'female stewardesses' and they didn't appear to be out of bounds to the MN Officers or St Helenian crewmen! (Women at sea, eh, there's another good dit!). The St Helenian crewmens' bar had also been put out of bounds to RNP2100 - well, it was good while it lasted. In other notes, they also published the lists of meal times for harbour and sea, personnel detailed for the storing parties - because now the storing ship had really got serious, and finally we had details of the opening times of the Clothing Stores in HMS NELSON, hinting to the boys to ensure their uniform was up to scratch!

When I arrived at my office it was full of people. Nobody appeared to be working but it appeared to be the centre of the universe! I decided to start as I meant to go on! I let them all know, diplomatically, that this was not a public meeting place and that I had work to do! So the crowd dispersed with a lot of muttering and grunting!

A lot of my work was 'classified' or 'in confidence' and due to the lack of facilities could not be easily locked away when I wasn't there, even though I did have a small safe for the cash. When they had cleared we were left with the RPO, the POMA, the FCPO Coordinator and myself. This was the first time we had all been in the office together and we found that if we all sat down and then somebody wanted to move, we all had to get up so he could get off his seat. As we pondered this problem, one of the MN Officers arrived red-faced and breathless at the door demanding immediate use of the Gestetner! For him to do this we all had to get up, move our chairs out of the way and stand outside the office! Not a good system! Things needed sorting! The POMA disappeared to the Sick Bay and promised only to come back to help with the issue of the JRs' Beer Ration (3 cans per man per day). The FCPO Coordinator also decided to work from his cabin in the future, so now the dog might be able to see the rabbit! I now had to learn to live with RPO - the ship's policeman!

As I was sorting the office into a useful work area, I received my first typing job from the SNO – 'Temporary Standing Orders' - the boys were going to love this! RN law and order had really arrived now!

Those 'ex-Andrew' types amongst you will have already noticed the deliberate mistake on Daily Orders - there was no entry for 'Secure' at 1600! Leave started at 1615 but who was going to tell you to stop working? Nobody, was the quick answer! Sure enough, unpaid overtime again! It was 2130 when I left the ship for yet another night at home with my family! No sign of a cabin party on the way though. The long arm of Pusser's law was obviously at work! However, the flow of adventurers heading for the bright lights of Pompey and the 'fleshpots' of Southsea, was steady! The whiffs of various expensive colognes and after-shaves were prevalent. The weather was wet and windy for the time of year but there was Jack striding out in his flashiest T-shirt and skin tight jeans with no jacket or other protection, looking macho and smelling like a Chinese brothel! Some things never change!

Lest we forget - British Government questions the lack of progress <u>FROM</u> San Carlos and <u>TO</u> Goose Green! (What a neck! Sat back there in their cosy offices!)
Lt. Bruin RM, a bomb disposal expert, persuaded RM Colour Sergeant Garwood to ferry him round the ships in 'Bomb Alley' in his landing craft, so he could entertain the knackered troops in San Carlos water with his violin and a good old sing-song! IT WENT DOWN A TREAT.

THURSDAY, 27 MAY 82 - DAY 4

0700*	Call the hands
0730	Hands to breakfast
0800	HMS VERNON & HMS COLLINGWOOD working parties arrive (30)
0800*	Out pipes
0805*	Both watches of the hands muster in the Stern Gallery
	Commence storing ship
1000*	Stand easy
1015*	Out pipes
1200*	Hands to dinner
1300*	Hands carry on with your work
1700	HMS DOLPHIN working party arrives
2230*	Pipe down

With all the other usual general information, we had two new items today - Sunrise/Sunset times and High and Low Water times. The first note was telling us about the urgency of the storing ship and how it would continue throughout the next 3 days. (More nights at home with the family!). Storing parties had to ensure they were in the right place at the right time, or chaos would ensue! (Some chance - it was already chaotic and had been all week). Then we had a note about where people had to send mail for it to reach us speedily - the official postal address. This was the third most important thing to Jack when he was at sea! First came his pay, then his food and then his 'mailies'! Talking of pay, I had already had queries about pay, so the third note was reminding everyone to bring their cheque books on board, otherwise they would not be able to get any money. Finally, an innocuous single line note at the bottom of the page, from the POMA, asking for anyone qualified in First Aid to contact him! Say no more!

My day started with a trip to the outlying RN establishments to finally complete my office. We visited HMS DRYAD at Southwick, HMS CENTURION, HMS DOLPHIN and HMS SULTAN at Gosport, the RN Hospital at Haslar and HMS COLLINGWOOD at Fareham. By then I had as much as I thought I needed but what a struggle I had had getting it! I returned onboard and started unloading. Midway through, I was interrupted by the SNO. Would I mind doing the Daily Orders as the FCPO Coordinator was busy on shore and they couldn't find anybody else who could get them out before leave started? It was all written out in the book, so all I had to do was type and print them, then one of the JRs would distribute them! What could I say - not a lot! However, I had the distinct feeling that this was the thin end of the wedge! I also completed the Temporary Standing Orders that day, so I distributed them with the Daily Orders later that afternoon. Funnily enough, I didn't hear a lot of cheering when the troops saw them!

TECHNICAL NOTE (TN) - Fitting for abeam Replenishment at Sea (RAS) was incorrect and was being modified. (More drilling and hammering!).

With the arrival of the FSU01 onboard, the numbers of SRs had drastically increased. With this sudden influx of 'mechanical and electrical technical types' living onboard, came the need for a SRs' Mess. This was 'top priority' because 'technical types' don't have proper jobs, therefore, they need somewhere to spend their time! (Their usual answer was "If it isn't broken, I can't mend it"!) Hence the SRs' Mess was born! The problem with this ship was, where to put it? The ship only had two lounges that could be used for recreation areas! The largest, the Stern Gallery, had been allocated to the RN JRs for their mess. The Stern Gallery was a large passenger lounge at the aft (back) end of the ship with wonderful panoramic views out to sea. These windows were 'steel-plated' like my office, much to the chagrin of the JRs! The MN St Helenian Crew Members had their own bar/mess already, down below where their cabins were. This left the SRs and the Wardroom to fight over the Forward Lounge, which contained the passengers bar! After much debate, the answer was to split the Forward Lounge down the middle, with the Wardroom keeping the bar half and the RN SRs getting the other half. (What a surprise!). The SRs had to fit a bar facility in one corner but this didn't prove too difficult for our 'technical types' and <u>by lunchtime</u> we were up and running. (So these boys could be useful when they tried!). The Lounge had a large curtain fitted down the middle from deckhead to deck and that was to be regarded, on the SNO's instructions, as a soundproof, solid brick wall! Any conversations taking place behind this 'wall' were totally private! This rule was severely tested on many future occasions, when disgruntled SRs, with a couple of beers in them, would tell the rest of the mess what they thought about the various officers onboard, especially when they knew the officers concerned were sitting on the other side of the curtain. Strangely, some of the officers played this game as well! I then went home again. However, having just typed Daily Orders for Friday, I knew I wouldn't be going home tomorrow night. I'd got my first duty with RNP2100. Just my luck to be Duty Senior Rate on a Friday night 'baby sitting' all those 'extremely happy' impending war heroes from over the border! What fun, I was really looking forward to it! It was definitely the RN now – overnight DUTIES!

Lest we forget - SBS land on Mount Kent.
Sea Harriers attack Goose Green and lose 1 aircraft.

FRIDAY, 28 MAY 82 - DAY 5

0700*   Call the hands
0730   Hands to breakfast
0800   HMS VERNON and HMS NELSON Working Parties arrive (30)
0800*   Out pipes
0805*   Both watches of the hands muster in the Stern Gallery. Continue storing ship
1000*   Stand easy
1015*   Out pipes
1200*   Hands to dinner
1300*   Hands carry on with your work
2230*   Pipe down

Note 1 was one of mine telling the RN Ship's Company to collect a Next of Kin Form, Will Form, Royal Naval Dependants Fund Form and an 'N' Trust Insurance Application Form if they wanted one, from the Ship's Office. All to be filled in carefully and completely then handed in by 1400 Saturday. When these forms were being distributed a lot of the younger sailors went very pale in colour and very quiet. It had suddenly begun to dawn on them that this wasn't a game after all. It was one of the few times in my RN career when I had no difficulty getting Jack to fill in a piece of paper properly.

Note 2 was from the RPO reminding the newer joiners to hand in any overdue Discharge Notes and Rail Warrant Record Cards from their last unit.

Note 3 was about more paperwork, reminding the boys to make financial provision for their wives and loved ones before they sailed, by starting weekly and monthly allotments of their wages to them. With all this paper flying around, the Ship's Office was now in full production!

Note 4 was from the medical world telling anyone knowing his blood group to let the POMA know for his records. (He was full of doom and gloom that one!).

Note 5 was a warning that the NAAFI shop would not open until we'd been at sea for 7 days, so everyone was to stock up on soap, toothpaste, etc, etc. (What NAAFI Shop?). The only shop onboard was the Pursers little gold mine, owned by the Curnow Shipping Company, therefore the NAAFI would not be coming onboard! The only problem with this was the Purser was now on his own - his lady assistants were not coming on this 'cruise'! What was Jack going to do if he couldn't get his daily quota of nutty and goffers? He'd never survive the hangovers without this! This looked to be a major problem as far as he was concerned. Not opening until 7 days out to sea - it sounded like the Yank Navy!

After all this 'good news', Note 6 got really serious. From today there will be NO SMOKING THROUGHOUT THE SHIP, other than in accommodation spaces. Yet another nail in the coffin as far as the 'cruise' was concerned. However, Jack was used to that on RN ships anyway. It had been pleasant not to have to bother up until now though. The MN Officers and crew weren't going to be pleased, as most of them lived with a duty free hanging out of their mouth and smoked where they wanted. RN Law and Order strikes again!

The last note of the day, Note 7, was another bit of RN Law. There had been murmurings about taking orders from 'long-haired civvy officers' and words had been exchanged in high places about familiarity between MN Officers and RN crew. So it had only been a matter of time before this already thorny problem went public. All RN personnel were reminded that, under RN Law, if they were serving on a civvy ship, they had to comply with the authority of the civvy Master of the Ship.

The Daily Orders looked a lot prettier today, having been produced and typed by an expert. The boss thought so too, so the expert was detailed off to do them permanently. Well, well, well, yet another surprise! Shot himself in the foot again! So from now on a large chunk of my day was taken up checking information and sorting the Daily Orders into a presentable package. They then had to be typed, printed and distributed round the ship. This was a seven days a week job! However, it was one of the main sources of information in the ship and therefore taken very seriously. The beauty of it was that everybody onboard read them just to make sure they weren't missing anything, never mind that it was orders from above and it was their duty to read them.

Being Duty Senior Rate that night meant that I wasn't allowed to leave the ship during my period of duty. This enabled me, however, to complete a lot of jobs in the office that I hadn't been able to fit in up until now. It also meant I had to sort my part of the cabin out for my first nights sleep onboard. Sleep - what a joke! The drilling and hammering were still going at full speed 24 hours per day and of course when I did get into my pit another 'drunken problem' would return onboard wanting to tell me all about his night in the local boozers! So, in the end, not a lot of actual sleep was achieved. However, everyone else appeared to have had a good time and were having a wonderful weekend! Especially the dockyard mateys who must have been on excellent money for the shiftwork and overtime they were putting in. For us 'Queen and Country' types who were paid for working 24 hours per day, 7 days per week, etc, etc, duties were just another part of life's rich pattern!

Lest we forget - 2 Para attack Darwin Hill and Goose Green – 17 British die and 250
            Argentines.
            Colonel H Jones killed in the attack.

SATURDAY, 29 MAY 82 - DAY 6

0700*	Call the hands
0730	Hands to breakfast
0800	HMS VERNON, HMS NELSON, HMS EXCELLENT Working Parties arrive (30)
0800*	Out pipes
0805*	Both watches of the hands muster in the Stern Gallery, continue storing ship
1000*	Stand easy
1015*	Out pipes
1200*	Hands to dinner
1300*	Hands carry on with your work
1700	HMS SULTAN and HMS COLLINGWOOD Working Parties arrive (15)
2030	HMS DRYAD and HMS COLLINGWOOD Working Parties arrive (15)
2230*	Pipe down

The notes were exactly the same as Friday's Daily Orders, with one addition. The POMA was still wanting to meet people with First Aid Training. (He doesn't give up does he?).

TN - Ammunition ship, concession granted by Flag Officer Portsmouth, storing continues concurrent with ammunitioning.

Those astute types amongst you will have noticed that, even though it was Saturday, nothing on the Daily Orders indicated this other than the date!! The routine was 'Daily Harbour', probably with overtime again! If we were paid for overtime we'd be bloody rich! What about those shore based boys from HMS SULTAN, HMS DRYAD and HMS COLLINGWOOD turning to at 5pm and 8.30pm on a Saturday night. They must have upset somebody to get 'volunteered' for that. I'll bet they were impressed with 'life in a blue suit'!

So we just worked like any other day. We were going to war in a hurry after all! I, of course, had the added bonus of not having had much sleep due to the return onboard of all the 'happy people'. So by the end of the day I was well and truly knackered and I very nearly fell asleep on the Gosport Ferry. This was to be our last night ashore, for definite this time, as we were under sailing orders and off to Portland tomorrow afternoon and then after various trials we would be off down south. After all the hard graft this was really it - we were off to war! The tension began to mount!

Lest we forget - ATLANTIC CONVEYOR sinks under tow.
Argentine surrender at Goose Green – 1400 prisoners-of-war taken and the imprisoned islanders released.

SUNDAY, 30 MAY 82 - DAY 7

0001	Continue storing ship throughout the night
0700*	Call the hands
0730	Hands to breakfast
0755*	Out pipes
0800*	Both watches of the hands muster in the Forward Lounge, continue storing ship. Mobile crane available.
0830	Cold move to the Promontory - mobile crane will be available for lifting stores
0930	Fuelling
AM	1. Check RAS rigging
	2. Carry out inclination tests
1000	Planning Meeting in the Wardroom Dining Space
PM	Move to compass swing buoy
1500	All personnel not sailing with the ship to Portland to proceed ashore
o/c	Compass swing - proceed to Portland
	DAILY SEA ROUTINE

NB - We expect to be on passage to Portland for approximately eight hours - on arrival it is intended to anchor for the rest of the night and to commence RAS trials AM tomorrow. The ship will remain on DAILY SEA ROUTINE until further notice. Remember, it may all change at short notice.

Note 1 read thus:- "Well done all onboard, the past week has been crammed full of activity and a tremendous amount of hard work has been completed. We have not finished yet, but may I take this opportunity of thanking the entire Ship's Company (RN & MN) for working so hard for long hours. Soon we should have completed our pre-sea checks and be on our way to Portland for a short 'work-up' period, of approximately 24 hours, then south!" (That made all of us RN types feel proud and thankful that our efforts had been noticed - who needed overtime pay anyway!?).

Note 2 was a cracker! "Missing Stores - yesterday, during store ship, a substantial number of cases of beer went missing. Considering that the intended role of the ship is to provide support to people down south, I hesitate to say that these stores have been stolen. However, the beer did disappear during its journey from the lorries on the jetty to the stowing place onboard. Maybe the cases have been overlooked and are obscured by other stores. It is my intention to call a beer amnesty, if the missing cans are returned to the Ship's Office by 1200 today, the matter will be forgotten. Unfortunately if not, then the only course left is to search the ship". (Funnily enough, we never did have to search the ship!).

Note 3 was yet another nail in the 'cruise' coffin - all the RN personnel had to return all the 'nice' MN bedding to the Ship's Laundry. (Back to the sleeping bag, yet another luxury gone!).

Note 4 reminded all the smokers that the newly issued 'Plastic Bins' in the cabins were not ash trays and all damage would be paid for by the offenders.

Finally, note 5 yet again reminded everyone about the "NO SMOKING THROUGHOUT THE SHIP" rule. (They were obviously having trouble with that one).

This was the first day the Daily Orders were countersigned by the Ship's Master. This was to reinforce Note 7 from Daily Orders of 28 May 82 reference the authority of the Master. (Law & Order was here to stay obviously!).

As you will have noticed again, yet another normal working day. It's a good job I hadn't planned to go to church! Today we were definitely sailing to war, so I had to do the 'goodbyes' again before leaving for work! With it being Sunday, all the neighbours came out to say goodbye as well - the embarrassment of it - it was a relief to get back onboard, I think?! I had spent all weekend chasing paperwork. I had to ensure that all personnel, RN and MN, had completed all the necessary forms for wills, insurance, next of kin, etc, etc. I then had to produce a 'Souls on Board' list prior to sailing. This was a full list of all personnel with their full personal details and next of kin details. This was in case we were sunk! It therefore had to be 100% accurate. To complete all this I had to find people hidden all over the ship storing, having meal breaks, loafing on the jetty, etc, etc. All this was not helped when it was mentioned from on high that we would have to sail with civvy workmen and dockyard mateys onboard, as they had not finished their work yet! Not an easy job - especially with no staff to help you. The ship's broadcast was antique and didn't help because it didn't actually go to all the many and varied places where Jack could hide, that was of course if you could hear it above the hammering and drilling which was now at full panic stations anyway. Also in the middle of this mayhem, I got a conscientious objector! Just what you need at a time like this! Was he serious or was he just working his ticket? Probably too young and homesick was more the problem along with being scared. His mess mates had obviously talked to him and reminded him that the penalty for desertion during time of war was still hanging - Jack will have his little joke! Anyway, he eventually changed his mind after 'counselling' and filled the forms in! It made you think though!

Life was now totally chaotic, as it normally is when you are setting off on a long trip. But this was different. There was a war at the end of this trip and the news emanating from it was not good. Again the thought was that if the Argies could sink real warships what chance had this overloaded rust bucket got?'

Then the 'buzzes' started. We weren't sailing. Then we were. Then we weren't. Then we were. So it went on. As I sorted out the Daily Orders for Monday, it became apparent that WE WEREN'T!

TN - The Commander in Chief Fleet's staff confirmed that stern RAS equipment was now going to be fitted to the ship. That put our Estimated Time of Departure (ETD) right by 7 days from 1400 hrs Sun 30 May.

The signal telling us this had been sent on Friday, 28 May 82! So where had it been for two days? Well, that meant more nights at home with the family and more goodbyes! What an organisation, the decision makers had struck yet again! At this point 50% of RNP2100 were given leave until 1200 Wednesday, 2 June 82. Those who could be spared that is, so guess who didn't get to go? They were given leave but had to keep themselves available for immediate recall. That evening when I went home again I got some strange looks from the neighbours and my family was totally baffled. However, I believe there was some heavy celebrating in Portsmouth and Southsea that night!

Lest we forget - 45 Cdo take Douglas.
        3 Para take Teal Inlet.

MONDAY, 31 MAY 82 - DAY 8

0001 - 0300	Working Parties continue storing ship
0700*	Call the hands
0730	Hands to breakfast
0755*	Out pipes
0800*	Both watches of the hands muster in the Forward Lounge
0800	RNDQ's Working Party arrives (10)
0800	Prepare to shift berth
0830	Cold move to promontory
0830 - 1600	Progress storing, Test RAS gear, Embark fuel (Dieso), Inclination Trial
1000*	Stand Easy
1000	Planning Meeting in Wardroom Dining Space
1015*	Out pipes, hands carry on with your work
1200*	Hands to dinner
1300*	Hands carry on with your work
o/c	Proceed to compass swing buoy, Engine trials en route
o/c	Alongside Fountain Lake Jetty No1, Complete loading programme
1700*	Return MN bedding to Ship's Laundry
2230*	Pipe down

We were back to 'Daily Harbour' Routine again!

Note 1 informed the RN Junior Ratings that Station Cards were to be handed in and collected at the Ship's Office, not given to the duty watchkeeper in the Lounge. (More RN law being sorted out - this ensured that we knew who was onboard and who wasn't!?).

Note 2 informed us of the new Stores Office situated on 'D' Deck Port Side.

Note 3 reminded us about cleaning and tidying the ship, stowing for sea, cigarette ends and ditching of gash now that storing was nearing completion.

Note 4 informed us that there would be no Radio Telephone Calls when the ship sailed due to operational commitments.

Note 5 was that old chestnut about NO SMOKING THROUGHOUT THE SHIP.

Finally Note 6 read thus:- "The additional stay at Portsmouth was caused by a further operational capability being required of the ship. We were ready to sail on time and may I thank you all for your tremendous efforts over the past week, this includes the dockyard work-force. Now that we have a few days in hand please don't waste them. We have now the opportunity to get the ship in all respects ready for sea before sailing next weekend and we will sail looking clean on the outside and well stowed inside." What more can you say, they never give up do they?

We had a new addition to the Daily Orders today - a Duty Radio Operator (RO) was now being nominated. The Radio Communications empire was obviously spreading. Also for you observant types, this was Day 2 of the 'Wardroom Dining Space', that was behind the curtain in the dining room, and they were the tables with tablecloths!

Whilst all this technical activity was going on, the 'white mafia' in the offices, etc, were busy with their paperwork. (As some old soldier once said "An army marches on its paperwork"!). A Divisional System was now in place for the RN personnel and a Watch and Station Bill was in production. So all the RN people knew their place of duty at all times - action stations, defence watches, emergency stations, etc, etc. It was just like being back in the real navy again! (The Divisional System was a tiered system within the various departments of the RN. An officer had so many SRs and JRs 'under his wing' for discipline, records, welfare etc etc purposes. The SRs would then cover so many JRs, so the SRs could maybe solve a problem on the way up the chain, or maybe represent the JR if it carried on upwards. It meant that all ratings were being fairly treated and had a system in place to complain with if they so needed. The system was invented after the Invergordon Mutiny in 1931, so as to avoid further mutinies – 'mushroom farming' was even worse in those days)!

After yet more overtime, I went home again.

Lest we forget - 42 Cdo take Mount Kent and Mount Challenger.

TUESDAY, 1 JUNE 82 - DAY 9

0700*   Call the hands
0730   Hands to breakfast
0800*   Out pipes
0800   RNDQ's Working Party arrives (10)
0805*   Both watches of the hands muster in the Forward Lounge
1000*   Stand easy
1015*   Out pipes, hands carry on with your work
1200*   Hands to dinner
1300*   Hands carry on with your work
1700   RNDQ's Working Party departs
2230*   Pipe down

Note 1 read thus:- "DISCIPLINE
a.   Service personnel are not under any circumstances to enter the cabins or recreation areas of the civilian crew.
b.   Service personnel are not permitted to entertain civilian crew members in their cabins.
c.   Service personnel are not permitted to entertain in their sleeping accommodation. All entertainment for Junior Ratings will take place in the Stern Gallery.
d.   Whenever possible the Merchant Navy crew will be controlled by the Ship's Officers and the Royal Navy Party by Service Officers and Senior Rates. However, any order given by a Merchant Navy Officer to Royal Navy personnel is to be considered that of the Senior Naval Officer (QR(RN) Article 1805 refers). Disciplinary action will immediately follow any insubordination."
(Not another cabin party problem - just because he was going to war Jack thought he could get away with anything!).

Note 2 read thus:- "SECURITY - all are reminded of the need to be extremely careful not to refer to operational matters, past, present or future in letters home. The media is alert to such information and puts families under great pressure to obtain news. Speculation on possible return dates in letters is to be similarly discouraged. Private film presents further security risk. Care must be taken that in either processed or unprocessed form it is not sent home in normal mail if it could disclose any classified information. Private film of possible Intelligence or other professional value should be handled in accordance with QR(RN) 3808.2."
(Say no more, nudge, nudge, wink, wink).

Note 3 read thus:- "DUFF BUZZ GENERATORS

a. Because it is impracticable to "Clear Lower Deck" I wish to say a few words about the Ship's Programme through Daily Orders. The RAS gear on the port side will be completed by AM Thursday - this means that we shall then be able to receive and give (L) & (S) stores from the port side and receive only from the starboard. The reason for our delay in sailing, to AM Sunday, is to provide a stern RAS capability. This will be completed AM Saturday.

b. All ships going South are required to submit to CINCFLEET a statement of how much extra stores and passenger carrying capability they have - just in case it is required - we have stated that we can provide a specified amount of each - the space will probably never be required.

I request that all DUFF BUZZ generators be switched off as from now."

(This note highlights the problem of communication. If Jack is not told what is going on all the time, he will make up his own version which will quickly spread doom and gloom around the whole ship).

Some heavy notes today!

Note 4 was a reminder of yesterday's note on cleaning up the ship or "Mother Goose" as the SNO liked to call her!

Note 5 was from the overworked producer of Daily Orders informing would be 'Note producers' that their little offerings had to be in the Ship's Office by 1030 on the day of printing. (Not when the POWTR was printing the bloody things on the Gestetner - there's always one isn't there? They must think you wave your magic wand and there it is done!).

Note 6, the last one today thank goodness, was again reminding people to sort out their financial problems before sailing. (Some chance! For a lot of them this trip was going to solve their financial problems - be they female, in a bottle, in a nappy, loan shark, etc, etc – you can't spend much at sea, and the prospect of foreign visits didn't look too bright – so it would be save, save, save!)

Yet another addition today with the arrival of the Duty Stores Accountant (SA). Yet another growing empire! (It must be nice to have staff!).

TN - (For the rest of the week). - Store ship, aided by RNDQ's Working Party until 2200 daily. Work on RAS rigs and Flight Deck progresses satisfactorily. 24 hour working maintained by dockyard.

WEDNESDAY, 2 JUNE 82 - DAY 10

0700*	Call the hands
0730	Hands to breakfast
0800*	Out pipes
0800	RNDQ's and HMS DRYAD's working parties arrive (1 + 20)
0805*	Both watches of the hands muster in the Stern Gallery
1000*	Stand easy
1015*	Out pipes, hands carry on with your work
1200*	Hands to dinner
1300*	Hands carry on with your work
1700	Working parties depart
1700*	Return MN bedding to Ship's Laundry
2230*	Pipe down

N.B.   Flight Deck helicopter flying operations will take place today. Listen out for the warning pipes.

Note 1 stated "PERSONAL EQUIPMENT - All members of the ship's company are to ensure that they have in their personal possession the following equipment:-
a. S6 respirator and spare canister (in date for test)
b. Anti-flash gear
c. Steel helmets and Flak Jackets (personnel manning exposed positions only - they will be nominated)
d. Life Jacket
e. Once-only suit tied to life jacket belt (these will be issued after Ascension)
f. Mug (plastic or tin)
g. Ear plugs
h. Field dressing
i. Geneva Convention ID Card (Form S2907 available from the Ship's Office) in respirator bag
Everybody must be in possession of this gear before sailing. Departmental Regulators are to compile check off lists and report to HODs any deficiencies by 1200 2 June."

Note 2 was on the same theme by stating " PERSONAL KIT - The following is the absolute minimum kit requirement:-

2 sets AWD (with name tape)	1 Beret	1 pair DMS boots
1 pair black shoes	1 pair sandals	2 pair overalls cotton
2 pair blue shorts	3 pair blue socks	2 pair white shorts
3 pair blue stockings	5 sets underwear (not nylon)	
3 White Fronts	2 sleeping bag liners	2 towels
2 pillow cases	No2 Blue suit and cap	Personal toilet articles
1 woolley pully	Housewife	Sports gear

To be stowed in the living accommodation, if you haven't got it, get it before 4 June.

Notes 3, 4 and 5 were reminders about Radio Telephone calls not being available when the ship sails, JRs' station cards and the site of the new Stores Office.

Notes 6, 7 and 8 were back to the paperwork! Problems of one sort or another arose every day, so reminders were sent out to try and nip them in the bud! One note reminded those involved with buying or selling houses at the present time, to grant 'Power of Attorney' to their wives or solicitors before sailing. Another reminded people to make a will before sailing if they hadn't already and also one about life insurance. Most life insurance policies required you to inform the company if you were under orders for active service. So, in order not to falsify their policy, they now had to tell them!

Note 9 stated:- "The Forward Lounge is now the Senior Rates Mess (Port) and the Wardroom (Starboard). It is out of bounds to JRs. Access around is possible by port and starboard Oerlikon Deck ladders." (Up until now the Forward Lounge had been the focal point of the whole ship, so this one came as quite a shock, especially to the JRs. This was one of the final acts in the conversion from cruise ship to RN ship and was also the start of many strange stories!).

Life onboard was now beginning to get tedious. The novelty had worn off and the hard work was beginning to take its toll. The drilling and hammering continued incessantly, as the Flight Deck, Gun Placements, RAS gear, etc, were fitted and sorted out. Also the longer we sat there, the more tasks their lordships dreamt up for us. This meant more stores to hump, more visitors to clean up for and of course more panic by the bosses! We would just get one problem sorted out and immediately another would be dropped on us. In fact the light at the end of the tunnel had now disappeared round a bend!

I, personally, was now in harness producing the full copy of the ship's Standing Orders (SOs). Other STUFT ships were sent a copy of a version of SOs from a similar sized and crewed RN ship and they quickly converted them. We, of course, had nothing to compare with! However, the SNO obtained an old copy of the SOs for the aircraft carrier HMS ARK ROYAL and we adapted them! Not easy I can tell you, but they did provide a few amusing bits! Between us we removed all the potential howlers and ended up with a reasonable set of orders, it was a lot of hard work though. I still had all the other office work to contend with, customers to sort, telephones to answer, Daily Orders, etc, etc, so life was hectic! However, I did get home at nights, eventually. The neighbours had given up asking me by now!

Lest we forget - 2 Para reach Bluff Cove.

THURSDAY, 3 JUNE 82 - DAY 11

0700*	Call the hands
0730	Hands to breakfast
0800*	Out pipes
0805	Both watches of the hands muster in the after gallery, FSU hands muster on the foredeck
AM	RN Slops Wagon available on the jetty
1000*	Stand easy
1030	Captain MCM visits. Met by SNO, Chief Officer, Chief Engineer, Chief Purser and Chief Steward
1200*	Hands to dinner
1300*	Hands carry on with your work
2230*	Pipe down

Only one note today and that was sorting the problem of tracing the whereabouts of SRs and Officers. As the JRs had station cards, we had a 'Tick Off Board'. Any SR or Officer, going off the ship for any reason, had to mark the board and leave a telephone contact number. The board was of course to be held in the Ship's Office! This meant that the Ship's Office throughout the day now resembled Waterloo Station at rush hour. This didn't help those trying to work in it!

Added to all the chaos today, was the visit of Captain MCM, who had come for a 'look round' and to check up on FSU01. Really helpful and a boost for the morale, especially for the cleaning parties!

HMS Victory – one of our near neighbours in Portsmouth Dockyard

FRIDAY, 4 JUNE 82 - DAY 12

0700*	Call the hands
0730	Hands to breakfast
0800*	Out pipes
0805*	Both watches muster on the foredeck
AM	RN Slops Wagon available on the jetty
0805	Working party arrives (1+10)
0930	RN & MN Heads of Department (HODs) Planning Meeting in the Wardroom
1000*	Stand easy
1015*	Hands carry on with your work
1200*	Hands to dinner
1300*	Hands carry on with your work
1600*	Secure
2230*	Pipe down

The first note was back on the 'cigarette ends'! It was 'unseamanlike' to stub them out on decks! (Perhaps somebody should have told the Dockyard mateys!).

Note 2 was a new one and an indication of worse things to come! It read:- "THINK WATER - SAVE WATER - The Osmosis Plant produces 20 tons of fresh water daily. This allows 40 gallons per day per person. HOWEVER out of this 30 gallons per person is required by the ship for: galley, flight cleaning, laundry, coffee boats, etc, etc. Responsible use of fresh water when we sail means we don't have to think of rationing. A close watch on water consumption will be kept." Say no more!

Note 3 was amending the telephone directory. "FSU stores module is now Ext 43."

Note 4 read thus:- "PHOTOGRAPHS - At 1400 Saturday 6 June 1982 a member of the Fleet Photographic Unit will be onboard to take photographs of all RN personnel. Personnel are to muster on the foredeck when piped. MN crew photograph at a time to be announced Saturday PM."

Note 5 was reminding anyone who hadn't collected a field dressing to get one from the Sick Bay today.

It was weekend again and the buzzes were going well. We were due to sail at 1400 on Sunday! Would we make it this time? Daily Orders had given no clues today - leave was normal night leave, nobody had mentioned being under sailing orders? Saturday's Daily Orders were therefore being anxiously awaited all over the ship! Talk about 'Hot off the press', you could feel the tension. Were we going or were we not? My neighbours were dying to find out!

Saturday's Daily Orders finally arrived and guess what? We weren't going! Again! Somebody high up had made another decision before going off for the weekend! Something else had to be fitted! What a surprise! There again, it was on Day 13's Daily Orders! My neighbours thought it was funny!

Lest we forget - 2 Para occupy Bluff Cove and Fitzroy.

SATURDAY, 5 JUNE 82 - DAY 13

0700*	Call the hands
0730	Hands to breakfast
0800*	Out pipes
0805	Both watches muster on the foredeck
1000*	Stand easy
1015*	Hands carry on with your work
1200	Secure
1300*	Duty part of the watch muster on the foredeck
1350*	Clear lower deck of all RN personnel, muster on the Flight Deck
o/c	MN ship's company photograph on the Flight Deck
o/c	RN/MN ship's company photograph on the Flight Deck
o/c	Non duty watch to night leave
2230*	Pipe down

Note 1 informed everybody of their responsibility to ensure that 'C' Deck Pantry was kept clean. If it wasn't, it would be closed.

Note 2 informed the RN contingent that haircut standards were to be maintained and failure to do so would lead to a visit to the 'new ship's barber', (the POMA), under the supervision of the RPO.

Note 3 told us that Duty Watch Lists had now been completed and were displayed on the Main Notice Board in 'C' Deck cross passage. So today on Daily Orders, instead of an Emergency Party, we had a Duty Watch - 1st Port.

Note 4 read thus exactly: - "For MN Crew
1.   The ship has been appointed to sail on Wednesday 9th June following completion of extra RAS fittings.
2.   NEWS MEDIA - If anyone is approached by news reporters of any kind, say nothing and refer to the Senior Naval Officer, Master or Mate."
(As it states, this note was only for the MN crew who obviously 'needed to know'! Jack as usual was 'mushroom farming' - i.e. being kept in the dark and fed loads of shit! So, what's new?).

The final note, Note 5, informed us that we now had an RN type Executive Officer - the 'Jimmy'! This of course meant more law and order for the RN personnel.

Leave was "As piped" and the routine was 'Saturday Harbour', this meant finishing work at 1200. However, we then had to await the arrival of the RN Photographer and leave would not be piped until the photographs had all been taken. As we waited we had dinner and then a few cans were opened and we waited. As the cans took effect, mutterings about stupid bloody photos were heard in the background and we waited. More cans passed through, still no photographer so we waited some more. Eventually we were informed that leave was now starting for those entitled - the photographer could not make it! Having wasted half of his afternoon off, Jack was not impressed to say the least! Along with all the other silliness he had to suffer, this was a classic. Again I think the local alehouses benefitted from this organisational cock up!

SUNDAY, 6 JUNE 82 - DAY 14

0700*   Call the hands
0730   Hands to breakfast
0800*   Out pipes
0805*   Both watches muster on the Flight Deck
1000*   Stand easy
1015*   Hands carry on with your work
1200*   Hands to dinner
1205   Non duty watch to night leave
1300*   Hands carry on with your work
1600*   Secure, non duty part to night leave
2230*   Pipe down

Note 1 was a new one. It read:- "LAUNDRY - It is apparent that the laundry facility onboard is being abused. Machines have been left full of dirty water and the compartment in a disgusting state. From today the laundry will be locked. Any member of the Ship's Company requiring to use the laundry facility is to draw and sign for the key from the Ship's Office. The POMA will be in charge of the laundry facility with a view to setting up a laundry service run by a Royal Navy crew of 2 volunteers. Names of volunteers to the POMA." (The question to be asked here is, why did we not have a Hong Kong dhobymen team onboard, like RN ships? Because as we now know their lordships are now trying to bin them! This would be a disaster to most matelots, as these men provide a wonderful service for the ship's company at very acceptable charges. Before they bin them somebody in high places should ask Jack what his opinion is on the subject! Leave them alone, they don't affect anybody's budget! Lest we forget, Hong Kong crew members also died in the Falklands War.).

It must have been Sunday as there were only two notes! The last one was a 'dress' reminder and another new one. "Shirts are to be worn at all times within the accommodation area (eg. recreation and dining spaces), this includes passageways." (Obviously some misguided individual still thought he was on a cruise. Must have been MN!).

The routine was 'Daily Harbour' but leave was down to start at 1200 - strange. Must have been a typographical error! Today, however, we actually got away at 1200! So we managed a bit of another weekend at home. My neighbours didn't know what to make of it and some of them were now volunteering for STUFT ships! There was a fear now, however, that with all this new gear they kept fitting and all the extra stores, etc, they kept cramming onboard, that the whole thing might just sink! This may sound jocular - but some people were becoming concerned!

MONDAY, 7 JUNE 82 - DAY 15

0700*	Call the hands
0730	Hands to breakfast
0800*	Out pipes
0805*	Both watches muster on the foredeck
AM	Continue securing for sea, touch up paintwork, top up stores as required
1000*	Stand easy
1015*	Hands carry on with your work
1015*	Loan clothing issue - foul weather gear, lifejackets, etc.
1200*	Hands to dinner
1300*	Hands carry on with your work
1600*	Secure
2230*	Pipe down

Note 1 was the big RN hammer coming down again and yet another nail in the 'cruise' coffin. It read thus:- "CABINS - In general, the state of the RN cabins is disgusting. Cabins are to be squared off and gash ditched by 0800 daily. The Ship's Coordinator and RPO will carry out cabin rounds daily at 0900."

Note 2 was a repeat of the FSU Stores Module telephone number and Note 3 was further to yesterdays Note 1. "The laundry service will commence on Thursday, 10 June 82. A price list will be available from the POMA."

Issued along with these Daily Orders were more bulky complex orders, known as Temporary Standing Orders, which would then be eventually incorporated in the Ship's Standing Orders. Ours were known as 'St HELLTEMS' - an appropriate name! 1/82 was born today - "Operation Corporate - Ships taken up from Trade (STUFT) Reports". Reports were to be rendered from all STUFT ships, covering "preparation, deployment and operation of the ships". There was a very comprehensive list of subjects to be covered and any useful extras would be most welcome. Everything from Aviation and Administration to Recommendations for future STUFT operations was required. So everybody onboard, who was required to raise a report, was being warned off early.

2/82 was also produced today. This was informing the boys about 'Family and Welfare' matters, including the MODMAIL system, concession telegrams and other ways of communicating with your family or vice versa. Also explaining the Welfare Service with useful telephone numbers and answering a lot of other questions under this banner!

There was an addition today! "THE SHIP IS UNDER SAILING ORDERS". Were they spinning a dit or was it for real this time? The buzzes began again and the tension started to build again! We must be going this time, surely! As can be seen from the Daily Orders, it looked serious this time as we were definitely securing for sea RN style! All the daily tasks were now geared towards sailing and the 'excitement' mounted!

TUESDAY, 8 JUNE 82 - DAY 16

0700*	Call the hands
0730	Hands to breakfast
0800*	Out pipes
0805*	Both watches muster on the foredeck
0830	Turn ship (To embark reel into Port Quarter)
0900	FOP stores party arrives (Store ship) (10)
0930	Planning Meeting in the Wardroom - HODs
1000*	Stand easy
1015*	Hands carry on with your work
1200*	SRs to lunch
1215*	JRs to lunch
1300*	Hands carry on with your work
1430*	MN Crew - individual ID Card photos on the Flight Deck
o/c	Group photo RN/MN Crew
1600*	Secure
1930*	Stand by for Rounds
2230*	Pipe down

Note 1 explained to the MN Crew that "the correct times and method of usage of the clothing and equipment issued by RN Stores will be explained at a later date". (Yesterday they had been issued with action working dress, anti flash gear, gas mask, etc. This had helped to bring a little reality to their situation, especially when they tried on the gas mask! Up to now they had still been 'cruising' and everything had been a novelty and a bit of a giggle! Various little occurrences were now beginning to get the message across however!).

Note 2 was different! "Helicopter operations - The Ship's Flight will embark PM Wednesday during our passage to Portland. Upper and weather decks abaft of the funnel will be out of bounds to all personnel not involved in Flying Stations. Gash is not to be ditched during Flying Stations (listen for pipes). Use of the Flight Deck will be restricted whilst we are at sea. Anybody wishing to use the Flight Deck contact the OOW."

Note 3 was another first! Sport! "Five aside soccer - HMS NELSON gym has been booked from 6pm - 8pm tonight. Anyone interested contact the Stores Office." (Could this be our last chance for a kick about before we went to war?).

Note 4 was informing us that, "Due to limited seating and facilities onboard SRs will go to lunch at 1200 and JRs at 1215." (Some people thought that this meant the JRs lost 15 minutes dinner break. Guess what? They weren't impressed! However, the following day it all changed again!).

Note 5 was an update on yesterday's official bollocking in Note 1. "There was an improvement in the standard of cleanliness in the cabins today, however:-
a. Stow/lash all loose gear for sea.
b. Dhobying is NOT repeat NOT to be hung in the cabins. The heads are quite sufficient for this purpose."

Note 6 read thus:- "The distribution of Daily Orders will now be restricted to RN & MN Officers, Notice Boards, Offices and Messes." (Paper rationing had started!).

Surprise, surprise - we're still under sailing orders! It must be serious this time! Was this going to be my last night at home - again? It seemed like it, so I had to go through all the goodbyes yet again. It was now getting past a joke! The boys living onboard had a bigger problem. They had their first evening 'Rounds'. Final Curtain for the cruise! The RN was now fully up and running! Funnily enough, there weren't a lot of JRs onboard to witness this wonderful RN tradition arriving! The buzz was that we were definitely going this time, so there was some serious celebrating, commiserating, partying, dit spinning, etc, etc, to be completed around the inns of southern Hampshire!

RFA Sir Tristram at Port Stanley after being bombed at Bluff Cove

Lest we forget - RFAs SIR GALAHAD & SIR TRISTRAM were bombed at Bluff
Cove – 51 die and 51 seriously wounded.
LCU F4 was sunk at Choiseul Sound.
HMS PLYMOUTH hit by 4 bombs in Falkland Sound.
3 Argentine Skyhawks shot down by Sea Harriers.

WEDNESDAY, 9 JUNE 82 - DAY 17

0700*	Call the hands
0730	Hands to breakfast
0800*	Out pipes
0805*	Both watches muster on the foredeck
0830	RAS gear tests
1000	Fuel - outboard CL4
1000*	Stand easy
1015*	Hands carry on with your work
1130*	MN Crew/RN SRs to lunch
1145*	Secure, RN JRs to lunch
1300*	Hands carry on with your work
1300	Inclination trials
1400	Slip CL4
1500	Proceed to 3 buoy for compass swing
1700	Sail
1900 -	
2000	Embark Wasp
1930*	Stand by for Rounds (XO/RPO)
2230*	Pipe down

Note 1 read:- "3 WRNS (Ex Liaison Team) embark during the day to sail to Portland. They will disembark on anchoring at Portland." (I'll not go into their task up until now, as it isn't for me to comment!! The question now was, aren't we extremely busy preparing for war? Have we not got enough things to sort out without carrying useless passengers for jollys? So the big question was - WHY? One of the buzzwords rammed down my throat for 22 years in the RN was - PRIORITIES! Say no more - as we now know things were only to get worse on the subject of WRNS at sea!)

Note 2 was to sort out the mess created by yesterday's Note 4! It stated:-
"The following are the revised meal times:-

Breakfast	0730 - 0800	MN Crew
	0730 - 0815	RN Ratings
	0730 - 0830	Officers
Lunch	1130 - 1230	MN Crew/RN SRs/ RN Watchkeepers
	1145 - 1230	RN JRs
	1130 - 1230	Officers
Dinner	1730 - 1830	MN Crew/RN Ratings
	1930 - 2030	Officers
	2015 - 2030	RN Watchkeepers (8)

Note 3 indicated that we were definitely sailing - "The RN ship's company will break into 4 watches at 1600 today and the Senior Rate of the Watch Roster will also be initiated."

TN - On completion of Inclination Trials and Compass Swing we sail for Portland.

St HELLTEM 3/82 'Rounds' was published. It fully explained the routine, route, what had to be reported and other points to note. (It also helped to set the MN minds at rest, they had thought it meant them as well!).

The new meal times extended the SRs lunch time by 30 mins and they also solved the previous problems, so we were now waiting for the catch! The routine was 'Daily Harbour/Daily Sea', so that was it, we must be off this time! And we were! BUT, when Thursday's Daily Orders came out, we found that HMS LEDBURY was having engine problems, so we were now going to be stuck in Portland when we got there!

So at last, the big moment came and we sailed from Pompey. There was a lot of hooting and cheering from the dockyard as we left and even a few families on the Round Tower at Old Portsmouth waved us off. It was very chaotic as we still had Dockyard mateys working onboard, all the RN people were familiarising themselves with their new surroundings on sailing and the MN people were all doing their best to impress with their ship handling skills. 'Hands to Panic Stations' was definitely appropriate. However, at last we were off. No more goodbyes. What a relief. As we left the Isle of Wight behind us, the thought did cross my mind that I might not be coming back! When the rest of the Task Force sailed off it was all singing and dancing as they didn't know quite what to expect. By now ships had been sunk and people had died - it was a different ball game. The war was in full flow and we were heading straight for it in this rust bucket! It was difficult to work out which emotion to follow, until a voice from on high started shouting about Thursday's Daily Orders! Yet again the work ethic took over! There wasn't enough time to feel sorry for yourself, to worry about your future or to decry the wages you were being paid for this! The troops sent to the First and Second World Wars had departed thinking that they would only be away for a matter of weeks, months at the most – and how long did those epics last?!
(NB The RMS ST HELENA conversion was the longest of any STUFT ship. The average time was 2 days – ours took 16 days !)

That evening we had more crap to contend with! First, we had to stop for a couple of hours because of an engine defect, then, even worse, we had the arrival of the WAAFUs with their 'budgie'! We had the dreaded pipe you become familiar with in the RN when you want go to sleep at night after a hard days work - "HANDS TO FLYING STATIONS". (All day long they lay in their beds. Then when the rest of the ship's company want to rest in theirs, after they have had a hard day's work - the Fleet Air Arm comes alive!)

THURSDAY, 10 JUNE 82 - DAY 18

0630	No2 Hatch opening and derricks raised
0700*	Call the hands
0730	Hands to breakfast
0800*	Out pipes
0805*	Both watches muster on the foredeck
1000*	Stand easy
1015*	Hands carry on with your work
1130*	MN Crew/ RN SRs/Watchkeepers to lunch
1145*	Secure, RN JRs to lunch
1300*	Hands carry on with your work
1915*	Duty part of the watch clean up messdecks and flats for Rounds
1930*	Stand by for Rounds
2230*	Pipe down

Before the normal notes we had a special item which read:- "PROGRAMME - HMS LEDBURY has to change both her engines. The FSU will be required to assist in this evolution which will take place at Portland. Obviously, our departure South will be further delayed. It is hoped that the engine change will be completed within 48 hours. We shall then carry out our RAS trials and proceed on our way South. Rough guestimate for completion - Friday evening."

Note 1 was as a result of our initial attempt at life on the ocean wave! Every time an RN ship went out at the start of a trip there were minor problems to overcome. New joiners would be learning their way round the ship, new entries who hadn't been to sea before would be learning the whole experience, etc, etc. This time we had an MN crew as well! The note read thus:- "MN CREW - Attention to instructions and advice piped over the PA system is TOO LAX. You are required to listen more attentively and follow any instructions given. This will make for a better run and effective ship."

Note 2 was an oddment - "Food is NOT to be taken from the Dining Halls. If food continues to be removed to cabins, the duty senior rate will be required to monitor the JRs Dining Hall at meal times."

Note 3 informed us - "The watertight door between 3/4 tween decks is to be kept shut at all times, except when passing through." (A little disconcerting this one!).

Finally, Note 4 was a further addition to the birth of the Rounds and read thus:-
"Duty part of the watch will clear up the following areas for evening Rounds:-
Captain's Flat (D Deck); Ship's Office Flat (C Deck) and ladder to B Deck; JRs Recreation Space; JRs accommodation flats (B Deck); Radio Room Flat and ladder (MSO duty rate); and the Night Pantry (C Deck Stbd side)."

TN - Carried out successful alongside trial of abeam RAS gear.
   0730 Arrive Coaling Jetty South at Portland.
   FSU/ HMS LEDBURY engine change.

Replenishment at Sea (RAS) is carried out between 2 or 3 ships whilst they are still moving and is a complicated and dangerous operation. In the RN, it has been developed into an 'art'. Fuel and water are passed through pipes from the supply ship in the middle out to the ships on either side, as they all sail alongside each other on the same course and at the same speed. Jackstays and lines are also used to pass stores and personnel backwards and forwards at the same time.

Two new additions to the Daily Orders duties were Duty Flight 1 (DF1) and Duty Flight 2 (DF2). The routine was 'Daily Sea/Daily Harbour' and leave would be "As piped". Our first ship's visit! How long were we staying? Not yet another chance to go ashore and say goodbye to the family on the telephone, go jogging, take our library books back, visit a museum or place of local interest, or simply get pissed before going off to war - again! A few 'snips' in Portland, then off to the bright lights of Weymouth. Just what the holiday makers needed - a drunken shower of would-be war heroes! The boys on the engine change weren't going to be happy though! Then Daily Orders for Friday came out and told us we weren't going until Sunday morning - so that meant two nights ashore! Bloody costly this going to war, couldn't be doing the liver much good either! After three weeks of "Are we or aren't we", we were beginning to wonder who actually was running this show! What was our destiny? While we were thinking about it we all went ashore and got pissed again, as you do when you're concerned about your destiny! The boys on the engine change worked all night! The Flight went home of course!

Lest we forget - Peru sends 10 Mirage jets to aid the Argentines.

FRIDAY, 11 JUNE 82 - DAY 19

0700*	Call the hands
0730	Hands to breakfast
0800*	Out pipes
0805*	Both watches muster on the foredeck
0830*	RAS Party muster on the Poop Deck - pass stern RAS to HMS LEDBURY
0900*	Group planning meeting in Wardroom. Attending - COs RMS ST HELENA, HMS BRECON, HMS LEDBURY plus Flight Cdr, MO, XO, RS & HODs
1000*	Stand easy
1015*	Hands carry on with your work
1130	MN Crew/RN SRs/Watchkeepers to lunch
1145*	Secure, RN JRs to lunch
1300*	Hands carry on with your work
1915*	Duty part of the watch clean up messdecks and flats for Rounds
1930*	Stand by for Rounds
2230*	Pipe down

"PROGRAMME - STOP PRESS. We shall now sail at 0800 Sunday. On sailing RMS ST HELENA intends to carry out engine trials for approximately 2 hours. At 1000 we RV with HMS BRECON and commence RAS trials. On completion (late PM) we RV with HMS LEDBURY and the group will then deploy South."

Note 1 was a repeat of yesterday's Note 1 about the MN crew being "TOO LAX"!!

Note 2 was also for the MN crew and read as follows:- "MN Crew are reminded that the equipment and clothing supplied to them by the RN is on loan only and should be returned at the end of the charter. Failure to do so will mean the individual concerned has to pay for items not returned."

Note 3 informed us that - "IT IS A DISCIPLINARY OFFENCE TO TAKE FOOD from the Galley and Dining Room areas." (Jack helping himself to late night snacks after cabin parties or runs ashore!).

Note 4 informed personnel who would be complementing the Standing RAS Party.

Note 5 was a 'Special Note' that read thus:- "Daily Orders Tombola will commence when we leave Portland. Tickets will be on sale from the Leading Cook in the Galley at 10p per ticket or a sheet of 6 tickets for 50p. (Sale of tickets will be piped). A snowball will be in operation and a set of numbers will appear in Daily Orders each day (10). The POWTR will act as Treasurer." (This was yet another way of aiding communications within the ship. When the snowball started growing, the boys would be fighting each other to read Daily Orders!).

Note 6 reminded us of the meal times and stressed the fact that the times referred to both sea and harbour routines. In the RN, supper in harbour is normally early and a snack, as most people, including the cooks, go home or ashore. At sea it is later and becomes the main meal of the day, with lunch becoming a snack. The limitations on this ship meant the routine would remain the same.

TN - HMS LEDBURY engine change progressing.

St HELLTEM 4/82 gave us more "Advice to Ship's Company". It contained a list of extra general information not fully covered by Daily Orders, eg. Daily Routine and Watchkeeping system, dress, personal equipment, rules for the upper deck in the War Zone, gash (ensuring that everything sunk), securing for action, mail censorship, etc.

"THE SHIP IS UNDER SAILING ORDERS" still.   Yeah, yeah, yeah, heard it all before - they're obviously looking towards knackering up another weekend for us! Most of us went and got pissed again. All this 'goodbye' stuff was costing us a fortune in phone calls, museum entrance fees, overdue library books, beer, wines, spirits, snips, etc. A lot of the boys were going to need a fairly long war to get their plastic cards back in credit! The Flight went home - again!

FSU01's Wasp – the 'Budgie'!

Lest we forget - The battle for Stanley began at Mount Longdon, Mount Harriet and
Two Sisters – 23 Paras and 50 Argentines die.
3 Islanders killed in British bombardment of Port Stanley.

SATURDAY, 12 JUNE 82 - DAY 20

0700*	Call the hands
0730	Hands to breakfast
0800*	Out pipes
0805*	Both watches muster on the foredeck
1000*	Stand easy
1015*	Hands carry on with your work
1100*	Hands secure. Clean into No2s.
1120*	Out pipes
1125*	Clear lower deck. Ship's Company fall in on the Flight Deck for Dedication Service
1130	Inter Denominational Ship Dedication Service on the Flight Deck
o/c	Secure. Hands to dinner
1255*	Duty part of the watch out pipes
1300*	Duty part of the watch turn to, square off the upper deck and secure for sea
1915*	Duty part of the watch clean up messdecks and flats for Rounds
1930*	Stand by for Rounds
2230*	Pipe down

Note 1 read: - "Volunteer/s is/are required to run a Ship's Raffle while we are away. The idea being to raffle a video recorder, with a selection of small prizes (eg. watch, camera, perfume, etc.), leading up to the draw for the VCR. Any offers to the POWTR, who will act as Treasurer."

Note 2 was yet another reminder about 'Power of Attorney' forms being available for people buying or selling houses.

Note 3 stated: - "SECURING FOR SEA - It is everybody's responsibility to ensure that their place of work and living accommodation is properly secured for sea. The RMS St Helena is a very lively lady in the most moderate seas. Make securing for sea your top priority over the next 24 hours. The Buffer will supply cordage for lashings if required." (This sounded ominous and we were still under sailing orders, so we might actually go this time! Nobody now believed this but you had to make the effort!).

Note 4 stated:- "SERVICE OF DEDICATION - Members of the Ship's Company, (RN & MN), may invite family and close friends to join us in our Service of Dedication. This is a traditional Royal Navy Service performed in all newly and re-commissioned ships. Names of guests to the Ship's Office." Note 5 instructed the MN crew what to wear for Note 4. "Officers - Reefer Jackets (Blues) and Crew - White open neck shirts, black trousers and black shoes."

<u>TN</u> - HMS LEDBURY engine change progresses. RMS ST HELENA final top up with victualling stores.

St HELLTEM 5/82 fully covered the "Organisation of Duty Watches". It explained who would keep duties and what the actual duties would consist of, as decided after the trip from Portsmouth. A few changes had to be made to cover the shortcomings discovered! It further explained how a 'communal party' was required for daily work in the Galley, duty watch emergency procedures, bridge sentries, damage control monitors and patrols, lookouts and lifebuoy sentries, SRs' duties, Flight duties, Communications Group duties and duty Stores personnel. This was the updated 'bible' for this subject.

The routine was 'Saturday Harbour'. Another half day off! Getting the afternoon off was a novelty, so just for a change we did the 'going to war' thing and got drunk earlier! You never know we might actually go this time! A lot of beer was drunk and a good time was had by all, I think! I woke up sleeping on the grass in the grounds of the RN Base, HMS OSPREY. I was not alone! Several of my mess members were there too! I lay there looking up at a lovely blue sky, the sun was shining and the birds were singing. England in summer! As I pondered our situation and what the devil had led up to it, I began to feel my aching bones and the headache!
Suddenly a voice shrieked "What bloody time is it?" We were sailing off to war at 0800! Oh my God, it was normally bad enough being adrift when the ship was under sailing orders. But going to war! Nobody had a watch on! (Sailors don't normally carry valuables with them when they go ashore, as mugging is a world wide pastime nowadays). What time was it then? Panic! Had the ship gone? Panic and dread! We started running towards the harbour. As we got onto the road and looked down into the harbour we could see the ship sitting there. Thank God it hadn't gone! It might at any minute though! The relief turned back to panic again and we ran down the hill towards the dockyard. This wasn't doing much for the hangover! We had to keep stopping to get our breath back, but then the panic would take over again and away we went. We raced through the Dockyard Gates with our ID Cards flashing for the MOD Plods, who of course wondered what the emergency was! When we turned the corner the ship was still sitting there but looked extremely quiet! In fact very bloody quiet! In fact - deserted! Not what you would normally acquaint with a ship about to leave harbour on a long trip! We scrambled up the gangway, shocking the QM into wakefuless! "What bloody time is it?" "Half past bloody five" replied the rather upset QM! What a beautiful morning we all thought as we made our way to our beds! Then the headaches and hangovers brought us all back to reality! Funnier things have happened at sea, so they say!

Lest we forget - HMS GLAMORGAN was hit by an Exocet missile (made in
France) – 13 die.
3 Para take Mount Longdon – 6 Paras and 50 Argentines die.
42 Cdo take Mount Harriet.
45 Cdo take Two Sisters.

SUNDAY, 13 JUNE 82 - DAY 21

0700*	Call the hands
0700	Mail closes onboard
0730	Hands to breakfast
0745*	SSD as detailed to your stations
0750*	Forenoon watch on deck and Lifebuoy Sentry close up
0800	Sail from Portland
0800	To 1000. Engine trials
1000*	Stand easy
1015*	Hands carry on with your work
1000	RAS trials with BLACK ROVER - prove reception. Then with HMS BRECON prove abeam and astern refuelling
o/c	RV with HMS LEDBURY and proceed South
1130	MN Crew/RN SRs/Watchkeepers to dinner
1145*	Secure, RN JRs to dinner
1300*	Hands carry on with your work
1915*	Duty part of the watch clean up messdecks and flats for Rounds
1930*	Stand by for Rounds
2230*	Pipe down

"PROGRAMME - Portland to Ascension Island is 3700 miles. At our planned passage speed it will take us approximately 13 days to get there. During this period the Ship's Company will be exercised in all sorts of evolutions eg. Emergency Stations, Abandon Ship Stations, Action Stations, RAS Stations, etc, until it is considered we are worked up enough to look after ourselves in any eventuality that may occur further south. It will be hard work, at times it will be extremely trying, I request everybody to really dig out and try and keep a smile on your face." (Not another 13 in the equation!).

Note 1 reminded nominated personnel to read the memorandum that had been produced concerning Duty Watches for the RN side.

Note 2 read thus:- "FALKLAND VICTUALLING STORES - Yesterday, late evening, we embarked approximately 20 tons of 'Comfort Stores' for the Armed Forces ashore and the Falkland Islanders. These stores are extremely difficult to obtain down south and are considered to be a luxury by those for whom they are intended. The stores are stowed in our holds, cannot be locked up and are easily accessible. I shall consider pilfering of these stores a serious offence in the prevailing circumstances."

Note 3 showed we were still having a lot of integration problems, reading thus:- "From now on Daily Orders will not differentiate orders by adding RN or MN. Daily Orders are for the RMS ST HELENA Ship's Company, that means all of us. It should be obvious within the context of an order to whom it specifically refers."

Note 4 was concerning a subject next to Jack's heart, after his pay and food as already mentioned! It read:- "Mail closes at 0700 today. While the ship is away, mail will be received and sent as often as possible, but it is likely that there will be extended periods where there will be no mail facilities. Depending on operation restrictions and communications, it may be possible to keep in touch with families using the MODMAIL system. A St Helltem will be issued in due course explaining the mail system we will use."

The routine was 'Daily Sea'. At last, we'd done it. The final 'Souls on Board' list had been sent to the Next of Kin Cell in HMS CENTURION and at 0815 we actually sailed, complete with hangovers! The hangover, however, was useful as it took precedence over the feelings of morbidity, panic, excitement, terror, etc, etc, that sailing off to war would normally have caused. After all the various trials had been completed it was time to start playing at warships! On this thing? Sailing on the 13th? With 13 days to go before going ashore again? Having taken nearly three weeks to 'get off the ground'? Thank God I'd got a hangover and wasn't capable of thinking about it!

In the late evening we had 'a bit of a snag'! We had a major fuel leakage in the Engine Room! Luckily, it was found and halted before it developed into something much worse! RN and MN Engine Room personnel worked together and quickly sorted it out. However, again, it didn't help the RN personnel build up their confidence in the conversion of this 'rust bucket' into a warship! In fact, it made us all very nervous!

HMS Brecon practising RASing

Lest we forget - start of the battle for Tumbledown, Wireless Ridge and Mount William – 15 British and 40 Argentines die.

PART THREE

THE TRIP SOUTH

or

SAILING ON THE 13TH - BETTER LATE THAN NEVER!

MONDAY, 14 JUNE 82 - DAY 22

0700*	Call the hands
0730	Hands to breakfast
0800*	Out pipes
0805*	Both watches muster on the foredeck
0845	Flying brief on Bridge
0900	Prepare for flying
0915*	Hands to Flying Stations
0945*	Clear lower deck. Ship's Company muster on the Main Deck for an address by MCM7
1130	MN Crew to Crew Bar to collect ID Cards and tags
1130	MN Crew/RN SRs/Watchkeepers to dinner
1145*	Secure, RN JRs to lunch
1300*	Action Stations
o/c	Abandon ship drill
1915*	Duty part of the watch clean up messdecks and flats for Rounds
1930*	Stand by for Rounds
2230*	Pipe down

Note 1 reminded everybody that "Daily Orders Tombola starts in the next issue of Daily Orders so GET YOUR TICKETS NOW from the Galley."

Note 2 informed us that the "Ship's Laundry will commence operations on Tuesday. All gear is to be clearly marked and handed in to the laundry by 0830."

Note 3 was where we started the serious work! It read thus:- "This afternoon the ship will go to Action Stations. Make sure you all know where your Action Station is, details are on the Watch & Station Bill displayed by the Ship's Office. Anti flash and life jackets should be worn, emergency suits carried by all personnel,"

Note 4 continued the theme - "Abandon Ship Stations. All personnel not on watch or involved in lowering boats, should muster by watches on the main deck."

Note 5 was an exercise in motivation, congratulating us on our previous days work.
"Today we have achieved:- a. RAS abeam starboard side receiving from RFA BLACK ROVER
b. RAS astern replenishing HMS BRECON
c. RAS abeam port side replenishing HMS BRECON
d. Jackstay transfer starboard to HMS BRECON
Well done, today the whole ship's company have completed successfully and creditably all these complicated evolutions, thank you."

TN - FLYEX; Exercises for Action Stations, Emergency Stations and Abandon Ship.

Well, as you can see, things had now changed. It was all starting to get serious. The routine was 'Daily Sea' now - how long before that changed again? Now there was no going ashore, no going home, exercises at all times of day and night and work, work, work. Our main source of amusement in an evening at sea, when not working of course, was the movies. Our first night's offerings were:- "JRs - 'The Wild Geese', Wardroom/SRs - 'The Island', MN Crew - 'Crescendo'.

My bit of 'good news' for the day was the position of my Emergency Stations! Along with a couple of St Helenian crewmen, I was to position myself in amongst the AVCAT stowage, underneath the Flight Deck! (There was no room for a sensible AVCAT stowage so the drums had been lashed together on the deck below the new Flight Deck!). Our job was to put out fires, etc, which would threaten the AVCAT! For those who don't know - aviation fuel is extremely delicate and highly flammable! Just the place to be, especially if we had a helicopter 'crash on deck'! What about 'Health & Safety in the Workplace'! I certainly wasn't being paid the correct rates for this job! Sitting on a huge potential bomb with a hose pipe in my hand. Wonderful, I must have upset somebody to get this one!

During the day I shut the window (big square porthole!) to my office and secured it for war! A large piece of metal was then welded over it and sunlight became a thing of the past! The Purser was most upset to find he couldn't see out of the window now!

Another little high spot of the day occurred that night as we were trying to sleep. It had got a bit rough and we were moving about a bit, when a strange knocking sound took our attention. It appeared to be coming from the heads. The noise quickly developed into a 'dull clank! Eventually we gave up and went to investigate. We found the toilet bowl had come loose from the deck. This appeared to be caused by old age and rust - the bolts holding it to the deck had disintegrated! We secured it for the night and went to sleep, eventually. The rust bucket theory took on a whole new life!

Lest we forget - 2 Para enter Port Stanley.
                  Argentine forces surrender in Port Stanley only after various
                  successful attacks on them (General Mario Menendez).
                  (The day some spotty Civil Servant in MOD London decreed that
                  this war had finished).

TUESDAY, 15 JUNE 82 - DAY 23

0001	Clocks retarded 1 hour - 'Z' time. We shall remain in 'Z' time, (Greenwich Mean Time), until Ascension Island
0700*	Call the hands
0730	Hands to breakfast
0800*	Out pipes
0805*	Both watches muster on the Fore Deck
0900* - 1100	STBD RAS + VERTREP
1130	RN SRs & Watchkeepers to dinner
1145*	Secure, RN JRs to dinner
1300*	Hands carry on with your work
1330 - 1600	Close up HQ2 and Forward DC Party - Section Training
1630	Fire Exercise
1915*	Duty Part of the watch clean up messdecks and flats for Rounds
1930*	Stand by for Rounds
2200* - 2330	Night FLYEX
2230*	Pipe down

Note 1 was for the technical types - "Any department that requires lead acid batteries filled or charged, contact the FSU01 MSM Module on the starboard side Fore Deck."

Note 2 was war bits - "Any personnel without Identity Tags and Geneva Convention ID Cards contact the RPO in the Ship's Office. The Identity Tags are to be worn around the neck at all times, day and night. The Geneva Convention Identity Cards and the Rules Sheet are to be placed in the plastic wallet and sealed to make a waterproof envelope. These are to be carried on your person at all times. The rules for the use of the Identity Cards are set out at the top of the card." (So now we'd got our dog tags round our necks permanently!).

Note 3 was sorting out problems from the day before's exercises:- "As a result of yesterdays internal exercises valuable lessons have been learnt. Some changes have had to be made to the Watch & Quarter Bill, therefore ensure that you double check your stations." (In short this meant that it had been a complete shambles and Plan B was now in operation!).

Note 4 was a bit of good news:- "The Ship's Shop will be opened on a daily basis from 1000 - 1030 and 1730 - 1830."

Note 5 was a bit of the other! - "Haircuts - 1930 to 2030 in the Surgery - Price 50p." (What an appropriate place!).

Note 6 was of great significance and importance! Something to look forward to every day, something that brought a purpose to living! (Nowadays, of course, we have the Lottery!). - "AND NOW - WHAT YOU'VE ALL BEEN WAITING FOR - THE FIRST TEN NUMBERS FOR THE TOMBOLA, DRAWN BY THE SNO:-
21, 88, 15, 14, 61, 66, 87, 51, 70, 26.
PRIZES:- Line - £6, House - £15, Snowball - £6, Welfare - £3, TOTAL - £30.
Claims for line to Ship's Office by 1200 today. The SNOWBALL will be claimable if you get a house within or including the first 40 numbers drawn."
(This may all seem a little silly, grown men playing bingo, but it gave a lot of people a little pleasure during long arduous days at sea! Little things like this all helped to take their minds off more ominous goings on!).

TN - AM - RAS/VERTREP
     PM - DCX, Night FLYEX

St HELLTEM 6/82 about "Compartment Kill Cards" was issued. This was a collection of cards containing detailed firefighting and damage control information for each compartment on the ship. It showed what firefighting gear was in the vicinity, what machinery, etc, etc, was in or near to the compartment. This was obviously of great value to firefighters in the dark fighting fires and several copies were held in different firefighting locations throughout the ship.

The Fire Exercise (DCX) was a cracker! It made the RN types really appreciate life on a 'grey job'! RN warships are sectioned and compartmented within decks and access is only through securable doors or hatches. So if one compartment or whatever is hit it can be closed down and the ship can survive. Also other compartments can be closed down to maintain stability etc, seats of fires can be isolated and flooded etc, etc. At certain levels of activity the ship can be closed down and access can only be through closed doors and hatches. This means the ship has a lot more chance of survival if bombed, torpedoed, rammed, etc. The curtains in the passages of this ship didn't seem to have the same effect, somehow?!

YOMP MARINES

Lest we forget - Argentine forces in outlying settlements surrender.
          Port Stanley shop destroyed by Argentine arsonist!

WEDNESDAY, 16 JUNE 82 - DAY 24

0700*	Call the hands
0730	Hands to breakfast
0745*	Time check
0755*	Out pipes
0800*	Both watches muster on the Fore Deck
0900 - 1000	NAVCOMEX Drill (RAS sequence by flags)
1000	Emergency Steering Procedures
1000*	Stand Easy
1015*	Hands carry on with your work
1130	RN SRs/Watchkeepers to dinner
1145*	Secure. RN JRs to dinner
1300*	Hands carry on with your work
1300*	Standing Fire Party muster on the Flight Deck for briefing
1345*	Brief for FLYEX
1400*	Prepare for flying
1415*	Hands to Flying Stations
1430 - 1600	FLYEX
1300 - 1315	Exercise Crash on Deck
1455	All 20mm Gun Crews muster by Starboard Oerlikon forward
1500 - 1600	20mm Non Firing Drills
1900*	First Dog Watchmen clean up messdecks and flats for Rounds
1925*	Stand by for Rounds
2000	JRs' Movie - "Star Trek"
2100	Wardroom/SRs' Movie - "Super Cops"
2200 - 2359	Night Screen Ex - No Radar/ Nav Lights
2300*	Pipe down
2315	Flying Brief
2330*	Prepare for flying
2345*	Hands to Flying Stations
0001 - 0130	FLYEX

"PROGRAMME - Now that Argentina has surrendered in the Falklands, our presence is required at Stanley as soon as possible to start our minehunting role. As yet we have received no firm instructions that modify our original orders. However, it is proposed by CINCFLEET that a minesweeping headquarters be established in RMS ST HELENA, that will assume duties as Mine Counter Measures (MCM) Commander Falkland Islands. The HQ Staff will probably consist of 1 Cdr, 2 Lt Cdrs, 1 Lt, 1 FCPO, and 2 SRs. This team would control the Minesweeping/Minehunting effort in the Falklands."

Note 1 was about Jack shooting himself in the foot again on the domestic front! - "The Tea/Coffee Boat stores in the night pantry are being withdrawn due to high consumption and the state the pantry is being left in. An urn of coffee or tea will be available in the pantry at Stand Easy and Watch on Deck will receive night issues. The watch on deck is responsible for cleaning the pantry before the end of the watch."

Note 2 was justifying the existence of the 'ship's policeman'! - "The RPO is now the Transfer Liaison Co-ordinator. He is to be informed of all passengers and stores required to be transferred to/from ships in company and will liaise with the Flight/CBM."

Note 3 was nice for those interested in that sort of thing:- "There will be opportunities for casual flights for both RN and MN crews during the passage. Anyone interested should see the Aircrewman."

Note 4 - Now the bad news! - "Hot Water - The ship is not capable of coping with the hot water demands of 105 ship's company all showering within a short period of time. To conserve hot water when showering, switch off the shower after you are wet, soap up, switch on, rinse off quickly, switch off. Nobody should require more than 1.5 minutes for a shower. If we are not more conscious in conserving the use of hot water, rationing will have to be initiated."

Note 5 was a BZ! - "Well done RAS teams:- 31 mins each ship - Fuel passed = 7 tons to HMS BRECON and 12 tons to HMS LEDBURY."

Note 6 was to let us know that summer was really going to hot up! - "Air Conditioning - all scuttles and screen doors are to be closed by 1200 today when the air conditioning will be switched on."

Note 7 was back to war stuff - "Result of our first darken ship exercise on Monday night showed only 4 light leaks:-
a. Compass Binnacle - Monkey Island (Roof of the Bridge)
b. Air conditioning intake - Stbd side funnel on 'E' Deck
c. Chef's Cabin - 'D' Deck Port side
d. RN Cabin B10 on 'B' Deck
The next darken ship exercise will be 2200 to 2359 tonight."

Note 8 read - "Tombola numbers drawn by the Ship's Master:-
13, 19, 67, 42, 24, 81, 7, 36, 80, 84.
Claims for line to Ship's Office by 1200 today."

TN - AM - NAVCOMEX, Steering Gear breakdowns
    PM - FLYEX, Exercise Crash on Deck, Gunnex

St HELLTEM 7/82 detailed off the "Standing Fire Party". It explained their individual duties and nominated the personnel concerned for the Control Group, Attack Party, Support Party, Containment Group and Electrical Party. It also explained the responsibilities of various duty personnel. This was a vital organ within the ship and was treated thus. My job was with the Containment Group.

Also today, St HELLTEM 8/82 explained the 'Naval Discipline Act' in an attempt to alleviate a few problems! It read - "A state of 'Active Service' was declared by the British Government, duration 3 months from 15 May 82, for all forces, service and civilian between latitudes 7 South and 60 South. This is roughly from and including Ascension Island to the Falkland Islands. The purpose of this declaration is to enhance operational efficiency by ensuring that all personnel involved in Operation Corporate are subject to one over-riding code of conduct. The principal practical effect is that civilian personnel in RN ships, RFAs and Merchant Ships attached to the Task Force within the declared area become fully subject to the Naval Discipline Act (NDA) vide NDA Section 118(1). MN personnel in ships that are subject are now under dual jurisdiction, as they also remain subject to the jurisdiction of their Ship's Masters who retain their disciplinary powers given by the Merchant Shipping Acts. The intention is for MN personnel to remain subject to their Ship's Masters jurisdiction under the Merchant Shipping Act for day to day discipline. The additional powers of the NDA only being used where necessary for the Operational Efficiency of the Task Force. Attention is drawn to Forms S282 (Articles of War) displayed outside the Ship's Office and outside the Ship's Shop. RN personnel appointed to RFAs or Merchant Ships are to comply with any instructions given to them by, or with the authority of, the Master for the proper working or management of the ship. Any breach of this regulation may be dealt with as conduct to the prejudice of good order and Naval Discipline under the Act." (Interesting stuff, eh?).

Then we had St HELLTEM 9/82, "Divisional Organisation". This detailed the Officers and Senior Rates tending the 6 divisions. (Flight, FSU SRs, FSU JRs, Medical, SRs and JRs). This was the RN's answer to looking after the troops, since various mutinies had forced their hand in years gone by!

Last but not least we had St HELLTEM 10/82 a "Survival Questionnaire". This gave us all some wonderful bedtime reading! It read - "This memorandum is issued for guidance if the worst should come to pass. Make sure you know the answers!!" Just the sort of morale booster we needed! Anyway, this is a condensed version. "On abandoning ship wear as much clothing as possible, your lifejacket and once only suit. You can wear the once only suit over the lifejacket but ensure the drawstring is drawn tight. Inflate your lifejacket fully as a partially filled lifejacket can cause injury and allow the head to flop forward underwater if unconscious. Don't jump onto a liferaft - you can injure yourself and others already on the raft, as well as damaging the raft. The first reactions on boarding a lifeboat are to cut the painter, stream the sea anchor when clear of the ship, close the door in cold climates and maintain the raft, checking for leaks, etc. The four principles of survival in this order are:- protection from the elements, check location aids and how they work, check water supplies and collect rain water if possible in saddle bags provided and finally ration yourselves to 2 packets of food per man per day. Do not eat seabirds, fish, etc, unless water is plentiful. Life rafts are fitted with Solas and Sarbe radios and each raft has six day/night flares and a heliograph mirror. Food and water supplies will last three days if rationed and started after 24 hours. (Injured people may start earlier). You are allowed 1 can (1 pint) of water per man per day with rainwater supplements. The duties of the senior person on the raft are to read the survival handbook, maintain discipline, have a roll call, set duties and routines, keep up morale. To keep the raft cool in warm climates douse water over the canopy and attach the sea anchor to lifeline adjacent to door to allow breezes into the raft. Three medical problems may occur - Hypothermia (exposure) - huddle together and keep warm; Immersion Foot (Trench Foot) - keep liferaft as dry as possible, empty water out of once only suit and elevate feet on central thwart; Frostbite - in cold windy conditions lookouts spend 15 mins max on watch and are checked by others on return inside the raft, numb or dull white areas treat with gentle warmth of others hands or body, don't rub or pat. If the raft is warm and dry you may take your once only suit off to distribute body heat and prevent sweating. In a full raft ventilate every half hour for 5 mins and to prevent CO_2 build up open the door only. Liferafts are launched thus: - check painter/operating line is attached to the ship, turn lever on hydrostatic release to left or right, push raft over the side, haul in on 85 ft operating line. Given time put extra clothing, blankets, water and 'nutty' type food in the raft. The floor of the liferaft is the only part which has to be manually inflated using the bellows. Etc, etc, etc."
(All good stuff, eh?).

Nobody really knew if the Argies had given up but the whole picture suddenly looked a bit rosier. Mind you it could only get better, couldn't it?! Goodness me it had been a busy old day!

Lest we forget - Defence Minister of State announces 255 British dead and
                  approximately 300 wounded.

THURSDAY, 17 JUNE 82 - DAY 25

0100	Night Screenex ends
0700*	Call the hands
0730	Hands to breakfast
0745*	Time check
0755*	Out pipes
0800*	Both watches muster on the Fore Deck
0815*	Flying Brief
0830*	Prepare for flying
0845*	Hands to Flying Stations
0900 - 1100	STBD RAS + VERTREP
1000*	Stand easy
1015*	Hands carry on with your work
1100 - 1200	Zigzag - 2 zigzag combined
1130	RN SRs/Watchkeepers to dinner
1145*	Secure, RN JRs to dinner
1300*	Hands carry on with your work
1300	Boat Transfer (TX) - MO to HMS BRECON (Medical Training)
1400 - 1500	V/S Exercise
1515*	Flying brief
1530*	Prepare for flying
1545*	Hands to Flying Stations
1600 - 1800	FLYEX o/c SOOTAX - MO from HMS BRECON
1600 - 1800	Visual Signalling (Light)
1900*	First Dog Watchmen clean up messdecks and flats for rounds
1925*	Stand by for Rounds
2115*	Flying brief
2130*	Prepare for flying
2145*	Hands to Flying Stations
2200	MN crew movie - "The Island"
2200 - 2359	FLYEX - HMS BRECON Guide - RMS ST HELENA to remain within 2 nautical miles of HMS BRECON

Note 1 was a bit of marketing from the Purser:- "SPECIAL SHOPPING NEWS - Today, on sale at the shop, is a full selection of 'T' Shirts & Sweat Shirts of RMS ST HELENA and Falkland Islands. Shopping times - 1000 to 1030 and 1730 to 1830. BUY NOW AND DON'T BE DISAPPOINTED."

Note 2 read:- "Cold water is plentiful at present. There is no restriction of the use of it." (What can you say, the pure luxury of it! Eat your heart out Kent and Essex!).

Note 3 was the law at work again:- "As some of you may have noticed 3 RN Ratings have had their hair cropped. This was done by a member of the crew in the Crew's Quarters. There are to be no more funny or exceptionally short haircuts amongst RN Crew Members. The Ship's Company are reminded that the Crew's Quarters on 'A' Deck are out of bounds to all RN personnel. Contravention of this order has already resulted in disciplinary action being taken."

Note 4 was for those with time on their hands! It read:- "For anyone wishing to use the ship's exercise bicycle, see the POMA." (Fitness was now very important with not knowing what the future held in store. So jogging on the Flight Deck and exercising were being done whenever possible, just in case! With all the work, it also helped you to unwind after a day at the office! However, the size of the Flight Deck was not conducive to long periods of jogging. It was so small that you could only run in circles and this put a strain on your ankles, because your body weight was on one leg all the time. It was, however, better than nothing!).

Note 5 gave us our first winner on the Tombola - A WE type would you believe, what a waste of good money! It read:- "Tombola numbers were drawn by one of the Mechanicians. They were 54, 71, 77, 3, 44, 45, 72, 46, 10, 69. Claims for the house and snowball to the Ship's Office by 12 noon today. The line, for £6, had been claimed by an LWEM(O) on the 20th number out." (Mechanicians later became 'Tiffs' (Artificers), in one of the RN's many cost cutting exercises. They didn't like that much!).

TN - AM - RAS/VERTREP, Zigzag Ex.
     PM - Boat Transfer, 2 x VS Ex, FLYEX - SOOTAX.

'Dress of the Day' gave us a choice of normal No8s or No10As (blue shorts and sandals). It was getting hotter. It was also my second duty today. At sea there wasn't much to it! You accompanied the OOD on Evening Rounds at 1930, normally a pretty boring task, however, it kept the boys on their toes and stopped them getting into bad habits! We inspected all the JRs' cabins, communal areas, passages, offices, etc, to ensure they were clean and tidy, also that all the JRs were in the correct rig. You also did security rounds at various times, ensuring there were no secure offices or workshops left open, no fires or other problems. As I completed the security rounds and looked out to sea, I had plenty to think about. These rounds reminded me of my days as a copper shaking door handles, in the middle of the night, in the Town Centre at Lytham. Now there was just one place I'd rather be than here!

Lest we forget - Argentine President Galtieri resigns.

FRIDAY, 18 JUNE 82 - DAY 26

0700*		Call the hands
0730		Hands to breakfast
0745*		Time check
0755*		Out pipes
0800*		Both watches muster on the Fore Deck
0900		HQ1, HQ2, Forward DC Comms Number close up - DC COMEX
0930		NBCDX - respirators and lifejackets to be carried (See Note1)
1130		RN SRs/Watchkeepers to dinner
1145*		Secure. RN JRs to dinner
1300*		Hands carry on with your work
1330 - 1500		RAS approaches for RMS ST HELENA, HMS BRECON guide
1500 - 1600		GPMG Small Arms Shoot (No target)
1515*		Flying brief
1530*		Prepare for flying
1545*		Hands to Flying Stations
1600 - 1800		FLYEX
1800 - 1900		NAVCOMEX towing sequence by Inter Code Flags
1900 - 2000		V/S Exercise
1900*		First Dog Watchmen clean up messdecks and flats for Rounds
1925*		Stand by for Rounds
2000		JRs' Movie - "Ashanti"
2115*		Flying Brief
2130*		Prepare for flying
2145*		Hands to Flying Stations
2200 - 2359		FLYEX. HMS LEDBURY guide. RMS ST HELENA to remain within 2 nautical miles of HMS BRECON

Note 1 started us off again with war stuff:- "NBCDX - Anti flash and flame resistant overalls rapidly lose their ability to protect you if they become contaminated by oil. Therefore, they are not to be worn during Damage Control Exercises. Once-only/survival suits are not to be carried during exercises to prevent them being damaged."

Note 2 was a lot better:- "Barbeque - On Saturday evening we shall hold a barbeque on the Flight Deck to entertain the X-polls." (These are visitors from other ships and are known as being cross-pollinated!). "Volunteers for cabaret acts to Purser Catering Officer. Rig will be relaxed (?). An extra issue of 2 cans of beer will be authorised at 1800." (My goodness, the debauchery of it all!).

Note 3 explained:- "Cross-Polling - 7 volunteers (preferably JRs) are required to visit HMS BRECON and HMS LEDBURY this weekend from 1100 Saturday to 1000 Sunday for a social visit. Names to the RPO as soon as possible."

Note 4 went domestic:- "Laundry - Do not leave laundry unattended in the tumble dryers. Any laundry discovered unattended is to be handed in to the RPO who will place it in the Scranbag. To recover an item from the Scranbag will cost the current Ship's Laundry charge per item. Proceeds to an Orphanage to be named."

Note 5, the law! "Dress - During working hours the correct dress of the day is to be worn. Cowboy combinations are not permitted eg. flip flops, trainers, gymshoes, emblazoned 'T' shirts, etc." (Still some 'cruisers' about, obviously).

Note 6 the law again! "Sunbathing - As bronzie weather approaches, ship's company are advised that it is the responsibility of every individual to avoid sunburn. Initial sunbathing should be no longer than forty minutes to an hour, less if fair skinned. Remember with shirts off on the upper deck the wind gives a false impression of coolness, you will burn if over exposed. To be incapacitated by sunburn is a disciplinary offence."

Note 7 yet more law! "It is apparent walking around the ship that the past few days of fine weather have lulled us all into a false sense of security. There is still far too much expensive equipment and gear sculling about on and between decks. Ship's company are advised that any gear lost or damaged through negligence caused by sloppy securing for sea will initiate individual C126 action. Ensure that everything is secured for sea, particularly during mealtimes and after secure."

Note 8 read:- "Tombola numbers today were drawn by one of the St Helenian crewmen:- 35, 1, 75, 65, 73, 41, 63, 57, 29, 28.
The underlined number is the last one for the snowball (40 numbers). Any claims for the house/snowball to the Ship's Office by 1200 today."

Note 9 equalled Day 10's record of 9 notes in one day! It read:- "MN Crew are requested to meet the Purser in the Crew Lounge this morning at 1130 to sign forms in connection with NI & IT UK."

TN - AM - DC Comex, NBCDX
       PM - RAS Apps, Gunnex, Night FLYEX, Night VS Exercise

St HELLTEM 11/82 about "SNO's Rounds" really blighted our weekends from now on! Rather than letting us rest after our labours, they liked to keep us on our toes with this sort of thing! "Starting Saturday, 26 June 82, mess deck rounds will take place every Saturday whilst the ship is at sea. The route will be as follows:- SRs' Mess, Cabin 26, 'C' Deck Toilet, 'C' Deck Pantry, JRs' Mess, Laundry, 'B' Deck JRs' cabins, Ship's Office. The senior rating in each cabin is responsible for ensuring that the cabin is clean for rounds and is reported to the Officer conducting rounds. The President of the SRs' Mess and the Leading Hand of the JRs' Mess should report their messes. The ratings detailed to clean Flats and Pantries are to report the areas they have cleaned. The POMA is responsible for reporting the Laundry." (At least we'll have a clean war!?).

'Dress of the Day' put everybody into blue shorts and sandals today. It was always a great sight to see. All those white legs, strange length shorts (Stanley Matthews style for those who remember!) and those bloody awful pusser's sandals! Until they were worn in, they gave you the most horrendous blisters. However, all the exercises in full action rig were now a different story as it got hotter. Running around in this heat in full action gear wasn't funny. We had to remember that when we got to the Falklands it would be winter, so it would all change again soon!

In mid-afternoon, as I passed by the Officers' cabins, I was confronted by a wonderful apparition! Fresh out of his bed and barely awake; purple overalls open down the front to his waist revealing his very hairy chest and macho gold chains; glass and bottle of tonic in one hand and ice bucket (with ice) in the other; with the query "Hi, Scribes, where's this afternoon's cabin party?" This filled one with confidence for our future, as this was the Chief Engineer! He must have gone down a treat as a 'Macho Sailor' with the ladies on the normal cruises! They obviously had a tough time of it these MN Officers! However, they'll come in handy if ever we have an official Cocktail Party onboard! This should have been a joke but as you'll see later it bloody wasn't! Purple bloody overalls, I ask you!?

Boss of the flight deck with his team hard at work!!!

Hunter RASing with 'Mother Goose'!

SATURDAY, 19 JUNE 82 - DAY 27

0001	- 0200	SCREENEX - Red shaded V/S
0700*		Call the hands
0730		Hands to breakfast
0745*		Time check
0755*		Out pipes
0800*		Both watches muster on the Fore Deck
0900	- 1100	STBD RAS (No VERTREP)
1000*		Stand easy
1015*		Hands carry on with your work
1100		Boat TX for stores and CROSSPOL
1130		RN SRs/Watchkeepers to dinner
1145*		Secure. RN JRs to dinner
1300	- 1400	20mm + GPMG shoot
PM		Prepare Flight Deck for Barbeque
1930		Barbeque

"PROGRAMME - We should arrive at Ascension Island next Sunday 26 June 82. Operationally we have achieved a great deal but a lot is still required if we are to achieve the minimum operational requirement. Well done so far, big effort next week. It's balls-aching but necessary."

Note 1 was a Royal BZ:- "PERSONAL FROM CINC - I have had the honour to receive the following message from Her Majesty the Queen and pass it to you all with great pleasure:- "I send my warmest congratulations to you and to all under your command for the splendid way in which you have achieved the liberation of the Falkland Islands. Britain is very proud of the way you have served your country." Signed Elizabeth R.".

Note 2 was back to our war games:- "Damage Control Exercise - Generally good, many useful lessons were learnt. It still took too long for reports to reach the bridge on closing up at action stations. Ship knowledge still needs to be improved. Procedures are being amended and will be practiced in further DCXs next week. We must get it right by Ascension."

Note 3 was something else to keep the troops amused:- "Designs are required for a Ship's Company crest, (incorporating - RMS ST HELENA, RNP2100, Falkland Islands Task Force, FSU01, etc.). Entries to the RPO, there will be a prize for the winner. The design can then be used for the following:- ties, 'V' neck jumpers, sweat tops, 'T' shirts. Check off lists will be sent round the messes for provisional orders of the above articles. If sufficient numbers are interested, a full order will be sent off."

Note 4 - not this old gag again! - "There is a NO SMOKING RULE throughout the whole ship, except in accommodation spaces and offices. Disciplinary action will now be taken against offenders."

Note 5 - the house goes on! - "Tombola numbers drawn by a member of the Flight were:- 82, 58, 76, 53, 90, 83, 59, 5, 31, 47. Claims for house to Ship's Office by 1200 today. Snowball not claimed, the £6 goes forward to next week."

St HELLTEM 12/82 about "Recreation and Entertainments" was produced explaining the whole sphere of leisure-time activities. A condensed version read:- "For physical training and outdoor activities the following facilities and equipment are available:- Bullworker, chest expanders, swingball, horseshoes, fishing rods, fishing lines, bicycle & rollers, exercise bicycle, volleyball and volleyball coaching, skeet shooting and .22 rifle shooting and karate. Indoor games are available:- Backgammon, Scrabble, Dover Patrol, Ludo, Buccaneer, Cluedo, Wembley, Yahtzee, Monopoly, Othello, Poker Dice, Draughts, Chess, etc. Educationally, the Ship's Library will open 1000 to 1030 daily, a linguaphone and a micro computer are also available. Films and videos will be shown throughout the week. Inter-Mess Entertainment is also being planned. This will include the St Helena Challenge Trophy. A continuing competition, the initial holders of the trophy will be decided by a four way crib match to be held on Sunday, 20 June 82 at 1400 in the JRs' Mess (WR, SRs, JRs, MN Crew). Challengers for the Trophy will then be chosen in rotation and the competition will be run as follows:- The holders will host the challenge, the challengers will name the game and the rules, which must be agreed before start of play. Any disagreements will be arbitrated by the Entertainments Committee. Any outdoor or indoor game may be chosen and the challenge must be made within 2 days of the last one or the challengers lose their place in the rota. The challengers may not choose an event which they have previously chosen as challengers. Any mess holding the trophy following four consecutive challenges will be awarded a crate of beer."

The routine was 'SATURDAY SEA' with a BBQ! Tropical seas, sun, flying fish, dolphins, sharks, whales - pure luxury! The Purser took charge of the entertainment, as he normally did on the cruises, so along with his expertise and Jack's natural ability to perform - a very good night was had by all! No trouble getting to sleep tonight!

HMS Ledbury practising RASing

Lest we forget - Argentine prisoners-of-war landed in Argentina by CANBERRA after being granted 'safe passage'!

SUNDAY, 20 JUNE 82 - DAY 28

0700*	Call the hands
0730	Hands to breakfast
0815*	Time check
0825*	Out pipes
0830*	Both watches muster on the Fore Deck
0930*	Secure
1000	Boat TX - return CROSSPOL teams
1045	Church Service in Forward Lounge
1100*	Pipe down
1130	Hands to dinner
1900*	First Dog Watchmen clean up messdecks and flats for Rounds
1925*	Stand by for Rounds

Note 1 showed that today was definitely a rest day. 'Tombola' had been promoted to Note 1 and the house still hadn't been claimed! "Tombola numbers drawn by the Purser were 89, 23, 55, 4, 62, 86, 17, 37, 52, 33, 34, 6, 22, 60, 38. Claims for the house to the Ship's Office by 1200 today. Tickets for next week are now on sale from the Galley at 50p per sheet. Buy now to avoid disappointment."

Note 2 was domestic:- "Drinking glasses are NOT to be left in the water IN THE SINK in the Servery."

Note 3 was legal! "Volleyball, deck tennis, etc, are played at your own risk - be careful as feet/ankles may easily be injured due to deck projections." (This was pusser ensuring they didn't waste good money from the budget for compensation!).

Note 4 was different! "The 3rd Mate has offered to start a PHOT FIRM, taking portraits in black and white to send home to mums, aunts, girlfriends, wives, etc. Cost - 7" x 5" Portrait 50p. Sitting by appointment, 10p to Welfare Fund."

TN - AM - Return CROSSPOL boat transfer.

So today we only worked for an hour as the routine was 'Sunday Sea'. So we were actually getting some more time off! This was standard RN practice to get you out of bed on a Sunday so you didn't waste the whole day sleeping! We had a pleasant day in the sun recovering from the BBQ hangover!

Lest we forget - British forces re-take Southern Thule (South Sandwich Islands) after Argentine surrender.
Britain FORMALLY declares end of hostilities (NOT Argentines).
Argentines still hold SAS/SBS prisoners.

MONDAY, 21 JUNE 82 - DAY 29

0700*		Call the hands
0730		Hands to breakfast
0745*		Time check
0755*		Out pipes
0800*		Both watches muster on the Fore Deck
0830*		Flying brief
0845*		Prepare for flying
0900*		Hands to Flying Stations
0900	- 1100	STBD RAS/VERTREP (CORPEN N Exercised)
1000*		Stand easy
1015*		Hands carry on with your work
o/c	- 1200	OOW Manoeuvres
1130		SRs/Watchkeepers to dinner
1145*		Secure, JRs to dinner
1245*		Flying brief
1300*		Hands carry on with your work
1300*		Prepare for flying
1315*		Hands to Flying Stations
1330	- 1500	FLYEX (Helo ditch HMS LEDBURY as crash boat)
1500	- 1600	Stream Astern RAS prove MODS
1600	- 1800	NBCDX
1900*		First dog watchmen clean up messdecks and flats for Rounds
1925*		Stand by for Rounds
1930*		Flying brief
2000*		Prepare for flying
2000		JRs' Movie - "Willard"
2000		Darken ship
2015*		Hands to Flying Stations
2030	- 2200	Night FLYEX
2200		MN Crew Movie - "Wild Geese"
2200	- 0100	SCREENEX (No lights/radar/darken ship)
2300*		Pipe down

Note 1 was mixed effort:- "All our thanks to the Chief Purser Catering/Galley Staff for the well organised BBQ on Saturday evening. We achieved the aim of having a relaxing evening and providing R & R to members of HMS BRECON/HMS LEDBURY on X-polls. Unfortunately one minor incident marred the evening and has been dealt with, I am pleased to say the offender was not a member of RNP 2100. Thank you all for entertaining our guests."

Note 2 was war work:- "Damage Control - The following lessons were learnt during the recent fighting:- anti-flash hoods should now be tucked inside clothing and a respirator will give you up to 90 seconds protection in a smoke filled compartment."

Note 3 was a reminder for the gambling fraternity that:- "Week 2 of the Tombola starts on tomorrow's Daily Orders. Have you got your tickets yet?"

TN - AM - RAS/VERTREP, OOW Manoeuvres
     PM - FLYEX, NBCDX, Night FLYEX, Screenex

As can be seen from the above, we were back to the normal working day with a vengeance! I solved a little mystery today. We had been eating salad since we left, which was not usual for us RN types, so I made a few enquiries and found we had a small refrigerated container full of lettuce and salad gear which was normally used on the cruises. Nobody had bothered about it so it had been filled up as normal. So not all the luxuries had been binned!

Since the RNP2100 had been formed a month ago, we'd had our fair share of 'buzzes' around the ship. On Day 9 the SNO had actually had to mention this in Daily Orders! However, it had not stopped, it had increased! Normally you could expect the odd 'buzz' from Jack but we were getting non-stop rumours flying about and nobody could understand why. A few days ago I had found the 'ship's policeman', with whom I shared the Ship's Office, going through my trays of work! They contained classified and 'In Confidence' material. This was paperwork that I had to work on but was not allowed to talk about to other members of the ship's company! Reports that had been in my tray had soon become common knowledge, so a few discreet enquiries were made and it was found that the 'Ratcatcher' was 'buzz-mongering'! I informed the bosses that because of the nature of the work I was now doing, I needed privacy and the ability to lock up my office when I wasn't in it! This was agreed and they decided the RPO was to move out of the Ship's Office and work from his cabin, where a temporary office would be built for him. Today, he moved out of my office and funnily enough, after that, the number of 'buzzes' dropped amazingly!

Some of the flight hard at work again!

TUESDAY, 22 JUNE 82 - DAY 30

0700*	Call the hands
0730	Hands to breakfast
0745*	Time check
0755*	Out pipes
0800*	Both watches muster on the Fore Deck. Hands as detailed clean flats and passageways. Paint Fore Deck with non-slip paint.
1000*	Stand easy
1015*	Hands carry on with your work
1130	SRs/Watchkeepers to dinner
1145*	Secure, JRs to dinner
1900*	First Dog Watchmen clean messdecks and flats for Rounds
1925*	Stand by for Rounds
2100	WR/SRs' Movie "Crescendo"
2300*	Pipe down

Note 1 was a BZ - "RAS Teams - A good RAS was had by all BUT now we all know our jobs we must not get complacent. Concentration is required to avoid errors which may result in serious injuries."

Note 2 was domestic:- "The Ice Machine has been unlocked for a trial period. If the ice continues to disappear by the bucketful the machine will be re-locked."

Note 3 read thus:- "Amended Ship's Shop times:- Daily 1000 – 1030/1700 - 1800." (The Purser had been having difficulty manning the shop along with all his other duties!? He claimed he needed help, so I volunteered. It got me out of the office for a break, so it wasn't all bad! There isn't a sadder sight than a queue of matelots waiting for their nutty in a morning and the shop shutter failing to lift! They were then required to return to work with nothing to aid their 'recovery'!

Note 4 was the first feedback from Day 27's St HELLTEM 12/82 on "Recreation and Entertainment". It read:- "Challenge Trophy - Winners of the Crib Match were the JRs. The first challengers are the MN Crew who should have made a challenge by today, the competition then taking place by Thursday."

Note 5 informed us that:- "Designs for the Ship's Crest Competition are to be handed in to the Ship's Office by 1600 today."

Note 6 was an exceptional bit of legislation that even now still makes me laugh:- "The Monkey Island (Bridge Roof) is for use by Officers and Stewardesses only, except during RASs when the RO(T) and MA close up." (See further comments below!).

Note 7 published the first Tombola house winners and started number two session:- "Tombola numbers for the start of Week 2 were drawn by an SR from FSU01:- 34, 21, 2, 59, 26, 66, 45, 63, 1, 9. Claims for the line to the Ship's Office by 1200 today. House for last week was won jointly by an MN Officer and a RNP2100 SR, on the 61st number out = £7.50 each. This week's prizes are:- Line £8, House £20, Snowball(41) £14, Welfare £4."

<u>TN</u> - Clean ship, paint decks.

Today they started telling us where we actually were in the world! A note was included at the top of Daily Orders stating:- "Estimated position at noon - 11 deg 37 min North, 17 deg 48 min West. Cape Roxo in Senegal is 80 miles NE." This helped to keep you sane, when everyday all you could see was mile after mile of water in all directions! Yet another attempt at keeping the troops happy and interested!

The reasoning behind note six was that the stewardesses sunbathed there! They were obviously regarded as 'safe' in their bikinis in the presence of the Wardroom! Who was trying to kid who? However, this may be a pointer to why we suddenly had to have the WRNS at sea in later years!? Surely it would have been a big boost for the troops morale, if they had been allowed to watch the stewardesses sunbathe, as well? Like they would normally ogle females on Southsea promenade, when they'd fought their way through all the retired officers sat in their deckchairs! Of course the stewardesses were allowed to lean on the rail and watch all the sailors sunbathing below!

Otherwise, today was a quiet day as far as exercises were concerned, so we were able to clear the backlog of every day work that builds up when you are away from the office playing war games!

A Hunt in the sun

WEDNESDAY, 23 JUNE 82 - DAY 31

0700*		Call the hands
0730		Hands to breakfast
0745*		Time check
0755*		Out pipes
0800*		Both watches muster on the Fore Deck
0900*		Flying brief
0900 - 1100		STBD RAS/VERTREP (Fuel & Water) Zigzag during RAS
0915*		Prepare for flying
0930*		Hands to flying stations
1000*		Stand easy
1015*		Hands carry on with your work
1130		SRs/Watchkeepers to dinner
1145*		Secure, JRs to dinner
1300*		Hands carry on with your work
1415*		Flying brief
1430*		Prepare for flying
1445*		Hands to Flying Stations
1500 - 1630		FLYEX (CASEVAC) from HMS LEDBURY
1630 - 1830		NBCDX/ Machinery Breakdowns
1900*		First Dog Watchmen clean messdecks and flats for Rounds
1925*		Stand by for Rounds
2000		JRs' Movie - "Island"
2000 - 2200		NAVCOMEX
2115*		Flying Brief
2130*		Prepare for flying
2145*		Hands to Flying Stations
2200 - 2359		Night FLYEX
2300*		Pipe down

Note 1 was a 'legal' reminder to the RN 'cruisers':- "Dress - Attention is drawn to 'Dress of the Day'. Too many members of the Ship's Company are interpreting the dress regulations in such a way as to suit themselves. The RPO will be intercepting cowboys and providing a dog watch hobby to occupy their time."

Note 2 was also keeping the troops amused! - "It would appear that a requirement exists for a Sales and Wanted/Swaps Column in Daily Orders. In future space will be set aside in Wednesday's Daily Orders to fulfil this need. The following are outstanding:- a. Purserchaser bargains - Solid Gold Charm of RMS ST HELENA (Ideal Xmas Gift) at £15. b. Support your local laundry, now in full swing, 10% to Welfare. c. Mug shots for Mummy, etc, contact CLIKKA SHUTTA Enterprises (Sparksee and Stutch)."

Note 3 was yet another of the same ilk:- "Skeet shooting - The Skeet Range will be in operation on Thursdays and Fridays at 1700 - 1800. Each round will cost 5p, proceeds towards the purchase of the VIDEO RECORDER for the Grand Draw at the end of the Commission. The Buffer will conduct the practice."

Note 4 read:- "MN Crew - who wish to send mail to the Island of St Helena are requested to hand their letters in to the Purser."

Note 5 was domestic:- "Scuttles and Screen Doors must be kept closed if the ship is to remain air conditioned."

Note 6 read:- "Tombola numbers drawn by St Helenian crewman were:-
74, 22, 18, 85, 77, 39, 44, 42, 8, 89. Any claims for the line to Ship's Office by 1200 today."

"Position at noon: - 7 deg 15 min North, 17 deg 0 min West. Freetown is 230 miles ENE."

TN - AM - RAS/VERTREP, Zigzag
     PM - FLYEX, NBCDX/Machinery Breakdowns, NAVCOMEX, Night
          FLYEX

Today we were back to war work! No time to go sneaking about looking for stewardesses sunbathing anyway!

Curnow Shipping Co. tie (l), with sweater and tie badge designed by a member of RNP 2100

THURSDAY, 24 JUNE 82 - DAY 32

0001	- 0200	SCREENEX (No lights/radar/darken ship)
0700*		Call the hands
0730		Hands to breakfast
0745*		Time check
0755*		Out pipes
0800*		Both watches muster on the Fore Deck
0800		HODS Planning Meeting in Wardroom
0900	- 1100	Astern RAS (token amount)
1000*		Stand easy
1015*		Hands carry on with your work
1100	- 1300	NBCDX (Action Messing) (NAVCOMEX 1100 - 1130)
1400	- 1600	'Crossing the Line' Ceremony
1600	- 1700	Gunnery (at Flares) (20mm, GPMG)/OOW Manoeuvres
1700	- 1800	Skeet shooting on the Fore Deck
1900*		First Dog Watchmen clean messdecks and flats for Rounds
1925*		Stand by for Rounds
1945		Flying brief
2000	- 2200	NAVCOMEX
2000		Darken ship
2000*		Prepare for flying
2015*		Hands to Flying Stations
2030	- 2200	Night FLYEX
2200		MN Crew Movie - "Star Trek"
2200	- 0100	Night SCREENEX (No lights/radar/darken ship by 2100) (Zigzag)
2300*		Pipe down

"PROGRAMME - We expect to arrive at Ascension Island at 1500 on Saturday, 26 June. Our earliest estimated time for departing AI is 0900 Monday, 28 June. Shore Leave is not permitted on the island except for organised sports parties. (See tomorrow's Daily Orders). Swimming is not permitted - SHARKS. Gash is NOT to be ditched within two miles of AI. The ship will be darkened each night at anchor." (Our second ship's visit! Bet we suddenly find we have lots of sportsmen tomorrow).

Note 1 read:- "NBCDX - The aim of today's Damage Control Exercise is to test the arrangements for Action Messing. The ship will go to Action Stations at 1130. Dress No8s, woollen socks, DMS Boots, carry life jackets, respirators, anti-flash (gun crews wear combat kit and steel helmets). It is intended to feed the whole Ship's Company within an hour, starting at 1200. Departmental and Section Heads are to arrange for one third of their men to go at 1200, when these return the next third leave (by 1220). The final third to dinner at 1240. Reports that all Departments have been fed are to be made to HQ1."

Note 2 was domestic:- "Laundry - The Ship's Company is reminded that NO laundry will be accepted after 0830 daily."

Note 3 was social:- "Crossing the Line Certificates - All those who have not crossed the line before, put your names on the list outside the Ship's Office to facilitate early printing of the Certificates. (Example outside the Ship's Office)." This was a sneaky way of checking that we hadn't missed anybody in the afternoon's ceremony. (There was also guaranteed to be some clown who would put his name down, thinking he had escaped a ducking!) The problem today was that we had too many 'victims', so we would have to finish them off on the way home! (Keeping our fingers crossed on that one, of course!).

Note 4 culminated the 'Crest Competition'. It read:- "Well done all who entered. The judging was made very difficult by the high standard of entries. The designs fell into two main groups and it was therefore decided that two winners should be chosen. One winner for a Sweatshirt/'T' Shirt design, the other for a jumper/tie design. The winning designs are displayed on the Notice Boards outside the Ship's Office."

Note 5 was more social stuff:- "Grand Raffle - Tickets are now on sale from FSU01. Hopefully, the 1st prize will be a video recorder, so start buying your tickets now. The more tickets sold the more prizes will be available. Tickets will cost 25p each or £1.25 per sheet."

Note 6 was even more social:- "Tombola numbers drawn by a JR were:-
54, 13, 17, 35, 6, 28, 88, 20, 33, 47. Any claims for line, house, snowball to Ship's Office by 1200 today."

Today's notes ended with a witticism from the SNO, in line with the day's programme! - "He who blows top only gets dandruff."

"Position at noon - 3 degs 10 mins North, 16 degs 20 mins West. Monrovia in Liberia is 380 miles NE."

TN - AM - SCREENEX, RAS astern, NBCDX
     PM - OOW Manoeuvres, Gunnex, Navcomex, Night FLYEX, Night SCREENEX

St HELLTEM 13/82 "Cleaning Resposibilities" read thus:- "The following areas are the cleaning responsibility of the Departments nominated:- Communications:- Bridge Flat and stairs, MCO, MSO. Stores:- Captain's Flat and stairs to 'C' Deck. CBM:- 'C' Deck (including toilet and pantry), stairs (fwd) to 'B' Deck, JRs' Recreation Space. FSU:- 'B' Deck and stairs (aft) up to 'C' Deck. Medical:- Surgery Flat and stairs. Laundry Crew:- Laundry. Stairs and 'C' Deck toilet are to be scrubbed. Flats swept out. Areas detailed are to be cleaned daily 0800 - 0900."

Still busy boys! We were definitely leading a 'full life', especially with all this extra cleaning added on! However, tonight we nearly had a bit of saucy entertainment?! A video donated to the ship was shown in the evening, it was called "Hot Racquets". It portrayed the life and raunchy goings on in an American Tennis Club, hence the title! It turned out to be 'soft core' pornography! The boys were all thoroughly delighted by this and it soon had a large, raucous and captive audience! All of a sudden, after about half an hour had passed, it stopped and the screen went blank! A fair amount of abuse and complaints could then be heard from all four messes where it was being shown. Then a broadcast was made by the 1st Lieutenant, explaining that he had stopped it, as it wasn't suitable for showing onboard!? He was later to learn what a hornet's nest he had opened up! These were grown men and well travelled sailors going to war and he was stopping them watching a soft core movie? Most of them had seen much worse round the world and in this day and age would definitely have seen worse at home on "Sky Movies"! It wasn't even in colour! More of this epic later!!!!!

Neptune's court ('Crossing the Line' ceremony – a dirty, smelly, wet affair!)

FRIDAY, 25 JUNE 82 - DAY 33

0700*	Call the hands
0730	Hands to breakfast
0745*	Time check
0755*	Out pipes
0800*	Both watches muster on the Fore Deck
0830	Flying brief
0845*	Prepare for flying
0900*	Hands to Flying Stations
0900 - 1100	VERTREP (MO to HMS BRECON)
1000*	Stand easy
1015*	Hands carry on with your work
1130	SRs/Watchkeepers to dinner
1145*	Secure, JRs to dinner
1245	Flying brief
1300*	Hands carry on with your work
1300*	Prepare for flying
1315*	Hands to Flying Stations
1330 - 1500	FLYEX (MO from HMS BRECON)
1600 - 1700	GUNNEX (20mm, GPMG) (Flares as target)
1700 - 1800	Skeet shooting
1900*	First Dog Watchmen clean messdecks and flats for Rounds
1925*	Stand by for Rounds
2000	JRs' Movie - "Crescendo"
2000 - 2200	NAVCOMEX
2100	WR/SRs' Movie - "Ashanti"
2300*	Pipe down

Note 1 continued yesterday's 'Programme' note:- "Ascension Island - Sporting facilities are limited, boat transport is limited. As soon as information is received re these problems, sports parties will be organised. This information will not be available until we anchor on PM Saturday, therefore, sport can only take place on Sunday. The only people allowed ashore will be organised sports parties."
(This visit looks a bit 'limited', doesn't it?!).

Note 2 read:- "No gash is to be ditched within two miles of Ascension Island. Sullage lighter will come alongside."

Note 3 read:- "Darken ship every night."

Note 4 referred back to yesterday's little epic:- "The Action Messing Exercise - was generally successful. The Galley & Catering Staff learnt important lessons. On future occasions all Ship's Company, RN & MN, are to collect their meal from the Main Servery and are to eat in the Main Dining Room." (But what will the stewardesses find to do then and as for the poor officers having to get their own food, well!?). "Watertight doors and hatches must be closed after you pass through them.

Don't leave them for others to close! The object of action messing is to feed as many people as possible in the shortest time. If you linger over your meal, your 'oppo' might not have time to eat!" (Action messing 'cruise' style was definitely different, it was binned after this attempt and done properly next time. Shame really!).

Note 5 referred back to Day 31's Fire Exercise:- "Standing Fire Party - Wednesday's fire exercise in the Fan Compartment showed marked improvements in every area. There are still lessons to be learnt:- Smoke control, close all doors and hatches in the vicinity of the fire and rig smoke blankets where required. Boundary cooling, use the minimum water required, eg compartment above 0.5 to 1 inch of water on deck is enough. Water, topweight = instability and capsized ships. Hoses, these will not work if kinked or tangled up when run out."

Note 6, in the middle of all this lot, helped to increase my workload! - "Pay queries and Requests - to the Ship's Office soonest, eg Badges due, LSP, etc.)."

Note 7 was advertising 'budgie' riding again:- "Jollies - Anyone who wishes to go flying in the Wasp should muster on the Flight Deck at 1115 for briefing, having obtained HOD's permission. Flying will take place between 1330 and 1430."

Note 8 was yet another Night Pantry dit:- "The Night Pantry was flooded yesterday. When topping up the boiler ensure the tap is off on completion."

Note 9 was social:- "Challenge Trophy - The JRs successfully defended at darts last night - the score being 10 - 5. The next challenge is from the WR and is to be in by 1600 on 25 June 82 and is to be played on leaving Ascension."

Note 10 was a record breaker, the first time 'Notes' on Daily Orders had gone to double figures! It read:- "Tombola numbers drawn by the Buffer were:-
41, 31, 70, 27, 67, 15, 82, 43, 36, 84. There were two claims for the line on the 27th number out = £4 each. All claims for the snowball (41 or less) to the Ship's Office by 1200 today."

"Position at noon - 01 deg 15 mins South, 15 deg 30 mins West. Ascension Island is 400 miles South by East."

TN - AM - VERTREP
        PM - FLYEX, Gunnex, Navcomex

Busy, busy, busy! Exercises coming out of your ears, the action messing 'picnic', in tray buried in paper and what do we get - bloody pay queries! I ask you! It's at the end of a week like this when you sit down and think of all those shops and offices you've been in where a smiling face tells you "Sorry, but we closed two minutes ago!" Bureaucratic swine, they should bring back conscription and let the useless bastards have a go at this lot, nine to bloody fivers!

RFA Sir Galahad at Fitzroy

Lest we forget - Governor Rex Hunt returns to Port Stanley.
                   RFA SIR GALAHAD towed out to sea and sunk by
                   HMS/M ONYX as an official war grave.

SATURDAY, 26 JUNE 82 - DAY 34

0700*	Call the hands
0730	Hands to breakfast
0745*	Time check
0755*	Out pipes
0800*	Both watches muster on the Fore Deck
0900 - 1100	STBD RAS (by flags)
1000*	Stand easy
1015*	Hands carry on with your work
1130	SRs/Watchkeepers to dinner
1145*	Secure, JRs to dinner
PM	373 to Wideawake (Ascension Island) with Liaison Officers. Time to be confirmed
1900*	First Dog Watchmen clean messdecks and flats for Rounds
1925*	Stand by for Rounds
2200	MN Movie - "Ashanti"
2300*	Pipe down

Note 1 was a novelty:- "Messdeck Rounds - for today are cancelled due to operational commitments." (My goodness these commitments must be something else - Captain's Rounds cancelled! In 22 years it's a new one on me!).

Note 2 read:- "Photex - It is hoped that we will carry out a 'Photex' today while the RAS is taking place. This will involve a light jackstay to STBD whilst fuelling to PORT. Listen for pipes to hear if you will be involved."

Note 3 was a repeat of Day 31's note 4 for MN Crew to give their St Helena Island mail to the Purser.

Note 4 was the Sick Bay making money again! - "Fishing Gear - Sea rods and reels plus hand lines are available from the Sick Bay."

Note 5 was more commercialism:- "Orders for ties/jumpers/sweatshirts/'T' shirts - are to be written on messdeck lists and returned to the Ship's Office by 1600 today, so that if enough orders are required we can send off before we leave Ascension Island. (Prices will be approximately:- Tie = £4, Jumper = £10, Sweatshirt = £7, 'T' Shirt = £3, if enough are ordered.)."

Note 6 read:- "Tombola numbers drawn by an MN Third Officer were:-
72, 83, 81, 57, 61, 12, 78, 86, 10, 56. Any claims for snowball/house to Ship's Office by 1200 today." (For any RN wives reading this, they have male Third Officers in the Merchant Navy!).

"Position at noon - 06 degs 50 mins South, 14 degs 35 mins West. Ascension Island is 65 miles South by West."

TN - AM - RAS/VERTREP
        1810 - Anchored at Ascension Island

Ascension Island is 33 square miles of volcano surrounded by volcanic ash, cinders and frozen lava. It is a harsh and unattractive place. There is only one small area of vegetation at Green Mountain. The population are workers from the RAF, USAF, Cable & Wireless, BBC and Composite Signals organisations. There are no native islanders, it is all British, American and St Helenian. There is no harbour, only an airfield at Wideawake. Ships anchor off and when the swell is minimal, use underwater pipelines and motor powered lighters to get their cargoes ashore. Because the island is a top security area, visitors ashore are restricted to organised tours by minibus. In fact visitors are discouraged normally and this is borne out by the fact that there are no hotels or other public places of entertainment available on the island.

Well it was nice to sit at sea looking at the land! What sort of visit was this going to be, we wondered? Looking over the side, we saw shark fins slowly gliding around! The locals didn't seem to bother - they were whizzing about in small boats looking extremely vulnerable! As we watched, we also noticed that if anything went in the water it immediately disappeared in a bubbling thrashing of the water!? Blackfish, a voracious eater, were in abundance in these waters. Jack was therefore able to spend his time throwing mustard sandwiches over the side and watching the sea 'boil'! Well, it helped pass the time! (It also explained why you can now buy mustard-flavoured mackerel in the shops!)

When I came to fill in the chit for the ties, jumpers, etc, it suddenly came to me - who gets them if we don't get back for some reason?! Makes you think doesn't it? It's these little things that get to you! I'd already binned any thoughts of Christmas Lists! There's only one thing to do when you realise you don't know what your future is - have another drink!

SUNDAY, 27 JUNE 82 - DAY 35

0700*	Call the hands
0730	Hands to breakfast
0745*	Time check
0755*	Out pipes
0800*	Both watches muster on the Fore Deck
0830*	Prepare for flying
0845*	Hands to Flying Stations
0900	HDS from Wideawake
1000*	Stand easy
1015*	Hands carry on with your work
1130	SRs/Watchkeepers to dinner
1145*	Secure, JRs to dinner
1300*	Hands carry on with your work
1600*	Secure
1900*	First Dog Watchmen clean messdecks and flats for Rounds
1925*	Stand by for Rounds
2300*	Pipe down

Notes 1 and 2 were trying to boost morale:- "Secure will be piped as soon as possible on completion of the days work, hopefully before 1600. Listen for the pipe." "Sports parties will be landed whenever possible as work allows."

Note 3 was back to work:- "Securing for sea - Rounds on the Upper Deck and between deck will be taking place to ensure we are secure for sea."

Note 4 read:- "Do not waste water, as no more will be produced until we leave AI."

Note 5 read:- "Tombola numbers drawn by the 1st Lt were:- 75, 38, 52, 90, 53, 80, 79, 62, 64, 58, 7, 68, 73, 49, 14.Claims for the house to the Ship's Office by 1200 ."

Note 6 was also social:- "World Cup - A full list of the Group 1 matches played is available from the Ship's Office for those interested."

TN - Engine defect rectification. Embark stores by VERTREP from Wideawake.

The routine was 'Daily Harbour', so that was another weekend ruined! However, my sports team managed to get some evening training in for our big international match the following day against the crabs who were stationed here! They had thrown out a challenge to us for a volleyball match! Obviously nobody had told them I was the RN Volleyball Coach! (See below). This was the only official ship's team match, the rest was all inter-part sport within the ship, so it took on a role of great diplomatic importance!

You may wonder how volleyball can be played on a ship! Many years ago the RN developed this art! A ball held in a small net is attached to a long string, this in turn is attached to the top centre of the main net on a swivel. This ensures that you don't lose balls over the side but means you do have to learn the skill of avoiding the flying string. A strange game but better than nothing!

RMS St. Helena's 'crab-conqueror'!

A picturesque view of Ascension Island

MONDAY, 28 JUNE 82 - DAY 36

0700*	Call the hands
0730	Hands to breakfast
0745*	Time check
0755*	Out pipes
0800*	Both watches muster on the Fore Deck
0830*	Prepare for flying
0845*	Hands to Flying Stations
0900	HDS from Wideawake
1000*	Stand easy
1015*	Hands carry on with your work
1130	SRs/Watchkeepers to dinner
1145*	Secure, JRs to dinner
1300	Sports Teams proceed ashore (Port Watch)
1900*	First Dog Watchmen clean messdecks and flats for Rounds
1925*	Stand by for Rounds
2300*	Pipe down

"Programme - The plan is to refuel about 1600 today and to top up with stores from a lighter alongside during the afternoon. If we complete these tasks it is possible that we shall weigh and proceed on passage to the Falklands at 2000ish. Things change quickly here so listen for the pipes and be prepared."

Note 1 was another explanatory effort for our colleagues from the other navy! - "The pipe "Clear lower deck" means EVERYBODY not actively engaged in watchkeeping duties. It is normally made in a situation when hands are urgently needed. Heads of Sections are to ensure that response is immediate."

Note 2 read:- "Upper and between deck Rounds - Securing for sea must be complete by 1100 today. The Master & Chief Officer will be conducting rounds after this time."

Note 3 read:- " Tombola tickets will be on sale again when we sail from Ascension Island. The house has been claimed by a St Helenian crew member on the 61st number out for a prize of £20. The snowball for next week will be £14 plus next week's percentage. Get your tickets as soon as possible."

TN - AM - Completed rectification of defect on Centre Auxiliary Engine.
            Embarked 150 bags of surface mail for the Falklands.
       PM - Refuelled from ALVEIDA.

We had a 'Saturday Sea' Routine today, so we regained an afternoon off. This was spent ashore participating in various sporting activities which culminated in the RAF bar, known as the Volcano Club - apt as the whole island had been created by a volcano. My volleyball team, having greatly benefited from the previous night's coaching session, thrashed the RAF team out of sight. We were then well 'looked after' by them in the bar! Not an epic ship's visit but it got us off the ship for some exercise, a few beers and the chance to let off a bit of steam! It was, in fact, a well-earned break!

I read a copy of the Rules of Engagement this afternoon (what we had to do before we could open fire on the enemy with our guns! GUNS???). Now there's a sobering read! Classified, of course, so that's the end of that dit!

I received a wonderful, heartwarming letter in the mail today! A letter from my bank telling me my account was overdrawn and I should visit the bank as soon as possible to sort it out! Watch my lips!

The innards of the Wideawake taxi! (Wasp cockpit)

Lest we forget - The Argentines released 3 British journalists imprisoned during the war for spying!

TUESDAY, 29 JUNE 82 - DAY 37

0700*   Call the hands
0730   Hands to breakfast
0745*   Time check
0755*   Out pipes
0800*   Both watches muster on the Fore Deck
1000*   Stand easy
1015*   Hands carry on with your work
1130   SRs/Watchkeepers to dinner
1145*   Secure, JRs to dinner
1300*   Hands carry on with your work
1600*   Secure
1800   Hands clean into night clothing
1900*   First Dog Watchmen clean messdecks and flats for Rounds
1925*   Stand by for Rounds
2300*   Pipe down

Note 1 read:- "Tombola tickets will be on sale this evening from the Ship's Office."

Note 2 read:- "The weekly programme will be promulgated as soon as it is received from HMS BRECON."

Note 3 was another first and was real glory stuff! - "Sports Result:-   Volleyball:-
RMS ST HELENA 4 -v- RAF Ascension Island 0"

On the end we had "Thought for the Day - Ignorance is blister, when one is sunburnt".

TN - 0230 Sailed from Ascension Island to the Falkland Islands.

That was our second ship's visit out of the way, wonder where the next one will be?
Will there be one? Will we ever set foot on dry land again? These and a lot of other
wonderful questions were now ever present in our minds! Now it was all really
serious, we were entering the war zone! Things could only get worse from hereon in!

WEDNESDAY, 30 JUNE 82 - DAY 38

0700*	Call the hands
0730	Hands to breakfast
0745*	Time check
0755*	Out pipes
0800*	Both watches muster on the Fore Deck
0805	RAS Stores Party muster at the Ship's Office
0830*	Flying brief
0845*	Prepare for flying
0900*	Hands to Flying Stations
0900 - 1100	RAS(Liquid) HMS BRECON & HMS LEDBURY
0915 - 1100	FLYEX
1000*	Stand easy
1015*	Hands carry on with your work
1130	SRs/Watchkeepers to dinner
1145*	Secure, JRs to dinner
1300*	Hands carry on with your work
1600*	Secure
1800*	Hands clean into night clothing
1900*	First Dog Watchmen clean messdecks and flats for Rounds
1925*	Stand by for Rounds
1930	Flying brief
2000*	Prepare for flying
2015*	Flying Stations
2030 - 2200	FLYEX
2300*	Pipe down

"Programme - Due to the present uncertain policy of the Argentine Government we must still maintain the ship to a higher condition of Operational Readiness. For the first half of our passage to the Falklands we shall remain in Cruising Watches. If, however, the indications are that the political situation is worsening between ourselves and the new Argentine Government, we shall complete the passage at Defence Stations. The ship will be darkened at night and radio restrictions are in force. Our greatest enemy will be the worsening weather conditions. Ensure that all departments are thoroughly secured for sea."

Note 1 reminded us that there's always one! - "Laundry - The Laundry was left in a disgusting state by whoever used it last night. Washing machines full of dirty water, spin dryers full of water. Therefore, the laundry will now be closed at 1930 daily after Evening Rounds."

Note 2 was a disciplinary reminder to the boys:- "Beer Hoarding - RN JRs are reminded that it is an offence to accumulate the daily beer issue. All beer must be consumed on the day of issue. The RPO will carry out locker searches from time to time without prior notice."

Note 3 read:- "Tombola numbers drawn by an FSU01 SR were 39, 60, 36, 1, 14, 53, 55, 19, 86, 33. Claims for the line to Ship's Office by 1200 today.
Line £8.80, House £22, Snowball(42) £22.80, Welfare £4.40."

<u>TN</u> - AM - VERTREP   PM - FLYEX

Today we had haircutting day! Now the 'threat' had increased, it was time to get the haircuts down to a minimum! A shaved head was cleaner and less likely to harbour infestations, etc, if you became a prisoner of war. Also nobody could get hold of it! The other problem was the beard! Anti-Gas Respirators (AGRs) were unable to make a seal with a beard, they had to be in contact with skin! So you could either shave off now or when a gas attack was imminent! Choices, choices!

A dit about communications within our Task Group was also published by the MN today! A few problems had occurred with communications between the three ships, where the RN way of doing things had differed to the MN way! The following was the solution to the problem:-
"One Thousand Code - This code has been devised to promote greater understanding between MN and RN personnel of each others customs:-
1001   If I had wanted your opinion I would have given it to you.
1002   Don't you ever get tired of being wrong?
1003   Don't you ever get tired of being right?
1004   If God had intended people to talk at breakfast he would have given them something intelligent to talk about.
1005   I will give you such a smack if you don't give my gunline back.
1006   I have a bone to pick with fate, come here and listen girlie, is my brain maturing late, or simply rotted early?
1007   We always try our hardest and are on friendly terms with external criticism.
1008   Golden Goose accepts that clever goslings know more than their parents but old geese produce golden eggs - occasionally.
1009   If you want to comment, think once, think twice, think three times, then say nothing.
1010   I know that you have made a mistake, you know that you have made a mistake, why signal and let the whole world know that a mistake has been made?
1011   This attempt doesn't really count.
1012   Happiness is ST HELENA shaped.
1013   Shall we try again next year?
1014   Suggest we try that again after reading the maker's instructions.
1015   "My word, I think you've got it".
1016   If at first you don't succeed, make damned sure that you do next time.

1017   If God had intended fibreglass ships, he would have made plastic trees.
1018   Please shake your:-   a. Dog b. OOW c. RO.
1019   Please wait - we are presently at luncheon.
1020   "Oh no, not CORPEN CUCUMBER time again".
1021   This game bores me, I want to 'Carry on Cruising'.
1022   The MIKE NOVEMBER request, GOLF ALPHA INDIA BRAVO.
1023   As good seamen go - you went.
1024   We admire your style but not your intentions.
1025   We admire your intentions but not your style.
1026   Thank you for the 'teach in'.
1027   Is this going to be the ten minute argument or the full half hour?
1028   I bet you are not lucky in love either.
1029   Vellee sorree, no speekkee Eengallish.
1030   We haven't received the script yet.
1031   Please stick to the screenplay.
1032   Don't get upset, we are only following the script.
1033   We are slowly getting used to working with 'prima donnas'.
1034   Please observe MIKE NOVEMBER recuperation time ie. 1400-1600 daily.
1035   You are interfering with my:- a.   Sunbathing
                                    b.   Eyeball analysis
                                    c.   Deck Tennis
                                    d.   Skeet shooting
                                    e.   Leisurely way of life.

1036   Hold out your wrists.
1037   Mother Goose likes you.
1038   Mother Goose is eggbound.
1039   Sorry, didn't see it, too busy navigating.
1040   You can't fool us, we are too stupid.
1041   There are three ways of doing this:- a.   The correct way
                                          b.   The incorrect way
                                          c.   Your way.

1042   Don't panic..Yet.
1043   We always stop at this time.
1044   Please pass on both sides.
1045   Reference Speed, our washing machine is not fitted with a tumble dryer.
1046   The newspaper hasn't been delivered yet.
1047   You might hate me, but you can't do without me.
1048   Please have mercy on us miserable offenders.
1049   So I said to this tart......................................!
1050   Come to mother, ALL is forgiven."

It had now gone quiet in the messes. Before beer issue, it was very, very quiet with little conversation. After a beer things loosened up a little but it was still difficult! Not a lot happened today, which made you think of the lull before the storm!

THURSDAY, 1 JULY 82 - DAY 39

0030		Retard clocks 1 hour (+1)
0630		OOW Navcomex
0700*		Call the hands
0730		Hands to breakfast
0745*		Time check
0755*		Out pipes
0800*		Both watches muster on the Fore Deck
1000*		Stand easy
1015*		Hands carry on with your work
1130		SRs/Watchkeepers to dinner
1145*		Secure, JRs to dinner
1300*		Hands carry on with your work
1345		Flying brief
1400 - 1430		OOW Navcomex
1400*		Prepare for flying
1400 - 1600		Forward Lounge out of bounds - carpet cleaning
1415*		Hands to Flying Stations
1430 - 1600		FLYEX
1600*		Secure
1600 - 1700		Skeet shooting (weather permitting)
1800		Hands clean into night clothing
1830 - 1900		OOW Navcomex
1900*		First Dog Watchmen clean messdecks and flats for Rounds
1925*		Stand by for Rounds
1930		Flying brief
2000*		Prepare for flying
2015*		Hands to Flying Stations
2030 - 2200		FLYEX
2200 - 2230		OOW Navcomex
2300*		Pipe down

Note 1 reminded us that we still had the 'policeman' on board and read:- "All personnel are reminded that items for transfer to HMS BRECON or HMS LEDBURY should be reported to the RPO, no later than secure on the day prior to the transfer."

The rest of the notes were socially orientated, so we were obviously trying to keep the boys happy again. Note 2 read:- "Crosspol - 1630 Saturday to 1000 Sunday - Names of volunteers to the Ship's Office by 1200 Friday."

Note 3 informed us that:- "St Helena Island's newspaper, "News Review", is available for anyone wishing to update their reading of this journalistic gem. Contact the Master."

Note 4 was down to the SNO again:- "Thought for the Day - The meek shall inherit the earth, they haven't the nerve to refuse."

Note 5 read:- "Challenge Trophy - The JRs maintained their winning run with a 23 to 20 win over the Wardroom at skeet shooting. The SRs have now challenged them at darts."

Finally Note 6 read:- "Tombola numbers drawn by one of the FSU01 JRs were:- 73, 11, 12, 28, 22, 2, 32, 15, 80, 62. Any claims for the line to the Ship's Office by 1200 today."

"Position at noon - 17 deg 10 min South, 22 deg 22 min West. Nearest point of land is the island of Ilhas Martinvaz 420 miles WSW. This island is 800 miles off the coast of Brazil."

TN - AM - OOW Navcomex
     PM - OOW Navcomex, FLYEX, Night FLYEX

St HELLTEM 14/82 "Welfare Committee" informed us that "A Welfare Committee is being formed to supervise the general recreational amenities and activities available to the Ship's Company and to administer the running of the Welfare Fund. There will be a total of six committee members: two from the SRs' Mess, three from the JRs' Mess and one from the MN Crew. Members of the Committee are to be elected by their respective messes and the names given to the 1st Lieutenant by 1600 Sunday, 4 July. The 1st Lieutenant will be the Chairman of the Welfare Committee. The POWTR will fill the post of Treasurer. A volunteer is required for the post of Secretary, names to the 1st Lieutenant by 1600 Sunday, 4 July 82."
(This was normal practice on RN ships and in shore establishments).

I was Duty Senior Rate again today. Bloody typical! We had the Challenge Trophy Darts Match against the JRs tonight in their mess, the Stern Gallery. Obviously I couldn't drink when duty, so I wouldn't be any use in the Darts Team - it's amazing how you can't throw the ruddy things properly until you've had at least two pints! It had been a busy day, so this was a very good way for the boys to let off a bit of steam. They did as well, with experience playing its part in the darts and the SRs ending the winning run of the JRs in the Challenge Trophy!

FRIDAY, 2 JULY 82 - DAY 40

0700*	Call the hands
0730	Hands to breakfast
0745*	Time check
0755*	Out pipes
0800*	Both watches muster on the Fore Deck
0815	HOD's Meeting in the Wardroom
0900 - 1100	20mm + GPMG Firings (Target Flares)
1000*	Stand easy
1015*	Hands carry on with your work
1100 - 1145	DC COMEX
1130	SRs/Watchkeepers to dinner
1145*	Secure, JRs to dinner
1300*	Hands carry on with your work
1400 - 1600	Stern Gallery out of bounds - carpet cleaning
1600*	Secure
1800	Hands clean into night clothing
1900*	First Dog Watchmen clean messdecks and flats for Rounds
1925*	Stand by for Rounds
2045	Flying brief
2100*	Prepare for flying
2115*	Hands to Flying Stations
2130 - 2300	FLYEX
2300*	Pipe down

Note 1 signalled the end of one of my 'little' tasks! It also finally confirmed 'Law & Order', RN style, had definitely arrived and could not now be ignored. It read - "Standing Orders are now out with HODs and DOs. Make sure you read a copy and sign to say you have read it by 30 July 82. The Regulating Department will not accept ignorance of the law as an excuse. HODs are to report to the 1st Lieutenant that all members of their department have read and signed Standing Orders."

Notes 2 & 3 were back to social: Note 2 read:- "Beards - From Sunday, only regulation beards are acceptable. A small competition is being arranged for Saturday evening to judge the best/original funny beard or moustache. Names of entrants to the Purser by 1200 Saturday. Saturday is shave off day - for funny growths only."

Note 3 read:- "Tombola numbers drawn by an RNP2100 JR were:-
74, 27, 17, 37, 26, 84, 16, 88, 75, 63. Any claims for the snowball/house (a total of £44.80) to the Ship's Office by 1200 today. Line claimed by the LSTD on the 20th number out = £8.80."

"Position at noon - 21 deg 10 min South, 25 deg 50 min West. The nearest point of land is Ilhas Martinvaz 175 miles west."

TN - AM - RAS, DC COMEX   PM - Gunnex, Night FLYEX

We had a bit of an internal contretemps today. One of the MHSCs claimed it had been sold 'out of date' confectionery by the Purser Catering, also, even worse, it had been overcharged! So it sent a brief but terse local signal to the said Purser demanding an explanation! The 'not happy' Purser immediately replied with his own 'brief but terse' signal, saying he would happily replace the 'out of date' stock and then informed the complainant to read his price list properly and he would no doubt find he had been charged correctly! This signal was sent off before the SNO knew about the incident. The Purser Catering then demanded that the SNO have 'a word in the ear' of the complainant, as his signal had virtually publicly inferred that he was 'on the fiddle'! The SNO, caught in the middle, was then forced to send a letter to the Commanding Officer of the MHSC concerned, asking that the complainant be advised to 'sort his life out' and in future, before opening his mouth and putting his foot in it, should first thoroughly check his facts! He should also be informed to ensure that future signals, generated by him, should be 'couched in more acceptable terminology'!

Yet another busy day. Thank goodness it's the weekend!
Silly me, weekend? Of course it was but it was also the first SNO's Rounds on Saturday morning as well, wasn't it? So we spent all Friday night cleaning the bloody cabin!

```
                              Fm LEDBURY

EXTRA FOR VERTREP TOMORROW

B41   SPARKLING ORANGE    3 CASES
C1    LIQUORICE ALLSORTS  1 CASE
C4    PICNIC              2 CASE
C14   MARS                1 CASE
C23·  FRUIT PASTILLES     1 CASE
C26   JERSEY TOFFEE       1 CASE
C56   PERSIL E2           1 CASE
C39   RIGHT GUARD DE-OD   6 CANS

TO SUPPLY OFFICER
1. MARS (C14) PURCHASED FROM YOU LAST WEEK WERE TOO OLD (''SELL
BY'' DATE WAS 8 MAY 82) AND I HAD COMPLAINTS OF QUEER TAST, WHAT DO
YOU ADVISE                                           B4'S
2. I ORDERED B45 COCA COLA AT £5 A CASE. YOU SENT PEPSI (
    AT. £4.20 A CASE YET YOU CHARGED ME £5. A CASE, WHAT NOW
GXUY DE GXAE INT QSL PSE KKK


FM RMS ST HELENA
TO HMS LEDBURY
BT
REF MARS. WILL EXCHANGE FOR NEW STOCK.
REF COLAS, COKE AND PEPSI ARE £5.00 ALWAYS HAVE BEEN £5.00
READ YOUR LIST PROPERLY. DIET PEPSI IS £4.20 YOU DID NOT GET
DIET PEPSI. THATS WHATS NOW.
D.A. PURSER CATERER.
BT
```

Illegal 'Operation Corporate' signal traffic!!

SATURDAY, 3 JULY 82 - DAY 41

0030	Retard clocks 1 hour (+2)
0700*	Call the hands
0730	Hands to breakfast
0745*	Time check
0755*	Out pipes
0800*	Both watches muster on the Fore Deck
1000*	Stand easy
1015*	Hands carry on with your work
1055*	Stand by for SNO's Messdeck Rounds
1100	SNO's Messdeck Rounds
1130	SRs/Watchkeepers to dinner
1145*	Secure, JRs to dinner
1630	Boat TX Crosspol
1715	Darken ship
1800*	Hands clean into night clothing
2300*	Pipe down

"Programme - HMS BRECON & HMS LEDBURY may RAS at short notice. If the weather is good they will RAS even though they only replenished in the last 24 hours. 20mm/GPMG firing practices may also be carried out at short notice."

All the notes today had a weekend theme! Note 1 was another attempt to 'educate' the troops. It was also the start of a 'series' and read:- "RN/MN History - RN - 3/7/40 British Fleet under Vice Admiral Sir James Somerville in HMS HOOD, attacked French Fleet at Mers-el-Kebir. MN - The youngest and eldest men killed on active service in WWII were MN. A 14 year old Catering Boy and a 76 yrs old AB."

Note 2 confirmed what a shower of super stars my mess contained:- "Challenge Trophy - The JRs suffered a very sad defeat on Thursday evening in their third attempt to defend the trophy. (Four are needed to win the beer). After leading 3 - 0 they slipped away into oblivion (no stamina), to eventually lose 9 - 6. The SRs are now awaiting their first challenge from the MN Crew, to be made by this evening."

Note 3 read:- "Thought for the Day - The Army is a projectile to be fired by the Navy. (Admiral John Fisher 1st Sea Lord)."

Note 4 read:- "Tombola numbers drawn by one of the Stewardesses were:- 42, 4, 9, 46, 25, 56, 72, 59, 66, 68. Claims for house/snowball to Ship's Office by 1200 today."

"Position at noon - 25 deg 4 min South, 29 deg 7 min West. Nearest land is the Ihlas da Trinidade 300 miles N."

TN - AM - Rounds, Crosspol

St HELLTEM 15/82 "Defence Stations" surfaced today! Briefly, it stated:- "Due to the continuing uncertain situation in the Falkland Islands area it may be necessary for the ship to go to Defence Stations for an indefinite period. It is envisaged that the following will be required:- NBCD - 2Y coveralls; Guns crews - closed up by day

(? night); Wasp - Daylight, Alert 8, 1 x AS12, Exocet Catcher; Course and speed - possible Zig Zag; Route - Direct, clear of threat or as briefed; Darken ship - yes; Nav lights - as ordered, probably off; Radar - as ordered, probably off; EMCON - as ordered. Defence Watches will be ordered if:- Intelligence changes, threat changes, at 400 nautical miles from Falkland Islands, RECCE observed, as ordered by CTG. The aim of Defence Stations is to provide an initial reaction to a threat with personnel on watch, whilst closing up to Action Stations. This normally entails approximately 50% on watch at any one time whilst the remainder rest and eat. The Flight Commander is responsible for devising a routine whereby the aircraft is maintained at Alert 8 during daylight, armed with 1 x AS12 and Exocet Catcher fitted. Engine Room Staff will maintain their present routine. OOWs will be MN Officers. The watchkeeping system to be employed will be:-

0200 - 0800	Meal times will be:- 0130 - 0230 (Snack)
0800 - 1200	0730 - 0830
1200 - 1600	1130 - 1230
1600 - 2000	1530 - 1630 (Snack)
2000 - 0200	1930 - 2030

Note:- Catering staff will take over 15 minutes before the Watch Change. The shop will be open 15 minutes before and after meal times.
Dress:- a. ALL personnel will wear coveralls (flameproof), anti-flash hood (tucked inside clothing) and gloves, steaming boots, woollen stockings, action working dress or equivalent, life jacket, identity tags around neck, Geneva Convention ID Card and carry 'Once-only' suit, respirator and field dressing.
b.   Personnel in exposed positions and guns crews will wear flak jackets, steel helmets and Arctic clothing (as ordered by XO). (Guns crews - ear defenders available).
c.   Personnel off-watch are to sleep fully clothed with only foot wear and lifejackets removed (but ready for instant donning). The Communal Party (Galley/Servery) - will be detailed by HQ1 and will consist of 2 hands from HQ2 and one from the Forward DC Party, Flight and First Aid Posts. Two of the hands will be required full time in the galley, the third hand will be returned to his section when the Dining Hall is clear. This St HELLTEM is issued in order to give the ship's company an idea of what is required. RMS ST HELENA cannot be manned as a warship at Defence Stations for obvious reasons but we must be fully prepared to fight the ship at very short notice. We haven't got much in the way of armament but we can give somebody a headache."

This was a Saturday routine with a difference! We didn't turn to at our place of work! We scrubbed out for perishing Rounds! I had to do the office as well as the cabin! In the cabin we found out about the disadvantages of having our own heads/bathroom - we had to clean them! Not that difficult normally but these had never been cleaned to RN Rounds standard before! A chisel came in very useful! Also on the doom and gloom side, Daily Orders had started publishing 'Sunrise/Sunset' again? Winter was obviously on its way back, that must have been the shortest summer I've ever had!

For the second time this week, we had been 'officially' informed of the 'uncertain situation' in the Falkland Islands area! So as they had told us this much, what was the full harsh reality, we wondered? Normally we were told nothing until it was on us, as in the mushroom farming mentioned earlier! Better have another pint and ensure I enjoy my weekend, it might be the last one for a while!

SUNDAY, 4 JULY 82 - DAY 42

0700*	Call the hands
0730	Hands to breakfast
0815*	Time check
0825*	Out pipes
0830*	Both watches muster on the Fore Deck
0930*	Secure
1000	Boat TX Crosspol
1045	Church Service in Forward Lounge
1100*	Pipe down
1130	Hands to dinner
1715	Darken ship
1900*	First Dog Watchmen clean up messdecks and flats for Rounds
1925*	Stand by for Rounds

Note 1 got rid of the serious stuff early:- "SNO's Rounds - generally good. Following points are relevant to ALL cabins:- Shower mats not lifted therefore decks insanitary; Sink overflows full of rubbish; Toilets - undersides of seats/rims not cleaned, drain covers not lifted and scuppers cleaned/disinfected; Overheads not thoroughly dusted; Woodwork (including outside of cabin doors) not polished; Gash bins not scrubbed out. The cake has been awarded to cabin B3. (An old RN tradition - the prize for the cleanest cabin or mess was always a cake!) Cleanliness is next to Godliness."

Things then lightened up and Note 2 read:- "Comic beards and moustaches - ALL non-regulation facial hair growths are to be removed by 0800 today. SHAVE OFF."

Note 3 was a BZ - "Gunnex - On Saturday, Gun Crews, Well done, good shooting." (This one may have been designed to give the rest of us a bit of a confidence boost!?).

Note 4 read:- "History - RN - 4/7/40 German aircraft attack on FOYLEBANK which was sunk at Portland. ALS J F Mantle won the Victoria Cross.
MN - 1922 King George V conferred the honour on the Merchant Service, of the title Merchant Navy in recognition of it sharing the hazards of the RN in WWI."

Note 5 read:- "Tombola numbers drawn by the Chief Officer were:- 43, <u>48</u>, 90, 77, 7, 83, 65, 10, 29, 8, 82, 69, 5, 64, 57. Number underlined is the last one for the Snowball. Any claims for house/snowball to Ship's Office by 1200 today."

"Position at noon - 29.3 South, 33.4 West. Nearest point of land is Cabo Frio, Brazil, 650 miles to the North West."

<u>TN</u> - Crosspol

There'd been strange looking attempts at growing beards, some were deemed passable and allowed to continue to a mature state! The rest had to shave off! But it had given us a few laughs, which was the point of the exercise. It was Sunday routine, I worked overtime in the morning, finishing in time for lunch and a few beers. That night we had the Challenge match - v - MN Crew, playing cribbage. The boys proved their skill at another 'pub' game and won handsomely, and a good night was had by all!

MONDAY, 5 JULY 82 - DAY 43

0700*	Call the hands
0700 - 0730	Navcomex
0730	Hands to breakfast
0745*	Time check
0755*	Out pipes
0800*	Both watches muster on the Fore Deck
0800 - 0830	Navcomex
0830	Flying brief
0845*	Prepare for flying
0900*	Hands to Flying Stations
0900	STBD RAS
0915 - 1100	VERTREP
1000*	Stand easy
1015*	Hands carry on with your work
1130	SRs/Watchkeepers to dinner
1145*	Secure, JRs to dinner
1300*	Hands carry on with your work
1300 - 1330	Navcomex
1330 - 1430	OOW Manoeuvres - The ship may alter course and roll violently, ensure that everything is properly secured for sea .
1430 - 1800	First Aid Lecture on survival in cold weather. There will be 2 lectures - ALL must attend at least one lecture
1730*	Darken ship
1800 - 1830	Navcomex
1800	Hands clean into night clothing
1830	HMS BRECON & LEDBURY retard clocks 1 hour to 1730P(+3)
1900*	First Dog Watchmen clean messdecks and flats for Rounds
1925*	Stand by for Rounds
1930	Flying brief
2000*	Prepare for flying
2015*	Hands to Flying Stations
2030 - 2200	Night FLYEX
2300*	Pipe down
2359	Retard clocks 1 hour (2259 (+3))

"Programme - A penumbra of uncertainty still enshrouds Argentinian actions, therefore, tomorrow we exercise full Action Stations, etc (Tuesday War). At 0900 on Friday, 9 July the ship will assume the Second Degree of Readiness Defence Stations until arrival at the Falklands on Sunday. St Helltem 15/82 refers."

The notes were all social again and after the day we'd just had we needed a bit of social! Note 1 read:- "Video - Only one video film will be available to be shown each day. If shown it will commence at 2100."

Note 2 hailed my mess's great defence at pub games last night:- "Challenge Trophy - the SRs defended the trophy for the first time last night. They drew 6 - 6 with the MN Crew at cribbage, thereby retaining the trophy." (OK, so it was a bit closer than I claimed!).

Note 3 read:- "Tombola numbers drawn by a Flight SR were:-
52, 71, 89, 54, 47, 44, 50, 31, 21, 79, 6, 70, 67, 24, 76. Any claims for the house to the Ships' Office by 1200 today."

"Position at noon - 33 deg 3 min South, 37 deg 2 min West. Nearest land - Cabo de Santa Marta Grande, Brazil, 625 miles NW."

TN - AM - Navcomex, RAS/VERTREP
          PM - First Aid Lectures, Darken ship, Night FLYEX

'Dress of the Day' gave us the option of wearing No8s or No10As, so winter was obviously closing in again! Busy old day again, especially when the typewriter started moving around the desk on its own during the OOW Manoeuvres! They forget about us mere office staff trying to work in the bowels of the ship! Typewriters are bad enough at sea when the ship is rolling so they don't need any extra help! It's also not funny when one slides off the desk and smashes - a C126 for a typewriter is no joke on these wages! I also went to a First Aid Lecture today - it was the first one in my whole life that didn't send me to sleep! I think thoughts of self preservation may have helped though!

Had some good news today! We were informed that, when we arrived at Port Stanley the 'Ratcatcher' would be working ashore! With his 'Mail Office' skills he was required to sort out and re-open the Post Office in Port Stanley!? When the Argies had invaded, they had taken over the Post Office and had been using it, during their short stay, as a public lavatory! So it had to be cleaned out, disinfected and then re-opened as a Post Office! I was shocked! It was the first time in my RN career, that I had ever known Pusser pick the right man for the right job!

TUESDAY, 6 JULY 82 - DAY 44

Today's Daily Orders looked ominous, they started with:- "Dress of the Day - (0800 - 1600) Flame proof coveralls , anti flash hood tucked inside clothing, gloves, DMS Boots, woollen stockings, Action working dress or equivalent, lifejacket, identity tags round neck, Geneva Convention ID Card and carry 'Once-only suit', respirator and field dressing. Today is 'War Day' and it is going to be as realistic as possible. Everybody to be dressed as above for action and everybody in the right place at the correct time. It will be a little boring at times but remember previous lessons learnt. All exposed personnel, lookouts, guns crews, etc, and bridge staff to wear steel helmets."

(Then we got back to normal!)

0700*	Call the hands
0730	Hands to breakfast
0745*	Time check
0755*	Out pipes
0800*	Both watches muster on the Fore Deck
0800	2nd Degree of Readiness Defence Stations (Port Watch to 1200)
0830 - 0930	GUNNEX ROF (Target Flares)
o/c	1 watch NBCDX (Port Watch)
1130	Stbd Defence Watch to dinner
1200*	Stbd Defence Watch close up - Port Defence Watch to dinner
1300 - 1400	GUNNEX ROF (Target Flares)
o/c	1 watch NBCDX (Stbd Watch)
1345	Flying brief
1400*	Prepare for flying
1415*	Hands to Flying Stations
1430 - 1600	FLYEX
1600	Secure from State 2
1630*	Darken ship
1800*	Hands clean into night clothing
1900*	First Dog Watchmen clean messdecks and flats for Rounds
1925*	Stand by for Rounds
2300*	Pipe down

Note 1 was business:- "Holds and Tweendecks - These compartments are now fairly well secured for sea. Do not leave gash or empty packaging lying around. These are a fire risk and could also block bilge pumps. If you see gash in the tweendecks - ditch it."

Note 2 was back to the:- "History - RN - On 5/7/42 nine Swordfish aircraft, from HMS EAGLE, sank the Italian Destroyer ZEFFIRO at Tobruk. MN - Over 36,000 Merchant Seamen were killed in World War II. Percentage wise, this was more than any other service."

Note 3 read:- "Tombola - House claimed jointly by a St Helenian crewman and an MN Officer - £11 each. Tickets are now on sale from the Ship's Office and the numbers will restart on Wednesday's Daily Orders."

"Position at noon - 37 deg 08 min South, 41 deg 02 min West. Nearest land is Albardao, Brazil, 639 miles NW."

<u>TN</u> - AM - Gunnex. 0800 Defence Stations to arrival Falklands. Action messing.
    PM - NBCDX, Night FLYEX, Darken ship until further notice.

Today we 'Assumed 2nd Degree of Readiness'! No joke, I can tell you! Thank goodness I didn't have to check my Tombola numbers as well! Hectic! Where's the Armed Forces Pay Review Board now?

A Warship?!

Lest we forget - PM Thatcher appoints an official commission to "EXAMINE THE CAUSES OF BRITISH FAILURE TO PREVENT ARGENTINE CAPTURE OF THE FALKLAND ISLANDS".

WEDNESDAY, 7 JULY 82 - DAY 45

0700*	Call the hands
0730	Hands to breakfast
0745*	Time check
0755*	Out pipes
0800*	Both watches muster on the Fore Deck
0830	Flying brief
0845*	Prepare for flying
0900	STBD RAS
0900*	Hands to Flying Stations
0915	VERTREP
1000*	Stand easy
1015*	Hands carry on with your work
1130	SRs/Watchkeepers to dinner
1145*	Secure, JRs to dinner
1300*	Hands carry on with your work
1430	All guncrews muster in the Stern Gallery
1600*	Secure
1645*	Darken ship
1800*	Hands clean into night clothing
1900*	First Dog Watchmen clean messdecks and flats for Rounds
1925*	Stand by for Rounds
1930	Flying brief
2000*	Prepare for flying
2015*	Hands to Flying Stations
2030 - 2200	Night FLYEX
2300*	Pipe down

Note 1 started off with work:- "Defence Watch Exercise - This went fairly well. Minor watchbill changes required and the 2 damage control bases were merged for Defence Watches only. In future, Action Stations will be closed up and the ship will then be 'relaxed' into Defence Stations. NB - Personnel off watch/day workers are all at instant notice for Action Stations and must dress accordingly. Remember the next time we close up at Action Stations/Defence Watches, it will NOT be an exercise."

Note 2 was old hat! - "History - RN - On 7/7/1913 a landing party from HMS EAGLE captured and destroyed a 5 gun Fort at Faresina. MN - National Sailors' & Firemen's Union of GB/Ireland founded by Havelock Wilson 7/7/1887 in a cafe in Sunderland."

Note 3 read:- "Tombola numbers drawn by an SR were:- 1, 86, 71, 17, 74, 21, 23, 43, 8, 35, 84, 82, 68, 30, 75. Any claims for the line to the Ship's Office by 1200 today. Line £10.10, House £25.25, Snowball (43) £32.90, Welfare £5.05."

"Position at noon - 40 deg, 10 min South, 45 deg 20 min West. Nearest point of land - Tabo Polonio, Uruguay, 550 miles NW."

TN - AM - RAS/VERTREP   PM - Night FLYEX

Another hard day at the office!

THURSDAY, 8 JULY 82 - DAY 46

0700*	Call the hands
0730	Hands to breakfast
0745*	Time check
0755*	Out pipes
0800*	Both watches muster on the Fore Deck
0900	SR's Mess Meeting
1000*	Stand easy
1015*	Hands carry on with your work
1130	SRs/Watchkeepers to dinner
1145*	Secure, JR to dinner
1300*	Hands carry on with your work
1400	Welfare Committee Meeting
1600*	Secure
1645*	Darken ship
1800	Hands clean into night clothing
1900*	First Dog Watchmen clean messdecks and flats for Rounds
1925*	Stand by for Rounds
2300*	Pipe down

Note 1 was worth reading:- "Arctic Clothing - Ship's Company are advised to take very great care of any warm clothing on issue to them. This is specialised clothing that comes very expensive if lost or damaged, if it's on your slop chit, you pay for it."

Note 2 was a BZ:- "RAS - yesterday's was the best yet. I think we've got it. Well done all concerned. Special chuck up for the Winch Driver."

Note 3 was a new one and spoke for itself:- "Survival - Question 1 - When unprotected by clothing, which part of the body will lose the most heat per unit surface area? (Answer tomorrow)."

Note 4 was another:- "First Aide-Memoires! - The first priority when going to the aid of any casualty is to avoid becoming the next casualty! So think before you act!"

Thank goodness for Note 5 and some good old:- "History - RN - 8/7/40 Motor boats of HMS HERMES and her Swordfish aircraft made abortive attacks against the French Battleship RICHELIEU at Dakar. MN - SS ATHENIA was sunk by U Boat on 3/9/39 just hours after the war had started."

Note 6 read:- "Tombola numbers drawn by one of the FCPOs were:-
53, 46, 33, 14, 25, 50, 4, 16, 31, 88, 2, 79, 76, 52, 54. Claims for the line to the Ship's Office by 1200 today."

"Position at noon - 44 deg 30 min South, 49 deg 05 min West. Nearest point of land - Cabo Corientes in a well known South American country!"

There was an extra dit on the bottom of the Daily Orders informing certain members of the Ship's Company to collect 'Cold Weather Gear' from the Stores Office at 0830. It was obviously going to get a lot colder yet! As you can see there was no TN today so that made life a lot quieter for a change!

However, it was Meetings day! The SR's Mess had a meeting in the morning because of the meeting that was being held in the afternoon! The meeting in the afternoon was the ship's first Welfare Committee Meeting. Therefore, the SRs had to call a meeting of the Mess, in the morning, to vote in their two Mess Representatives for the Welfare Committee meeting that afternoon! Logical it may have been but also a bit late as St Helltem 14/82 had asked for the names by 4 July 82?! However, they did the dirty deed in less time than it took me to type this paragraph!

The Welfare Committee Meeting was another story! It lasted 1 hour 10 minutes and started with the Chairman, the Executive Officer, explaining the reasons for having a Welfare Committee and reading the relevant articles in Queen's Regulations (RN). The Treasurer then gave a report with a financial statement. (Receipts from Tombola, Laundry, JRs' Beer, Photographs and mess subscriptions were covering the Payments owed to the RN Film Corporation for the movies we had been watching. The Tombola was going well and the Snowball was building up. The Grand Draw had made £86.40 so far and two prizes had been obtained to start the 'ball rolling' - A pocket calculator from the RPO's Lost Property and the video cassette "Hot Racquets"!). One of the FSU01 SRs was given permission to start a Ship's Magazine with the proceeds going to the Welfare. Volunteers to sell Tombola tickets were required. A Grand Draw Committee was required. A list of Welfare property was to be drawn up so that at the end of the commission this property could be disposed of correctly. A query about the sale of JRs' Beer would be looked into. It was approved that an MN Officer should be allowed to sit in at these meetings in the future and also that the MO should become Vice-chairman. There was a query about videos and it was decided to do some swapping with other ships when the opportunity arose. Further to the "Hot Racquets" video fracas, the committee thought that the video should be screened. The Chairman would investigate and report back! A query was also raised about the Laundry crew which would also be investigated. In 'Any other business' suggestions were required for money raising, more information was required by the ship's company about the latest news from the Falklands and a negative answer to the question about if the Welfare was subsidising the cost of the jumpers, ties, etc. Next meeting to be held 1 Aug 82, we hope!

Lest we forget - Argentines release their ONLY 'acknowledged' British prisoners of war!

FRIDAY, 9 JULY 82 - DAY 47

0001	Retard clocks 1 hour to Quebec time (+4)
0700*	Call the hands
0730	Hands to breakfast
0745*	Time check
0755*	Out pipes
0800*	Action Stations
0815*	Fall out from Action Stations. Stbd Watch remain at Defence Stations
	RAS Party (Port & Stbd Watch) muster at No2 Rig - prepare for RAS
0830	Flying brief
0900	RAS
0915	VERTREP
1130	Port Watch to dinner
1200	Port Watch close up at Defence Stations. Stbd Watch to dinner
1600	Stbd watch close up at Defence Stations
1930	Port Watch to supper
2000	Port Watch close up at Defence Stations

Note 1 was nearly a shock:- "Beards - We have received instructions that all new growth sets of under 1 month duration must be shaved off. Established full sets may remain depending on local Falkland Island Orders." (All those with beards knew that if we were threatened by gas/chemical/nuclear attack they had to immediately shave off. The gas mask cannot make a perfect seal on the face with a beard in the way!)

Note 2 read:- "First Aid - An unconscious casualty is most likely to die from a blocked airway. In such a case take the following action:- remove any debris from the mouth, extend the neck to clear the airway, ie lie him on his side so that blood, secretions or vomit are not inhaled."

Note 3 was our answer from yesterday on:- "Survival - The head suffers the greatest heat loss per unit surface area, so don't forget to keep it covered. Question 2 - Why is alcohol dangerous to someone suffering from hypothermia?"

Note 4 was sweet! - "A Flight JR is 18 years old today - Happy birthday to you!"

Note 5 read:- "Tombola numbers drawn by a St Helenian crewman were:- 15, 7, 26, 66, 87, 63, 40, 38, 62, 42, 81, 89, 41, 9, 45. All claims for the snowball (House in 43 numbers or less) or house to Ship's Office by 1200 today. Line claimed by the Master and a JR on 46 the 17th number out for £5.05 each."

"Position at noon - 48 deg 40 min South, 54 deg 12 min West. Nearest land is Cape Carysfoot, Falkland, 222 miles SW."

TN - AM - Action Stations, VERTREP.   PM - Night FLYEX

The 'Routine' was now Defence Watches. Life had just got hard! The beauty of this system was that when I came off watch I then had to go and have a go at my 'In Tray' or man the shop! 'Life' kept on going without realising there was a war on! The other funny thing was how our Defence Watches had managed to start on a weekend?!

SATURDAY, 10 JULY 82 - DAY 48

0200   Stbd Watch close up at Defence Stations
0800   Port Watch close up at Defence Stations
1200   Stbd Watch close up at Defence Stations
1600   Port Watch close up at Defence Stations
2000   Stbd Watch close up at Defence Stations

"Programme - The ship was detached last night to rendezvous with the Carrier Battle Group to transfer mail. We are now proceeding to Port Stanley where we will anchor. We have been ordered to transfer all remaining mail to HMS AVENGER and stores to AVALONA STAR and GEESTPORT. The Hunts will now prepare for their minehunting role. It is unclear at present whether we will be ordered to operate from another safe anchorage closer to the Hunts area of operations. At present it appears that the Hunts may first be tasked with locating and marking the wreck of HMS COVENTRY on the north coast."

Note 1 was more doom and gloom:- "First Aid - Bleeding - the best way to stop a wound bleeding is to apply direct pressure and elevate the injured part."

Note 2 continued the theme:- "Survival - Answer to Question 2 - Alcohol dilates the outer blood vessels and increases the blood flow and stops shivering, therefore increasing the cooling effect and making the temperature drop even faster. Question 3 - What are the signs of hypothermia?"

Note 3 didn't help:- "History - RN - 9/7/1917 HMS VANGUARD destroyed by internal explosion at Scapa Flow. MN - Miss Victoria Drummond was the only woman engineer to serve at sea during World War II. She earned the MBE and Lloyd's Silver Medal for bravery at sea."

Thank goodness for Note 4:- "Tombola numbers drawn by an FSU01 JR were:- 64, 70, 5, 20, 73, 57, 61, 60, 44, 83, 59, 80, 78, 90, 49, 36, 10, 34, 67, 69. Any claims for the house to the Ship's Office by 1200 today."

Finally, Note 5 read:- "When opening and closing doors DON'T LET THEM SLAM."
(Was this because of the damage to the door, the threat of heart attacks at the thought of being shot at or even the threat of restarting the war by somebody opening fire when they thought they were being shot at?).

TN - Falkland Islands - 1030 Anchored Port William. VERTREP stores to
                                          AVELONA STAR.
                                          1930 Air Raid Warning Yellow.

In the middle of this mayhem, I had a rather silly letter to type! In normal times, RN ships are loaned 'newish' films for screening whilst the ship is at sea. They are then charged by the distributors, the RN Film Corporation, and usually the fees are paid by the ship's Welfare Fund. We had been issued with some films by the RN Film Corporation whilst in Portsmouth Dockyard! At the beginning of this month we had received a letter from them demanding payment 'as soon as possible'! Again, normally, the Welfare Fund onboard would collect monies from the NAAFI Shop profits and the Chinese Laundry profits and with mess subsidies etc, they would be well able to pay these type of bills! However, in our particular case we had no NAAFI Shop, only the Shipping Company Shop onboard, and no Chinese Laundry, only our own 'amateur' effort! In fact, we had virtually only set up a Welfare Committee to deal with this correspondence! This letter was being sent to explain all this and to claim "special circumstances amounting to financial hardship", in accordance with the relevant rules! In the meantime, not expecting much charity, the laundry and tombola had started raising money for a Welfare Fund, just in case! A Welfare Meeting had been called to explain all this and to look into the possibility of mess subscriptions etc. So here we were, fully prepared and ready to go to war and we were pratting about with silly little bills for movies! A Welfare Committee had been forced into being to waste valuable time, plus time and money were also being wasted on correspondence! These trivial payments could have been written off along with the rest of the cost of this war! Must have been a different budget, I suppose!

There was no 'Position at noon' any more - we were there! What a miserable looking hole! All this way and all this fuss over this? The weather was cold, wet and windy. The view, of what was the main inhabited part of the islands, was bleak! It was weekend in the middle of summer - talk about the bleak mid-winter, we'd sailed all this way to find it! What the devil were we really doing here?

A Hunt in Port Stanley

PART FOUR

THE SPOILS OF WAR!

or

NOT ANOTHER BLOODY WINTER

SUNDAY, 11 JULY 82 - DAY 49

0700* Call the hands
0730   Hands to breakfast
0745* Time check
0755* Out pipes
0800* Both watches muster on the Fore Deck
0800   Inflate fenders
AM   HMS BRECON & HMS LEDBURY berth on RMS ST HELENA
1000* Stand easy
1015* Hands carry on with your work
1130   SRs/Watchkeepers to dinner
1145* Secure, JRs to dinner
1300* Hands carry on with your work
1600* Secure
1600* Darken ship
1800* Hands clean into night clothing
1900* First Dog Watchmen clean messdecks and flats for Rounds
1925* Stand by for Rounds
2300* Pipe down

"Programme - We will be at anchor in Port Stanley for several days, while the Hunts prepare for their minehunting role. As well as defect rectification they have to set their sonars to work, carry out diving training and land all magnetic items to us. We still do not know what jobs they will be tasked with but they are thought to include:-
Find the wreckage of HMS COVENTRY, find the wreckage of HMS ARDENT, locate an anchor, check the minefield off the entrance to Port Stanley (ten miles have yet to be found). I hope we will know more in the next few days. Shore leave details will be promulgated when known."

Notes 1 & 2 reminded us about the basics:- "First Aid - Bleeding - if bleeding will not stop with direct pressure, apply a shell dressing. If this does not stop it, DO NOT remove the original dressing but put another one on top." "Survival - Answer to Q3 - Unexpected, unreasonable, uncooperative behaviour, physical and mental lethargy, uncontrolled shivering, complaining of numbness and cramp, plus failure of vision. Question 4 - What is the initial treatment for hypothermia?"

Note 3 read:- "Tombola - House claimed by a St Helenian crewman on 78, the 58th number out, for £25.25. Tickets will be on sale again in the next few days and the SNOWBALL is growing."

TN - HMS BRECON & HMS LEDBURY berthed alongside.

For the berthing of the two minehunters alongside us, we used the two inflatable fenders for the first time. They covered the full length of the ship down both sides and enabled the minehunters to come alongside and berth on us. The fenders were bright orange in colour, which must have looked strange from a distance.

The 'Routine' was still 'Daily Sea' even though we were anchored and not going anywhere. The 'Dress of the Day' reminded us to keep our 'Defence Watch Dress' handy! It was all very strange and sort of eerie! It was July and it was freezing! The view was of bleak countryside similar to the remote parts of the West of Scotland. We could also clearly see the bombed out ships just across the water, a stark reminder of what we were here for! Anchored alongside us down the water was a mixed variety of larger ships - warships and STUFT ships, the ship holding Argie prisoners, stores ships, tankers etc! A strange collection - they all looked dark, dirty and forlorn! The only signs of life were the activity of the helicopters and small boats of various types which were rushing backwards and forwards from ship to ship or ship to shore! Other than this background noise, there was an overall atmosphere or feeling of silence and gloom over the whole area!

That evening on the Flight Deck, whilst taking a breather from the office, I was surveying the scene around us and thinking that this place must be very close to being the arsehole of the world, when I remembered the film "Tora! Tora! Tora!" for some strange reason! The film about the Japanese bombing the US Fleet in Pearl Harbour, without warning! I looked down the line of anchored ships and decided that I'd better go and see if the bar was open!

'Mother Goose' and her goslings with 2 big orange balloons
(apologies for picture quality-the fenders are floating between the ships – note the weather!)

Lest we forget - CANBERRA arrives back at Southampton with 40, 42 and 45 Cdos. Britain drops its condition that "Argentina formally acknowledge the end of hostilities before repatriating the remaining prisoners of war". (So they still hadn't stopped!)

MONDAY, 12 JULY 82 - DAY 50

0700* Call the hands
0730 Mail closes onboard
0730 Hands to breakfast
0745* Time check
0755* Out pipes
0800* Both watches muster on the Fore Deck
1000* Stand easy
1015* Hands carry on with your work
1130 SRs/Watchkeepers to dinner
1145* Secure, JRs to dinner
1300* Hands carry on with your work
1400 Operations brief in Wardroom - All HODs
1400 2nd of Port Leg Stretch Party muster on the Fore Deck
1600* Secure
1600* Darken ship
1800* Hands clean into night clothing
1900* First Dog Watchmen clean messdecks and flats for Rounds
1925* Stand by for Rounds
2300* Pipe down

"Programme - We expect to remain here, at anchor, in Port Stanley for 4 to 5 days. After that we shall probably move to San Carlos to enable the Hunts to locate and mark HMS COVENTRY, HMS ANTELOPE and HMS ARDENT."

Note 1 spoke for itself:- "Personnel ashore - Personnel are to be in organised parties controlled by a SR and are restricted to the roads. Do not touch abandoned equipment, it may be booby trapped. Thousands of small round anti-personnel minelets were indiscriminately scattered by the Argentinians in their panic. These explosives were put in gardens and on all areas of waste ground. Only metallic road surfaces can be considered safe. BE WARNED. Parties for a leg stretch ashore will be organised, leaving the ship at 1400, returning from shore at 1600. Dress for leg stretch parties will be either full combat clothing or full foul weather clothing with berets. NO COWBOY RIGS. The OOD will inspect each party prior to it proceeding ashore."

Note 2 did the same:- "Looting - You are warned, possession of any Argentine Military Equipment is strictly forbidden, if any is found in your possession Military and Civil charges will be brought against you. DON'T COLLECT SOUVENIRS."

Note 3 was the start of another war! - "Water - Due to the marine environment the water making machine, Ossie Mosis, cannot function efficiently. This means we only have a limited amount onboard. All onboard are requested to use the minimum."

Note 4 read:- "Tombola will start again tomorrow - get your tickets now."

TN - Continue FSU maintenance on MHSC.

The QHM in Port Stanley had produced the "Port Stanley Information Pamphlet" for the information of visiting ships. It contained all the relevant information about anchorages, air bookings, boat routines, Ceremonial, Communications, Guard ships, HQ Land Forces, helicopter requests, mail and stores, Port Services, a map and guide to the town plus a list of "Dos and Don'ts" for libertymen! The 'Dos' went:- "Pay proper marks of respect to all Tri Service Officers; use clearly defined paths and roadways; a reasonable standard of Uniform dress is to be worn by all Service Personnel (includes combat/foul weather clothing, berets/caps are to be worn by all. Cold weather hats may be worn if applicable); see the sights, take pictures, stretch your legs and enjoy the feel of firm ground under your feet." The 'Don'ts' went:- "Do not wander over fields or stray from clearly defined paths; drinking and smoking in uniform in the streets is forbidden; do not touch any unusual objects or even common objects as they are liable to be booby trapped; large military equipment is <u>not</u> repeat <u>not</u> to be vandalised for souvenirs; no unoccupied property is to be entered without authority from HQLFFI; do not exceed the speed limit of 25 mph in Port Stanley; do not miss your liberty boat back to the ship, you will spend the night ashore sleeping rough if you do so and temperatures can and do fall below freezing point!" The Port Stanley guide informed us that there were two churches, 10 shops and 2 hotels, (one of which was only open to residents!).

Went ashore and had a look! What a mess! The aftermath of battle is not a pretty sight or smell! We could only walk around the roads. The pub was shut and we weren't allowed in it anyway! The shop we went in was gloomy and pretty bare! That was it, nothing else to do but walk and the weather did not encourage too much of that! Port Stanley was only the size of a large village so once we had walked around for half an hour we were ready to get back onboard, incredible as it may seem! When you can only walk inside the tapes on the roads and everything is such a mess and a dangerous mess at that, you soon lose interest! The boys had got bored and it was bloody snowing now! The only problem was that the boat wasn't going back to the ship until 1600! We had over an hour to wait, we were stone cold sober, it was snowing and windy and there was nowhere to shelter! What a happy little group we were!

Port Stanley from above

Lest we forget:- This was the last day for qualification for the South Atlantic Medal??

TUESDAY, 13 JULY 82 - DAY 51

0700* Call the hands
0730   Mail closes
0730   Hands to breakfast
0745* Time check
0755* Out pipes
0800* Both watches muster on the Fore Deck
0800* Prepare for flying
0815* Hands to Flying Stations
0830   373 + 1st Lt to recce trisponder sites
1000* Stand easy
1015* Hands carry on with your work
1130   SRs/Watchkeepers to dinner
1145* Secure, JRs to dinner
1300* Hands carry on with your work
1400   1st of STBD Leg Stretch Party muster on the Fore Deck
1600* Secure
1600* Darken ship
1800* Hands clean into night clothing
1900* First Dog Watchmen clean messdecks and flats for Rounds
1925* Stand by for Rounds
2300* Pipe down

"Programme - On Thursday, we shall weigh anchor, probably at 0800, and proceed to top up with fresh water from FORT TORONTO and then dieso from a tanker. We may also VERTREP fresh fruit and veg from GEESTPORT. On completion we overnight passage to Port San Carlos where we anchor until the Hunts complete their task, possibly two weeks. On completion we return to Port Stanley and anchor. Hunts sweep Port William/Stanley approaches."

Note 1 explained our new "Boat Routine - A ship's lifeboat will run the following routine from RMS ST HELENA to Government House Jetty daily:-

From RMS ST HELENA		From Shore	
0900		0915	
1115		1130	
1300		1315	
1530		1545	

The Gemini is NOT to be taken away without permission of 1st Lt or OOD in his absence."

Note 2 read:- "Photographs - One of the JRs has a selection of colour photos of our recent passage. He is taking orders for copies. Anyone interested visit his cabin."

Note 3 was back to:- "Survival - Answer to Q4 - Remove wet outer clothing if possible, warm patient up and if conscious give warm, sweet drinks and food. Question 5 - With a water temperature of 5 deg C, what is your life expectancy if you fall overboard not wearing a survival suit?"

Note 4 was also back to:- "First Aid - The following are signs and symptoms of fractures:- Pain, a fracture nearly always hurts, swelling and bruising of the affected part, deformity and unnatural movement of the part, loss of function, crepitus - the sound of grating when the ends of two bones rub together."

Note 5, the old favourite, read:- "Tombola numbers drawn by a Flight SR were:- 40, 68, 66, 65, 31, 79, 29, 50, 16, 1. Prizes this week are:- Line £11.20, House £28, Snowball (44) £44.10, Welfare £5.60. Any claims for the line to the Ship's Office by 1200 today."

TN - Trisponders placed for MHSC in Port San Carlos area.

As soon as we had settled in here, the converted trawlers, who had been doing the minesweeping job, were sent home. They were HMS CORDELLA, HMS NORTHELLA, HMS FARNELLA, HMS JUNELLA and HMS PICT. They had been heavily armour-plated and looked nothing like trawlers! In fact, as they sailed out of Port Stanley in line past us, they looked quite grim and spooky, to use a modern term! However, the boys onboard were making a lot of happy noises and seemed as if they had been looking forward to going home!

So now we had settled into this strange routine! We could see all sorts of activity going on around us from our anchorage and we could now go ashore in a 'Leg Stretch Party'. BUT it still wasn't normal!

We were now getting visits from members of other ship's companies who had been here since it started. So the stories we were hearing were grim to say the least! However, nobody could say with any conviction that it had all now ended! Some of these younger sailors we talked to had become very old, very quickly and certainly wouldn't forget all this in a hurry!

More STUFT ships in Port Stanley

WEDNESDAY, 14 JULY 82 - DAY 52

0700* Call the hands
0730 Mail closes
0730 Hands to breakfast
0745* Time check
0755* Out pipes
0800* Both watches muster on the Fore Deck
0800* Prepare for flying
0815* Hands to Flying Stations
1000* Stand easy
1015* Hands carry on with your work
1030 Operations brief in the Wardroom - HODs, OOWs, & RS to attend
1130 SRs/Watchkeepers to dinner
1145* Secure, JRs to dinner
1300* Hands carry on with your work
1300 1st Port Leg Stretch Party muster on the Fore Deck
1600* Secure
1600* Darken ship
1800 Hands clean into night clothing
1900* First Dog Watchmen clean messdecks and flats for Rounds
1925* Stand by for Rounds
2300* Pipe down

Note 1 was bad news:- "Water - Ossie Mosis is now defunct and producing nothing. It is, therefore, imperative that we use water sparingly from now on. You have been warned - RATIONING will be the next step." (Reverse Osmosis desalination plant was fitted to STUFT ships at very short notice and some of it was 'not specifically designed for marine use'! (These were the actual words from on high!) Therefore, many defects occurred and heavy maintenance loads were imposed on the ships. Stores were difficult to obtain as they had to be ordered direct from the manufacturers incurring all the inherent delays. In our particular case, we had severe problems with the lack of depth of water around the Falkland Islands and especially with the high content of sea krill in the water. Each STUFT ship was requested to complete a questionnaire about their plant on their return to UK.).

Note 2 was back to:- "Survival - Answer to Q5 - Life expectancy in water at 5 degrees C is approximately 15 - 18 minutes. The water temperature NOW is 3.3C. Question 6 - How many once only suits are carried in a life raft?"

Note 3 was also back to:- "First Aid - Treatment of a fracture - Stop any severe bleeding, cover any wounds on or near the fracture, immobilise the broken ends of bone, also joints above and below the fracture site, finally treat for shock."

Note 4 read:- "Tombola numbers drawn by one of the St Helenian crew were:- 78, 63, 3, 85, 8, 49, 34, 64, 20, 89. Line claims to the Ship's Office by 1200 today."

TN - Progress maintenance on MHSC.

I had a change of scenery today - the Head of our Task Group, the Commander on

HMS BRECON, needed an urgent typing job done! As I was the only scribes around - I got the job! I was transferred to HMS BRECON by small boat at the crack of dawn. Strange little trip! The previous evening there had been the usual rumours about Argentinian air attacks! It occurred to me that this was not the place to be if this was going to happen! I had also typed the Daily Orders yesterday with the note about how long you could survive in these waters! At least it wasn't snowing or raining. It was, however, extremely cold and crisp and very quiet, sort of eerie! The only noise was sea birds and the chugging of the engine! We were surrounded by bleak countryside and no signs of life! Why would anybody want to have a war here? Strange world!

Once onboard, I got a brief tour of the ship so that I could find my way off, if needed! I was given a compartment deep down the fore end to work in and left to get on with it. Ridiculous, I know, but I actually felt better back on a Pusser's grey job - safer! I had to type a very long report that day, as it was required for an Inquiry the following day. As can be expected in these circumstances, things didn't go quite according to plan! Half way through the morning we had an Air Raid Warning Red! So I had to leave my little hole and go up and sit in the pokey little messing area until the threat disappeared. Everybody else went rushing off to their Action Stations, closing the ship down on the way and there I was, dressed in all the war and survival gear, sat on my own in the dining room, helpless and jobless! I had forgotten the way out and was stranded in 'no man's land'! I now knew the real meaning behind that old saying:- "Feeling like a spare p***k at a wedding"! As luck would have it, it was a false alarm again, so we all went back to work after about half an hour of this! Talk about stress, this was no joke, I can tell you! Other than this, I was looked after well and I got the job completed that afternoon and returned back onboard to my own in tray, which of course was full again! However, I now felt glad to be back onboard, where I knew where to go and what to do in an emergency! Funny old world isn't it?

The trawlers/minesweepers going home

Lest we forget - Final 593 Argentine prisoners-of-war repatriated.

THURSDAY, 15 JULY 82 - DAY 53

0700* Call the hands
0700   Mail closes
0730   Hands to breakfast
0745* Time check
0755* Out pipes
0800* Both watches muster on the Fore Deck
0800   Weigh anchor proceed to GA WALKER to fuel, o/c water from FORT TORONTO
o/c   Passage to Port San Carlos
0800* Prepare for flying
0815* Hands to Flying Stations
0830   373 with 1st Lt to PSC deploy Trisponder chain
1000* Stand easy
1015* Hands carry on with your work
1130   SRs/Watchkeepers to dinner
1145* Secure, JRs to dinner
1300* Hands carry on with your work
1530* Clear lower deck - muster in the Stern Gallery for Ops Brief
1600* Secure
1600* Darken ship
1800* Hands clean into night clothing
1900* First Dog Watchmen clean messdecks and flats for Rounds
1925* Stand by for Rounds
2300* Pipe down

Note 1 carried on the lessons for:- "First Aid - Shock - is increased by pain, loss of body fluid, exposure to extremes of temperature, mental anxiety and fright. Shock is present to some degree in every wound, illness or injury."

Note 2 did the same for:- "Survival - Answer to Q6 - 2 once only suits in a life raft. Question 7 - How much water is allowed per man per day whilst in a life raft?"

Note 3 read:- "Tombola numbers drawn by the RS were:- 11, 22, 48, 56, 84, 86, 74, 88, 35, 25. The line was claimed by a St Helenian crew member for £11.20, on 89 the 20th number out."

TN - Passage from Port Stanley to Port San Carlos.
        0730 MHSC slipped.
        0800 Weigh and proceed to Port San Carlos. First refuel from GA WALKER. 373 deploying Trisponder chain. MHSC minehunting in Sound.

I, personally, received a signal from our Task Group Commander today! A BZ for my typing effort in Port Stanley yesterday. It made a change to have your efforts noticed at that level!

I was Duty Senior Rate again, which was good in a way, because it gave me another chance for a change of scenery from the office. Life can get dull in the same old rut.

We had the "Clear lower deck" for an 'Ops Brief'. In reality, it was to stop the 'buzz-mongers'! Some of the boys had got themselves wound up for action, so life at the minute was not what they expected! Little did they know that, the most excitement they were going to get for the minute was the Tombola numbers!

Another STUFT ship

Trig point

FRIDAY, 16 JULY 82 - DAY 54

0700*	Call the hands
0730	Hands to breakfast
0730*	Prepare for flying
0745*	Time check
0745*	Hands to Flying Stations
0755*	Out pipes
0800*	Both watches muster on the Fore Deck
0800	Mail closes
0800 approx	Anchor at Port San Carlos Water, 3 cables from Ajax Bay Jetty
0800	373 & 1st Lt set up Trisponders
1000*	Stand easy
1015*	Hands carry on with your work
1130	SRs/Watchkeepers to dinner
1145*	Secure, JRs to dinner
1300*	Hands carry on with your work
1600*	Secure
1600*	Darken ship
1800*	Hands clean into night clothing
1900*	First Dog Watchmen clean messdecks and flats for Rounds
1925*	Stand by for Rounds
2300*	Pipe down

"Programme - After today's brief you are fully up to date (?)."

Note 1 was the start of another idea to give the boys something to do:- "Ship's Magazine will be printed next week. This weekend we need stories, dits, cartoons, crosswords, etc. If you don't do it, nobody else will! All articles to the Editor."

Note 2 was back to:- "Survival - Answer to Q7 - 18 fluid ounces per man per day of water after the first 24 hours have elapsed. Nil for the first 24 hours. Question 8 - What food is contained in survival packs with a 25 man life raft?"

Note 3 was:- "First Aid - Shock signs and symptoms - pallor, skin cold and clammy, rapid weak pulse, rapid and shallow respiration. Complaints of nausea and giddyness, may also complain of thirst, dazed confused and feeling cold. If the patient is left untreated he will become unconscious and die."

Note 4 read:- "Tombola numbers drawn by the Sick Bay JR were:- 57, 67, 14, 83, 45, 24, 76, 2, 52, 61. Claims for the snowball/house to the Ship's Office by 1200 today."

TN - Port San Carlos - 1030 - alongside TIDEPOOL taking on fresh water
1530 - anchored in well protected anchorage 062
Ajax Bay Jetty 1.2 miles.

San Carlos Water was a nice place! We got a better view of the wildlife and penguins here, even though it was from a distance! It reminded me very much of the West of Scotland! Roll on weekend, there again maybe not, we've got to clean up for Rounds again!

SATURDAY, 17 JULY 82 - DAY 55

0700*   Call the hands
0730   Hands to breakfast
0730*   Prepare for flying
0745*   Hands to Flying Stations
0745*   Time check
0755*   Out pipes
0800*   Both watches muster on the Fore Deck
0800   Mail closes
0800   373 to check Trisponders
1000*   Stand easy
1015*   Hands carry on with your work
1055*   Stand by for Master's Messdeck Rounds
1100*   Master's Messdeck Rounds
1130   SRs/Watchkeepers to dinner
1145*   Secure, JRs to dinner
1600*   Darken ship
1800*   Hands clean into night clothing
2300*   Pipe down

We then had another innovation to Daily Orders:- "Daily CHUCK UP (CU) and Daily KICK IN THE CRUTCH (KITC) - nominations to be in the Ship's Office by 1030 daily. Today's CU - Flight for setting up Trisponders in adverse weather conditions. Today's KITC - Those who used all the water yesterday."

Note 1 continued:- "Water Rationing - Until it is confirmed that Ossie Mosis will function satisfactorily at this anchorage, water will only be available during the following times:- 0630 to 0730, 1130 to 1300, 1600 to 1800, 2100 to 2200."

Note 2 was another attempt at normal living:- "Field Gun 82 - Competitive runs start on 17 July 82. Practice runs so far:- Run 1 Guzz beat Pompey, Run 2 Air beat Guzz, Run 3 Air beat Pompey, Run 4 Guzz beat Pompey. When the real runs start full details will be printed in Daily Orders." (These were the annual Field Gun Competition Runs from the Royal Tournament at Earl's Court in London. Every day the results are signalled out to the whole of the Royal Navy ashore and afloat. The competition is between the teams from Portsmouth, Plymouth and Naval Air Commands, so all RN personnel have allegiance to their home command.).
NB. They've now binned the Royal Tournament!

Note 3 was back to reality:- "First Aid - Treatment for shock - Lay the patient down if possible, slightly elevate legs and treat the condition causing shock. Maintain body temperature and loosen tight clothing at the waist and neck. Give warm sweet drinks if conscious, has no internal bleeding and will not require anaesthetic within 3 hours. Try to reassure patient."

Note 4 ditto:- "Survival - Answer to Q8 - 150 packets of glucose sweets (barley sugars, butterscotch, spangles). 2 packs per man per day for 3 days. Question 9 - Why should the raft floor be fully inflated immediately after you board?"

Note 5 read:- "Tombola numbers drawn by the Purser were:- 47, 13, 43, <u>77</u>, 5, 75, 23, 87, 39, 41. Any claims for snowball/house to Ship's Office by 1200 today."

<u>TN</u> - 0830 Called on Guardship - HMS SOUTHAMPTON.

The Master did the Rounds this morning! It was not quite the same as when the SNO did them, thank goodness! However, nobody told us about the change until we'd done the cleaning, so a lot of effort was put in that could have been glossed over! Cute, eh? It was more of a walk around and a chat as opposed to inspecting <u>inside</u> lavatory bowls like the SNO would have been doing!

It didn't seem like weekend, it was dank and wet outside and all was quiet. So in the afternoon I went back to the office to clear my 'in' tray in peace. I was busily typing away when there was a knock at the door and a voice asked where he could find the Ship's Office. The voice sounded familiar and I turned round to find an old shipmate, scribes and golfing partner of mine standing there looking war-torn and haggard! Our shock at seeing each other in this backwash was soon dispelled as we stood at the mess bar and he started annihilating my mess bill for the rest of the day! (In the RN there is a silly custom that dictates that a visitor to a mess, does not buy any drinks whatsoever! His host foots the bill with other mess members helping him out! This can be a very costly custom!). The war dits flowed and so did the beer as a few other SRs from HMS SOUTHAMPTON arrived in the mess. They were most amazed by our little ship, especially at teatime when we took them to the dining room and they had salads and saw the stewardesses! Goodness me, it's a small world isn't it?

HMS Southampton looking busy – a real ship!

SUNDAY, 18 JULY 82 - DAY 56

0700*	Call the hands
0700*	Prepare for flying
0700	Watch on deck transport Trisponder batteries to Flight Deck
0715*	Hands to Flying Stations
0730*	Hands to breakfast
0730	Mail closes
0730	Launch 373 for Trisponder maintenance
0815*	Time check
0825*	Out pipes
0830*	Both watches muster on the Fore Deck
0930*	Secure
1045	Church Service in the Forward Lounge
1100*	Pipe down
1100 approx	Scots Guardsmen from Ajax Bay visit. (10 junior ranks - remaining overnight and 10 senior ranks/WOs/officers for dinner only.
1300	Leg Stretch Party to shore
1600*	Darken ship
1900*	First Dog Watchmen clean up messdecks and flats for Rounds
1925*	Stand by for Rounds

"CU – 'Air' for being unbeaten in the 1982 Field Gun. (Ed. 'So far')
KITC - Crew of the lifeboat who tried to 'ROCK' the boat this afternoon - literally!"

Note 1 was nearly a BZ! - "Master's Messdeck Rounds - were good overall. Overheads require attention and those heads with black mould on the bulkheads are to be painted with white top coat (Action Senior Hands of Cabins). Cabins B7 and B12 were judged to be the best cabins."

Note 2 read:- "Mail - Due to the adverse weather conditions in the South Atlantic no Stores/Mail have left Ascension Island since 14/7/82. It is hoped the weather will improve and that mail will arrive at Port Stanley tomorrow."

Note 3 was a warning to the sightseers:- "Personnel going ashore - are to stick to the tracks and not touch Ordnance left lying around, as it has not yet been made safe."

Note 4 read:- "Boat Routine - to Ajax Bay Jetty:-

From RMS ST HELENA		From Ajax Bay	
	0900		0915
	1115		1130
	1300		1315
	1530		1545"

Note 5 was about housekeeping! - "Gash - Burnable gash will be taken ashore and burnt by the Ship's Boat each morning. Dry burnable gash is to be stowed on the Fore Deck at the Port RAS Point. Non-burnable gash (tins, bottles, etc) is to be stowed STBD side Fore Deck No4 hatch in waterproof bags. This will be taken to sea and dumped by MHSCs as the opportunity arises. This gash must be properly bagged."

Note 6 was the result of yet another mess from pre-RNP days! So why had I got lumbered with it? - "Pay queries - All FSU personnel with problems on their Pay Balance Statements please hand same in at Ship's Office, where a letter will be concocted and forwarded to HMS CENTURION, to solve all problems at one go!"

Note 7 was more domestics:- "Cups/Mugs - There will be a 48 hour civvie cup/mug amnesty. ALL MN cups/mugs are to be returned to the servery by 1200 Monday and thereafter, IMMEDIATELY after use, otherwise polystyrene cups will be used."

Note 8 read:- "Survival - Answer to Q9 - The floor is inflated to add insulation between it and the sea. Question 10 - Where can you find detailed instruction of action to be taken on boarding a life raft?"

Note 9 read:- "First Aid - Asphyxia - is the prevention of breathing. The causes are numerous but can be grouped under the following headings:- obstruction internal or external, chest wounds, inhalation of poisonous substances or gases - disease (tetanus or polio), electric shock. (Tomorrow - signs of asphyxia)."

Note 10 equalled Day 33's record and read:- "Tombola numbers drawn by an FSU SR were:- 21, 19, 10, 38, 33, 28, 26, 82, 55, 27, 81, 58, 53, 62, 46. Claims for house to the Ship's Office by 1200 today."

TN - Crosspol Scots Guards x 10

It was Sunday Routine, I had a hangover and I'd got a 'Call Round' to the SRs' Mess on HMS SOUTHAMPTON at lunchtime! (An invite to another ship or mess). A real ship with CSB! There wasn't going to be much overtime worked today! (CSB is Courage's Sparkling Bitter, which is the strong export beer served in SR's messes throughout the fleet. Because it is made for export, it travels and keeps longer. It's also very tasty and creeps up on you!). So, later that morning I and several others were all ready to go and get even for some of the damage that had been done to our messbills yesterday! However, on looking around when we went to catch the boat, we found the bloody RN had shot through! HMS SOUTHAMPTON, as Guardship, had been sent away that morning for some task or other! "The shoot through bastards" was the immediate response from the assembled victims! We never saw them again while we were down there and I never caught up with my fellow scribes until many years later! The lengths some people will go to, to avoid getting the beer in!

We all went back to the mess to commiserate! After a few pints of commiseration, I got caught again! I ended up back in the office for the afternoon, typing the first edition of the ship's magazine! Talk about a soft touch, well we all need a hobby!

The Royal Tournament at Earls Court – Field Gun run

'Flying Angels'

MONDAY, 19 JULY 82 - DAY 57

0700* Call the hands
0715   Mail closes
0715* Prepare for flying
0730   Hands to breakfast
0730* Hands to Flying Stations
0745* Time check
0745   373 to HMS BRECON to take Task Group Commander to Port Stanley
0755* Out pipes
0800* Both watches muster on the Fore Deck
1000* Stand easy
1015* Hands carry on with your work
1030   Boat to Ajax Bay Jetty with gash and Crosspol Team
1130   SRs/Watchkeepers to dinner
1145* Secure, JRs to dinner
1300* Hands carry on with your work
1600* Secure
1600* Darken ship
1800* Hands clean into night clothing
1900* First Dog Watchmen clean messdecks and flats for Rounds
1925* Stand by for Rounds
2300* Pipe down

"CU - The Editor, for all the hard work put into producing your magazine at the weekend. (Available for only 10p per copy - A real snip).
KITC - From the LSTD - To the JR who beat him to the house by 1 number."

Note 1 was for information:- "The Scots Guards ashore took part in the final battle for Port Stanley, after which they had various tasks including the guarding of Argentine prisoners at the abandoned Refrigeration Plant at Ajax Bay Jetty. 100 Scots Guards guarded 500 Argentine prisoners. The war graves of 3 Commando Brigade (42/45 Royal Marine Commandos), the Parachute Regiment (2 Para Brigade), Colonel H and Captain Wood plus the men killed on HMS COVENTRY are here, also the Memorial Cross on the hill. Opportunity exists for up to 10 members of the Ship's Company to spend 24 hours ashore with the Scots Guards. This is an opportunity to hear at first hand about how the battle was waged and also to realise what it is all about in any case - in short why we are here!"

Note 2 was a reminder that even in our new role as a 'hotelier', life in the RN went on as normal:- "Evening Rounds - JRs' cabins are on the Evening Rounds route and should be squared off prior to Rounds."

Note 3 read:- "Field Gun 82 - 17 July 1982
          Run 1 Pompey 025406/025406   1   Guzz   025205/025205 2
          Run 2 Guzz   024501/024501   2   Air   025306/025306 1
          Total Runs:- Air 1, Guzz 2, Pompey 1.
          Total points to date:- Air 1, Guzz 4, Pompey 1.
          Aggregate times:- Air 025306. Guzz 053706, Pompey 025406.
          Fastest times:- Air 025306, Guzz 024501, Pompey 025406."

Note 4 read:- "Tombola - House claimed by a JR on 55, the 59th number out, for £28. Tickets are now on sale for next week. Buy now to avoid disappointment."

TN - Providing 'Hearts and Minds' to San Carlos Settlement - MO and MN Caterer carrying out School Teaching duties to children at Settlement (13 from 5 - 13). Crosspol Scots Guards x 10.

Life had changed again! We were now busy trying to run the normal routine as well as being hosts to Crosspols! It was a strange situation! Strange people wandering around the ship! Strange goings on by men who had been to war! Drunken strangers all over the place! But what could you say - if I had seen some of the things that they had seen, I would be acting pretty strangely and be getting pretty drunk!

Today saw the 1st edition of the Ship's Magazine on sale, all proceeds going to the Welfare Fund. A literary masterpiece! The idea was to give the troops a chance to air their grievances and get all their little complaints out in the open. Otherwise their drips and moans would only fester and grow out of all proportion! I have copied the front cover of this epic for your entertainment but the rest of the contents I am unable to divulge, as I may be infringing copyright laws! (There are also a lot of names mentioned, some good some bad, libel laws may be infringed!) The magazine covered such diverse subjects as editorial comment on the lack of copy for the first issue, letters to the editor, two poems, some items of world shipping news, local Falkland Islands knowledge, a sports quiz, a sports page and a crossword. However, one article was my own work, so I've decided that it can be reproduced!

With some of our ship's company having such a thirst for knowledge and their ability to invent their own news, I thought this article might amuse!

GOOD BUZZES.

1. This week - Sunday will be a Sunday - NOT Day 63.
2. "Hot Racquets" was written by Hans Christian Anderson.
3. RPO does not stand for Robotic Person in Orbit.
4. The Forward Lounge does not have a split personality.
5. FSU does not stand for Fleet Sleeping Unit.
6. The Flight are not on drugs.
7. MN Officers will now work in the afternoons.
8. Stocks of Xmas Trees have run out in the Ship's Office as we need the paper to print Standing Orders.
9. The RS knows a good buzz.
10. Starting 1 August 1982 they will be darkening ship on the Torpoint and Gosport Ferries.
11. The Osmosis Plant Maintainer cannot walk on water.
12. Neither can the POMA. (He got ducked by the Flight on a transfer!).
13. The Pilot and the Aircrewman are due jabs. (POMA's revenge?).
14. Electricity and Water Bills are due. (A joke played on new joiners on ships, they are presented with a water or electricity bill and sent round the ship to pay it!).
15. There will be a meeting of the 'CB Club' on the Bridge next month – 'Get your ears on Anus'.

16. The Flight are now giving Squash lessons in the hangar.
17. The Buffer is alive and well and living in Bangcock!
18. There were 2 halves to the 'Crossing the Line' Ceremony - we have only had one of them!
19. Re-conditioned safe for sale - apply Flight Commander. (We lost a file and guess where it was found, even though he swore blind he hadn't got it!).
20. The Ship's Shop is a non-prophet making organisation.

Cover of 'SEE-DIT' Magazine

TUESDAY, 20 JULY 82 - DAY 58

0700* Call the hands
0730* Prepare for flying
0730   Hands to breakfast
0745* Hands to Flying Stations
0745* Time check
0755* Out pipes
0800* Both watches muster on the Fore Deck
0800   Launch 373
1000* Stand easy
1015* Hands carry on with your work
1130   SRs/Watchkeepers to dinner
1145* Secure, JRs to dinner
1300* Hands carry on with your work
1600* Secure
1615* Darken ship
1800* Hands clean into night clothing
1900* First Dog Watchmen clean messdecks and flats for Rounds
1925* Stand by for Rounds
2300* Pipe down

Note 1 was still going strong:- "First Aid - Asphyxia - Signs and symptoms - shortness of breath and dizziness; rapid pulse; swelling of veins in the neck; blueness of lips, ears and fingers; respiration and pulse become slow and irregular and finally stops. Death rapidly ensues."

Note 2 was also surviving! - "Survival - Answer to Q10 - BR1329(Handbook for Survivors) found in survival pack in life raft. Question 11 - What colour box is the emergency radio kept in?"

Note 3 read:- "Tombola will start again tomorrow - get your tickets now."

Note 4 was an oddment resulting from the Ship's Magazine. It revealed the answers to the Crossword Puzzle Competition which was won by one of the MN Officers.

TN -   Crosspol Scots Guards x 10
       HMS LEDBURY alongside - defect rectification by FSU

Today we received a newspaper clipping from back home! It got some of the details right (see below).

The buzz was that we were going to be down south a lot longer than expected! Surprise, surprise!! This is what caused the change at the top of today's Daily Orders - instead of the day and date, we had 'DAY 58'! It was widely regarded as being similar to counting off the days of your sentence, in a prison cell! Never forgetting, of course, that conditions in prison were normally far superior to conditions for ratings at sea in the Royal Navy - we would have to fit at least twenty people in a normal sized cell!

Tuesday 13th July 1982
 # Still is by all accounts!

MOTHER ROLE FOR LINER

By JOHN PETTY
Shipping Correspondent

WHILE the big ships come home in triumph, one of the smallest and most romantic British passenger liners will spend many more months in the Falklands, "mothering" minesweepers and bomb disposal squads still facing a long and dangerous task.

She is the 76-passenger St Helena, 3,150 tons, which normally makes sedate voyages from Avonmouth to Ascension Island, St Helena and Cape Town.

Now, equipped with a flight deck conversion and guns, she has gone south with a fleet of five trawlers and two 615-ton Hunt class minesweepers, the Brecon and the Ledbury, to clear away the debris of war—a case of "cleaning up after the big show."

Unexploded bombs as well as mines have to be shifted and made safe.

Moored hotel

Also being retained by Government is the Rangatira, 9,387 tons, which is under the British flag but owned by Union Steam of New Zealand. She was working in North Sea oilfields when requisitioned and has also seen service as a moored hotel.

It is likely that these will be the last merchant ships to be handed back. Curnow Shipping, of Portleven, Cornwall, will certainly be surprised if the St Helena is back before the New Year.

Meanwhile, the company is seeking to charter another ship to stand-in for the St Helena. At present it is having to use

WEDNESDAY, 21 JULY 82 - DAY 59

0700*   Call the hands
0715   Mail closes
0730   Hands to breakfast
0745*   Time check
0755*   Out pipes
0800*   Both watches muster on the Fore Deck
1000*   Stand easy
1015*   Hands carry on with your work
1130   Boat with sports parties to Ajax Bay Jetty (See Note 1)
1130   SRs/Watchkeepers to dinner
1145*   Secure, JRs to dinner
1300*   Hands carry on with your work
1600*   Secure
1615*   Darken ship
1800*   Hands clean into night clothing
1900*   First Dog Watchmen clean messdecks and flats for Rounds
1925*   Stand by for Rounds
2300*   Pipe down

Note 1 was a shock:- "Sports Make and Mend - Football matches with the Scots
Guards have been arranged. If you can be spared by your Head of Department give
your name to the Sports Representative as soon as possible."

Note 2 read:- "Tombola numbers drawn by one of the FSU SRs were:- 55, 16, 62, 78,
81, 32, 67, 52, 35, 12. Prizes this week are:- Line £8.40, House £21, Snowball (45)
£52.50 (making a total of £73.50), Welfare £4.20."

TN -   Crosspol Scots Guards x 10
       HMS LEDBURY alongside

It was nice to see the FSU working for a change! They could normally be found
supporting the mess! It was nice to go in the mess and have a choice of chairs for a
change! Of course, their standard answer to this was - "If it isn't broken, I can't mend
it and I've done my user checks!!" Loafing bastards!

Life was getting bitchy and was not helped by the continual flow of visitors to our
'hotel'. It was the same every day, strange faces milling about the ship in various
stages of drunkeness, it was getting tedious! Some of the JRs who had let them use
their cabins had had gear stolen and damaged! One even had photographs of his
girlfriend pinched from his bedspace! To be fair, the majority of them were good
news but there's always the odd rotten apple in every barrel who spoils things for the
rest! OK, so they'd had a hard time but there are limits when you are a guest in
somebody else's house!

THURSDAY, 22 JULY 82 - DAY 60

0700* Call the hands
0715   Mail closes
0730   Hands to breakfast
0745* Time check
0755* Out pipes
0800* Both watches muster on the Fore Deck
1000* Stand easy
1015* Hands carry on with your work
1130   SRs/Watchkeepers to dinner
1145* Secure, JRs to dinner
1300* Hands carry on with your work
1600* Secure
1615* Darken ship
1800* Hands clean into night clothing
1900* First Dog Watchmen clean messdecks and flats for Rounds
1925* Stand by for Rounds
2300* Pipe down

Note 1 was good news for a change:- "Mail - Serials missing, due to bad weather, had now been received and we are up to date again".

Note 2 read:- "Tombola numbers drawn by an FSU SR were:- 48, 47, 15, 13, 44, 71, 74, 89, 38, 39. Any claims for the line to the Ship's Office by 1200 today."

Note 3 was good news for the Flight:- "Field Gun 82.
19/7/82 Run 1 N/A   Run 2   Air   024909/024909 2
             N/A   Guzz 030301/030501 1
20/7/82 Run 1 Air   024802/024802 2 Run 2   Pomp 030706/030706 1
                  Pomp 025804/030204 1   Guzz 025705/025705 2
Total Runs: Air 3, Guzz 4, Pompey 3.
Total Points: Air 5, Guzz 7, Pompey 3.
Aggregate: Air 083107, Guzz 114002, Pompey 090406.
Fastest: Air 024802, Guzz 024501, 025406."

TN - 0830 HMS LEDBURY slip.

We had a day off from Crosspolling today! You can have too much of a good thing! "See-Dit" had gone down well with the troops. It raised a few eyebrows and got a few laughs, that was the point of the exercise! Anybody could air a grievance in print, for all to see, without getting into trouble. There obviously had to be limits and guidelines had been set so as not to upset the libel laws! In short the boys could have a good drip legally - within reasonable limits! What more inspiration to put pen to paper could Jack need! Now they knew what to do and had seen it in print, the next edition should be very interesting indeed! The only problem I had with this was the Editor was now flushed with success and couldn't wait to start on the next edition - which meant more bloody typing and printing for me! It's nice to have another hobby isn't it?

Lest we forget - Britain lifts the Total Exclusion Zone.

FRIDAY, 23 JULY 82 - DAY 61

0700* Call the hands
0715 Mail closes
0730 Hands to breakfast
0745* Time check
0755* Out pipes
0800* Both watches muster on the Fore Deck
1000* Stand easy
1015* Hands carry on with your work
1130 SRs/Watchkeepers to dinner
1145* Secure, JRs to dinner
1300* Hands carry on with your work
1600* Secure
1615* Darken ship
1900* First Dog Watchmen clean messdecks and flats for Rounds
1925* Stand by for Rounds
2300* Pipe down

"CU - The ship's company for their tolerance and patience whilst watching the Wednesday night video. (It was a load of rubbish!).
KITC - For the SR who selected this abysmal video."

Note 1 gave us:- "Amended Boat Times:-

Leave RMS ST HELENA		Leave Ajax Bay Jetty	
	0900		0915
	1115		1130
	1315		1330
	1515		1530"

Note 2 read:- "Tombola numbers drawn by an FSU JR were:- 61, 76, 31, 83, 9, 60, 17, 10, 88, 87. Line claimed by an FSU SR on 38 the 19th number out for £8.40. Claims for snowball/house to Ship's Office by 1200 today."

Note 3 was more WAAFU propaganda:- Field Gun 82:- 21 July 82

Run 1	Guzz	024705/024800	1
	Air	024500/024500	2
Run 2	Air	024805/024805	2
	Pompey	025703/025703	1

Total Runs:- Air 5, Guzz 5, Pompey 4.
Total Points:- Air 9, Guzz 8, Pompey 4.
Aggregate:- Air 140502, Guzz 142802, Pompey 120109.
Fastest:- Air 024500, Guzz 024501, Pompey 025406."

TN - Crosspol Scots Guards x 10.

The boys in kilts were back again! It was like living in a Service Station on the M6! In the SRs' mess, life was hectic as usual, with visiting Army Sergeants, SRs from other ships and MHSCs, etc. One army member actually got so drunk he couldn't get out of his seat to go to the toilet, so he just did it where he sat! This may sound like petty whingeing after what these people had been through BUT there comes a time!

SATURDAY, 24 JULY 82 - DAY 62

0700* Call the hands
0715   Mail closes
0730   Hands to breakfast
0745* Time check
0755* Out pipes
0800* Both watches muster on the Fore Deck
0800* Uncover guns
0930* Prepare for flying
0945* Hands to Flying Stations
1000   Launch 373
1000* Stand easy
1015* Hands carry on with your work
1130   SRs/Watchkeepers to dinner
1145* Secure, JRs to dinner
1600* Cover guns
1615* Darken ship
1900* First Dog Watchmen clean messdecks and flats for Rounds
1925* Stand by for Rounds
2300* Pipe down

"CU - FORT GRANGE STO(N) - See Note 3.
KITC - Water wasters again!"

Note 1 was the latest:- "SITREP on MCM Ops - HMS BRECON and HMS
LEDBURY have had a very good week of Hunting. The wreck of HMS ARDENT
was quickly found by HMS LEDBURY and a survey carried out by divers. Very
little of the ship remains aft of the Bridge. HMS COVENTRY was harder to find and
HMS APOLLO, who was called in to search the deeper water, located a contact
yesterday. The Hunts investigated the contact last night and by using PAPS (those
yellow submarines) positively identified the wreck as HMS COVENTRY. It will be
impossible for them to dive on her as she is in 100 metres of water. A large part of
San Carlos Water has been searched for unexploded bombs and several pieces of
ordnance have been countermined including 2 Sea Cats. HMS LEDBURY has found
wreckage of an aircraft including an ejector seat complete with Argentinian pilot. A
number of other contacts have been dived on and have proved to be empty cans and
general gash. Our immediate programme is not known but we expect to be at anchor
in San Carlos for several more days."

Note 2 was a wrap on the knuckles:- "Gemini is to be used for official trips only."

Note 3 was one of the best Notes yet! - "A gallon bottle of rum has been issued to
the ship by FORT GRANGE STO(N). It is intended to keep the rum for 'Splicing the
Mainbrace' when we sail for the UK."

Note 4 was dire:- "Watering times:- 0700 to 0730, 1130 to 1215, 1630 to 1730 and
2030 to 2130." (This meant that I had to finish work early, in order to get a shower
before the water stopped for the day! Some may think I'm joking!).

Note 5 was Saturday afternoon stuff:- "Sports Party - 1115 Boat ashore, to play/support ships teams at 5 aside soccer and volleyball. 50% leave will be granted. Names to the Sports Representative."

Note 6 was yet more FAA glory:- "Field Gun 82 - 22 July 82
Run 1 Pompey   025705/025705 1   Guzz   025104/025304 2
Run 2 Guzz   025106/025106 1   Air   024309/024309 2
Total Runs:- Air 6, Guzz 7, Pompey 5.
Total Points:- Air 11, Guzz 11, Pompey 5.
Aggregate:- Air 164901, Guzz 201302, Pompey 145904.
Fastest:- Air 024309, Guzz 024501, Pompey 025406."

Note 7 read:- "Tombola numbers drawn by the MO were:- 90, 85, 79, 86, 80, 41, 51, 63, 56, 37, 24, 34, 72, 3, 53. Claims for house/snowball to Ship's Office by 1200."

TN - 1610 HMS LEDBURY alongside.
      Crosspol Scots Guards x 10.

One good thing about this Crosspolling was that it got rid of SNO's Rounds, so it couldn't be all bad! In the SRs' Mess today we had a 'Pub Lunch'! Something silly and trivial to normal people but to us it was a major event and a brilliant idea! We had food in the mess, music and plenty of beer and a thoroughly good lunchtime was had by all! Sad isn't it?!

Bomb Alley from Ajax Bay

SUNDAY, 25 JULY 82 - DAY 63

0700* Call the hands
0730   Hands to breakfast
0815* Time check
0825* Out pipes
0830* Both watches muster on the Fore Deck
0930* Secure
1045   Church Service in the Forward Lounge
1100* Pipe down
1130   Hands to dinner
PM   Recover Trisponders
1615* Darken ship
1900* First Dog Watchmen clean messdecks and flats for Rounds
1925* Stand by for Rounds
2100   Weigh anchor - proceed to Port Stanley

Note 1 was an old favourite:- "Securing for sea - make sure everything is stowed correctly and secured for sea. No gash is to be left loafing."

Note 2 was becoming another:- "Water - remember to switch off all taps and showers so that when the water is switched on during rationing, it is not wasted."

Note 3 was more FAA boredom:- "Field Gun 82 - 23 July 82.
Run 1 Air   024807/024807 2   Pompey   025200/025200 1
Run 2 Pomp 025500/025500 2   Guzz   025604/025804 1
Total Runs:- Air 7, Guzz 8, Pompey 7.
Total Points:- Air 13, Guzz 12, Pompey 8.
Aggregate:- Air 193708, Guzz 231106, Pompey 204604.
Fastest:- Air 024309, Guzz 024501, Pompey 025200."

Note 4 read:- "Tombola numbers drawn by one of the stewardesses were:-
69, 7, 77, 5, 36, 28, 18, 68, 29, 70, 11, 43, 4, 8, 46, 57, 65, 50, 40, 82. Claims for the house to the Ship's Office by 1200 today."

Note 5 read:- "Boat Routine - There will be one boat only to Ajax Bay Jetty at 0900, this is the last boat to Ajax Bay so no personnel are to disembark. The boat will then carry on to the Settlement where all leg stretching will take place. There will be 2 other boats to the Settlement for leg stretching at 1315 and 1515."

TN -   0700 HMS LEDBURY slipped.
        Overnight passage to Port Stanley.

It was nice to have the ship to ourselves again! A night at sea, what bliss! You wouldn't believe it would you, actually wanting to get back to sea?!

MONDAY, 26 JULY 82 - DAY 64

0700*   Call the hands
0700   Anchor at Port Stanley
0730   Hands to breakfast
0730   HMS DUMBARTON CASTLE alongside - receive stores
0745*   Time check
0755*   Out pipes
0800*   Both watches muster on the Fore Deck
0800   Mail closes
0800*   Uncover guns
0830*   Prepare for flying
0845*   Hands to Flying Stations
0900   Launch 373 to set up Stanley Trisponder chain
1000*   Stand easy
1015*   Hands carry on with your work
1130   SRs/Watchkeepers to dinner
1145*   Secure, JRs to dinner
1300*   Hands carry on with your work
1600*   Secure
1600*   Cover guns
1615*   Darken ship
1900*   First Dog Watchmen clean messdecks and flats for Rounds
1925*   Stand by for Rounds
2300*   Pipe down

"CU - Sports Rep., we missed his birthday yesterday and he never dripped once!
KITC - The French (We'd just found out where the Argies got their Exocets)."

Note 1 read:- "Programme - Work in Port San Carlos and Falkland Sound is now
completed. Hunts will berth alongside us this morning and are expected to remain
overnight. They sail tomorrow to start work on the minefields at the entrance to Port
William/a route survey into Port Stanley/clearance of bombs that missed the runway."

Note 2 started off so well:- "Field Gun 82 - 24 July 82
Run 1 Guzz   025402/025402 2   Air   024503/025503 1 (Ho!Ho!)
Run 2 Air   025205/025205 2   Pomp   030209/030209 1
Total Runs:- Air 9, Guzz 9, Pompey 8.
Total Points:- Air 16, Guzz 14, Pompey 9.
Aggregate:- Air 252506, Guzz 260508, Pompey 234903.
Fastest:- Air 024309, Guzz 024501, Pompey 025200."

Note 3 read:- "Tombola - House claimed by an MN Officer on number 8 the 59th
number out. Tickets are now on sale for next week. (The £100 mark is getting near.)."

TN - 0750 HMS DUMBARTON CASTLE alongside, transferred stores.
    1000 HMS LEDBURY alongside, portside.
    1020 HMS BRECON alongside.

HORIZONTAL SNOW, ALL BLOODY DAY!

TUESDAY, 27 JULY 82 - DAY 65

0600   HMS BRECON & HMS LEDBURY slip
0700* Call the hands
0730   Hands to breakfast
0745   Mail closes
0745* Time check
0755* Out pipes
0800* Both watches muster on the Fore Deck
0800   Uncover guns
1000* Stand easy
1015* Hands carry on with your work
1130   SRs/Watchkeepers to dinner
1145* Secure, JRs to dinner
1300* Hands carry on with your work
1330* Leg Stretch Party ashore. (Return by last boat at 1600).
1415* Flying brief
1430* Prepare for flying
1445* Hands to Flying Stations
1500   Launch 373
1600* Secure
1600   Cover guns
1615* Darken ship
1900* First Dog Watchmen clean messdecks and flats for Rounds
1925* Stand by for Rounds
2300* Pipe down

"CU - Sports Rep. again, for beating the Tombola sales record, PLUS FORT TORONTO and QHM for the kind offer of a drop of water on Thursday AM.
KITC - The person who piped "hot water has been turned on" - it didn't reach 'B' Deck!"

Note 1 was the other war again:- "Water rationing - Due to the operational requirement to carry out necessary repairs to the main engine, the ship is immobilised and we cannot move to FORT TORONTO until Thursday to top up with fresh water. This means of course that water rationing is here for a couple more days. Revised water on times are:- 0700 to 0900, 1130 to 1300, 1600 to 1830 and 2000 to 2130. These times could change if pipes burst, etc, in this event a pipe will be made!!!! Wednesday will be a non-rationing day and the laundry facilities will be available, Thursday we top up. From Thursday on we will top up every 5 days. If consumption is kept below 20 tons a day water rationing will not be introduced. Daily consumption will be promulgated in Daily Orders. Please be sensible and use water sparingly thus avoiding the inconvenience and unpleasantness of rationing."

"Note 2 read:- "Boat Routine:-

From RMS ST HELENA		From Government Jetty	
	0900		0915
	1115		1130
	1315		1330
	1545		1600"

Note 3 read:- "Tombola numbers drawn by an RNP2100 SR were:- 68, 21, 53, 17, 31, 39, 66, 37, 41, 83. Any claims for the line to the Ship's Office by 1200 today. The prizes this week are:- Line £11.80, House £29.50, Snowball(46) £64.30, Welfare £5.90. (Total for House and Snowball is £93.80)."

TN - 0100 Gale force winds 45-50 kts.
MHSCs slipped and anchored independently.
RMS ST HELENA dragged anchor.

Life was getting silly again due to the water shortage, the lousy weather, not knowing when we were going home, etc, etc, etc. However, another edition of the magazine was due, so life could only get better! As a contributor to "See-Dit", the water rationing gave me my theme for this edition! So here you are:-

GOOD (WET) BUZZES

1. The Chief Stoker uses 100 tons of water to wash his overalls - 'cos he's a big boy!

2. Heard on the Bridge recently - "Water, water everywhere and not a drop to drink - or wash in, or dhoby with, or brush my teeth with, mank, mank, mank, mank, mank!"

3. The POSA has ordered some desert boots and 4 camels.

4. The Padre will be visiting next week to see if he can perform a reverse miracle on the wine.

5. Its a pity the taps onboard are not like the Ship's Company - CONSTANTLY DRIPPING!

6. The POMA has washed his hands of the Laundry (or he would if there was any water).

7. There isn't a clean tablecloth onboard!

8. The Welsh are going to buy the RMS ST HELENA - it must be because of the leaks.

9. The South Atlantic has now been thoroughly washed with fresh water so our task is now complete and we can go home.

10. The water shortage onboard was due to EBD. (Engineering Branch Disaster).

11. RNP2100 is to adopt the town of Windermere - we aren't sure why.

12. There is to be no more water wasted in whisky, this is pure extravagance and must stop.

13. Your Water Bills are available for collection from the Ship's Office.

14. First Prize in the Grand Draw will be a glass of fresh water.

15. The LSTD was caught in the Servery trying to melt down the water biscuits!

16. The ship's boat will be going ashore for snow tomorrow, for melting.
    (Typing error it should be SNOW - Senior Naval Officer Water).
    (Another typing error it should be 'a meeting' not 'melting'.).

17. Save water - shower with a friend!

18. WANTED - Water diviner - regular hours, lots of overtime, top MN salary, with enormous bonuses.

19. The TOR CALEDONIA ran out of water as well!

20. 'Good Buzzes' in the next issue will not mention WATER, honest!

Well it seemed funny at the time!

Another STUFT Ship

WEDNESDAY, 28 JULY 82 - DAY 66

(WASHING DAY)

0700* Call the hands
0730   Hands to breakfast
0745* Time check
0755* Out pipes
0800* Both watches muster on the Fore Deck
0800   Mail closes
0800   Uncover guns
1000* Stand easy
1015* Hands carry on with your work
1130   SRs/Watchkeepers to dinner
1145* Secure, JRs to dinner
1300* Hands carry on with your work
1315* Leg Stretch Party ashore (Return on 1600 boat)
1600* Secure
1600   Cover guns
1615* Darken ship
1900* First Dog Watchmen clean messdecks and flats for Rounds
1925* Stand by for Rounds
2300* Pipe down

"CU - All the boys involved on the upper deck last night when the anchor dragged. KITC - Aeolus - God of Wind (Greek - what'd you expect). PLUS the Chlorifier destructor."

Note 1 - how low can life sink:- "Laundry facilities for today - 2 volunteers are required for today to run the Laundry. They will not be paid but it is hoped to reward them in some way through the Welfare, if that is possible. They will only be required to wash and dry articles (no ironing), and will work from 0800 - 1600. (Make sure you can be spared before volunteering). The reason for this is to try to save water and get everyone's laundry done as quickly as possible. There will be no charge to individuals." (What more can you say!).

Note 2 read:- "Mail - The next mail expected onboard will be Thursday AM."

Note 3 was good news, one of the JRs had had a successful operation for appendicitis and was recuperating in Port Stanley hospital.

Note 4 read:- "Tombola numbers drawn by a St Helenian crew member were:-
46, 74, 45, 48, 1, 24, 58, 57, 72, 64. Any claims for the line to the Ship's Office by
1200 today."

Note 5 was more doom and gloom:- "Field Gun 82 - 26 July 82
Run 1 Nil
Run 2 Pomp 025605/025605 1   Air   025106/025306 2
Total Runs:- Air 10, Guzz 9, Pompey 9.
Total Points:- Air 18, Guzz 14, Pompey 10.
Aggregate:- Air 281902, Guzz 260508, Pompey 264508.
Fastest:- Air 024309, Guzz 024501, Pompey 025200."

I went to the hospital today to visit our JR who had just had the operation. I had to go
and sort out some paperwork for him. At the hospital, I saw some more of the results
of this wonderful war! What a waste of good young lives! All for what? So a few
British people could go and live on remote islands on the other side of the world! Did
nobody tell them, before they went, that we had some virtually identical remote
islands off the West of Scotland, which were much safer and much easier to
access/leave when a problem arose! They also had similar weather!

Yet more STUFT Ships

THURSDAY, 29 JULY 82 - DAY 67

0700* Call the hands
0730   Hands to breakfast
0745* Time check
0755* Out pipes
0800* Both watches muster on the Fore Deck
0800   Mail closes
0800   Uncover guns
0800   Weigh, shift anchorage to SH5, just off Government Jetty
1000* Stand easy
1015* Hands carry on with your work
1130   SRs/Watchkeepers to dinner
1145* Secure, JRs to dinner
1300* Hands carry on with your work
1315   Leg Stretch Party ashore (Return on 1600 boat)
1600* Secure
1600   Cover guns
1615* Darken ship
1900* First Dog Watchmen clean messdecks and flats for Rounds
1925* Stand by for Rounds
2300* Pipe down

"CU - The Osmosis Plant Maintainer for dedication above and beyond the call of duty keeping Ossie Mosis alive and producing 1000 tons of fresh water to date.
KITC - For the Instructors on the Hydrographers Trisponder Maintenance Course."

Note 1 was funny, they were paying us for all this? "Pay (RN) - Anyone wishing to know what pay is going in the bank in July see the POWTR in the Ship's Office 1000 - 1030 today. Paylists have been sent from HMS CENTURION for information." (I won't comment any further, other than to say it was a rip off, whatever it was!).

Note 2 was another novelty:- "Sports Enquiry - Name the current World Number One sportswoman for Freestyle Swimming. One of the JRs is attempting to win £50,000 in a crisp packet competition, so he needs some answers!"

Note 3 didn't get any better:- "Field Gun 82 - 27 July 82
Run 1 Guzz   025707/025707 1   Pomp 025304/025304 2
Run 2 Air   024507/024507 2   Guzz 030206/030206 1
Total Runs:- Air 11, Guzz 11, Pompey 10.
Total Points:- Air 20, Guzz 16, Pompey 12.
Aggregate:- Air 310409, Guzz 320601, Pompey 293902.
Fastest:- Air 024309, Guzz 024501, Pompey 025200."

Note 4 read:- "Tombola numbers drawn by an FSU JR were:-
38, 49, 13, 71, 88, 87, 15, 70, 75, 10. Any claims for the line to the Ship's Office by 1200 today."

<u>TN</u> -   Weighed and proceeded further up harbour to SH5 anchorage.
          1615 Weighed alongside FORT TORONTO for water, remaining overnight.

We had the reply to our letter to the RN Film Corporation today, reference the payments for the films on loan to us (see Day 48). They suggested that as we could not manage Welfare Fund payment, the cost "should be met by individuals" and "early payment would therefore be appreciated"! So now we had to go back over the last two months and ascertain who had watched the movies! (No doubt when we ask the boys, I'm sure they'll all own up!) In future we'll have to have somebody collecting admission money at the mess door! Of course some mess members will want to enter the mess for a drink etc, so we'll only be able to collect money from those actually watching the movie in the mess, not the ones at the bar or playing games! We'll have to incorporate collecting money into the duty projectionist's terms of reference or have a duty mess member collecting money - the Duty Mess President would be ideal! What about those sneaking in late when the projectionist is showing the film and those who finish their game and decide to watch, will they have to pay a percentage fee for the amount they watch? Will we have to have tickets for the accounting side of all this? We don't want any fiddling with the cash, do we? We'll also have to sort the window out in the loo to stop people sneaking in without paying, like some people used to do when they were children! (I didn't of course, as we didn't have any cinemas near where I lived in Westmorland as a kid! We didn't even have electricity or running water but that's another story!). Good job we had got the Tombola and Laundry making money for us in anticipation of this outcome!

And still it goes on, this strange routine we are in! We were still getting threats of war but thankfully nothing concrete was coming of them, other than air raid warnings! The weather was still horrendous! We'd got rid of the pain of the Crosspolling and gone to the other extreme and were now bored to death with life 'down south'. It was only a small ship after all, so we were in need of more than just a couple of hours leg stretching! The mess was the only escape and we were getting sick of seeing each others faces! We needed a break from this boring routine! Most of all, however, we needed to know when we were going home!

Drip, drip, moan, moan! Just think of all those poor people back home with no jobs at all! Don't forget there's always somebody in the world worse off than you! Bollocks, came the reply!

FRIDAY, 30 JULY 82 - DAY 68

0700* Call the hands
0730   Hands to breakfast
0745* Time check
0745* Prepare for flying
0755* Out pipes
0800* Both watches muster on the Fore Deck
0800   Mail closes
0800   Uncover guns
0800* Hands to Flying Stations
0815   Launch 373
0830   Leave present anchorage and proceed to SH5 anchorage
1000* Stand easy
1015* Hands carry on with your work
1130   SRs/Watchkeepers to dinner
1145* Secure, JRs to dinner
1300* Hands carry on with your work
1315* Leg Stretch Party to shore (Return on 1600 boat)
1600* Secure
1600   Cover guns
1615* Darken ship
1900* First Dog Watchmen clean messdecks and flats for Rounds
1925* Stand by for Rounds
2300* Pipe down

"CU - The SRs for offering the use of their Mess to Senior Naval Officer Falkland Islands (SNOFI) for an official Cocktail Party on Saturday in exchange for 70 tons of freshwater for the Ship's Company.
KITC - The Sick Bay JR for letting the blood rush to his head. (Private joke!)."

Note 1 was a reminder of a previous cautionary tale:- "Loan Clothing - Once again, I must advise all members of the Ship's Company, both MN and RN, that the Naval Store Loan Clothing on issue must be paid for if it is lost. The charge rate is 100% cost price plus 30% for negligence - this is the standard charge for clothing held less than 6 months. "But it was pinched, Chief" is not an excuse for failure of return! It is common knowledge that kit bartering goes on inter/ship and inter/service and it isn't necessarily a persons own kit that he exchanges. BE WARNED, WHAT YOU LOSE YOU PAY FOR AT 130% COST!"

Note 2 continued the theme:- "Lost property - During the afternoon of Day 67 dhobying was removed from the top right hand dryer - when the owner collected it he found one white thermal vest missing. Could it be returned to B7 Cabin, especially in the light of Note 1."

Note 3 was an amendment to the last edition of the "See-Dit":- "Crossword correction - 14 Across should read "Fifth Root of 59049". No correct answers have yet been received yet oddly enough!."

Note 4 didn't get any better:- "Field Gun 82 - 28 July 82
Run 1 Pomp 024905/024905 1   Air   024808/024808 2
Run 2 Guzz 024900/025100 2   Pomp 025306/025306 1
Total Runs:- Air 12, Guzz 12, Pompey 12.
Total Points:- Air 22, Guzz 18, Pompey 14.
Aggregate:- Air 335307, Guzz 345701, Pompey 352203.
Fastest:- Air 024309, Guzz 024501, Pompey 024905."

Note 5 read:- "Tombola numbers drawn by an FSU SR were:-
27, 22, 77, 26, 59, 52, 25, 78, 65, 67. Any claims for snowball/house to Ship's Office by 1200 today. The line was claimed by an FSU JR on 13, the 23rd number out, for £11.80."

"Programme - Hopefully, now that we have topped up with water plus stringent water rationing we may be able to remain at anchor off Government Jetty for 5 to 6 days. During this period everybody onboard should have been ashore in Stanley and possibly become sick of the sight of the place. When we have only 2.5 days water left we shall consider sailing from Stanley and anchoring in Berkely Sound, a change is as good as a rest! But remember it may all change."

"Stop Press - Watering times are as follows:- 0700 - 0900, 1130 - 1300, 1600 - 1800, 2000 - 2130. (Unless the Chief Engineer (MN) thinks of any more devious ways of putting the stops on.)"

TN -   0815 Proceeded to SH5
        1015 HMS LEDBURY alongside
        1045 HMS BRECON alongside

As you can see, water was still one of the main topics of conversation! Life here was already a boring routine, not helped by the fact that everywhere you went you were loaded down with war gear, survival gear, etc. Was the ruddy war over or wasn't it, nobody was letting on! However, life goes on! Or it does in the Wardroom, anyway! We've got a Cocktail Party onboard tomorrow night for the local 'aristocracy' - some bloody war this!

SATURDAY, 31 JULY 82 - DAY 69

0700*	Call the hands
0730	Hands to breakfast
0745*	Time check
0755*	Out pipes
0800*	Both watches muster on the Fore Deck
0800	Mail closes
0800	Uncover guns
1000*	Stand easy
1015*	Hands carry on with your work
1130	SRs/Watchkeepers to dinner
1145*	Secure, JRs to dinner
1200	His Excellency the Civil Commissioner, Rex Hunt visits for lunch
1315*	Leg Stretch Party to shore (Return on 1600 boat)
1600	Cover guns
1615*	Darken ship
1800	2 Duty Gangway attendants close up in night clothing (See Note 1)
1830 - 2000	SNOFI Cocktail Party in Forward Lounge
1900*	First Dog Watchmen clean messdecks and flats for Rounds
1925*	Stand by for Rounds
2300*	Pipe down

"CU - MCMs for almost completing their task in record time.
KITC - Designer of the orange fenders. (One burst!)"

Note 1 was another of those horrendous tasks encountered in a war zone! - "Two volunteers are required to act as gangway attendants for the CTP, aiding female guests over the gangway. (If no volunteers - Duty part of the watch will provide same)."

Note 2 was very appropriate and extremely good news for a lot of people but caused me more work! - "Voluntary Release - Early release is now again possible in the branches/categories already forecast to be in surplus."

Note 3 warned:- "Water - in the last 24 hours we have used 8 tons."

Note 4 was another attempt to entertain the troops:- "Return to UK Lottery - Those wishing to pick a day report to the FSU Office today. This is your last chance.
£1 per go, winner takes all."

Note 5 made the mood onboard even blacker, except the Flight deck:- "Field Gun 82, 29 July 82:-
Run 1 Air   025105/025105 2   Guzz   031506/031506 1
Run 2 Pomp 025700/025700 1   Air   024701/024701 2
Total Runs:- Air 14, Guzz 13, Pompey 13.
Total Points:- Air 26, Guzz 19, Pompey 15.
Aggregate:- Air 393203, Guzz 381207, Pompey 391903.
Fastest:- Air 024309, Guzz 024501, Pompey 024905."

Note 6 read:- "Tombola numbers drawn by the Purser Catering were:- 76, 18, 3, 69, 12, 14, 85, 35, 34, 20. Any claims to the Ship's Office by 1200 today."

Note 7 was yet another amendment to "See-Dit":- "Crossword further correction - 26 Across should read "Eight down fourteen left (hint - lat, long)." Still no correct answers received."

TN - 0630   HMS BRECON slipped
     0830   HMS LEDBURY slipped
     1830 - 2000   SNOFI CTP in RMS ST HELENA

It's supposed to be bloody weekend! Well as you can see, it was for the privileged members of the Ship's Company! For the rest of us, nothing changed. The JRs still had Rounds in the middle of the CTP, carried out by an officer in his 'party gear'! They also had to provide gangway staff to leer at the females in their tight dresses, nylons and stilettoes as they struggled up the gangway flashing their parts! So they had fur coats on, so what!? After two months of complete non-contact with the opposite sex, even the sheep and penguins on the distant shores were beginning to look good! What a way to motivate the troops! The SRs lost their Mess and access to the upper deck and fore end of the ship were all restricted. We could either sit in our cabins or in my case get in the office and do some more work! Just to top it all, I was bloody Duty Senior Rate again, with all this crap going on around me! Where were the forms to fill in to request 'Early Release'? So far, this must have been the high point of my time in the South Atlantic! It couldn't get any worse, could it?

Chinook lifting damaged Chinook at Stanley

SUNDAY, 1 AUGUST 82 - DAY 70

0700* Call the hands
0730   Hands to breakfast
0815* Time check
0825* Out pipes
0830* Both watches muster on the Fore Deck
0930* Secure
0930   First boat leaves (Church Service ashore - See Note 1)
1100* Pipe down
1130   Hands to dinner
1900* First Dog Watchmen clean messdecks and flats for Rounds
1925* Stand by for Rounds

"CU - The Master from the SRs for getting a round in. (He is now to be known as Flag Officer Rounds).
KITC - 'Air' for being a boring shower of bastards. (Field Gun!)"

Note 1 read:- "Boat Routine - There will be no church service onboard, however, a service will be held at 1000 in the Cathedral, boat leaves at 0930 (instead of 0900)."

Note 2 read:- "Tombola numbers drawn by an FSU JR were:- 79, 2, 63, 29, 16, 36, 54, 30, 62, 32, 55, 23, 4, 9, 19. Claims for the house to the Ship's Office by 1200."

Note 3 boringly read:- "Field Gun 82 - 30 July 82
Run 1 Guzz 025200/025200 2   Pomp 025405/025405 1
Run 2 Air   024903/024903 2   Guzz 025100/025100 1
Total Runs:- Air 15, Guzz 15, Pompey 14.
Total Points:- Air 28, Guzz 22, Pompey 16.
Aggregate:- Air 422106, Guzz 435507, Pompey 411308.
Fastest:- Air 024309, Guzz 024501, Pompey 024905."

Note 4 was the now usual doom and gloom:- "Water - In the past 24 hours we have used 12 tons." (I wonder how much was used in preparation for the CTP – all that bloody ice? I suppose that's another of the many great unanswered questions of this war!?).

TN - 0500 HMS LEDBURY slipped
     0630 HMS BRECON slipped

Well, what can I tell you? Weather - nil points, surroundings/view - nil points, social life - nil points (Wardroom not included in this one), leisure time - nil points, future - nil points, water supply - nil points, peace settlement - nil points, war action - nil points, motivation - nil points, job satisfaction - nil points, quality of life - nil points, etc, etc, etc. (We won't even think about sex life!). It's Sunday and the most interesting thing you can look forward to is going back to work! The 'buzz-mongers' are having a field day! Talk about bloody sad! Please, just lead me to the bar!

MONDAY, 2 AUGUST 82 - DAY 71

0700* Call the hands
0730   Hands to breakfast
0745* Time check
0755* Out pipes
0800* Both watches muster on the Fore Deck
0815   Mail closes
1000* Stand easy
1015* Hands carry on with your work
1130   SRs/Watchkeepers to dinner
1145* Secure, JRs to dinner
1300* Hands carry on with your work
1315   Leg Stretch Party to shore (Return on 1600 boat)
1600* Secure
1900* First Dog Watchmen clean messdecks and flats for Rounds
1925* Stand by for Rounds
2300* Pipe down

Note 1 read:- "Mail - Closing date for the airfield is 14 August 82. Then mail coming in will be air dropped. Mail going out, however, will be sent by boat to Ascension Island and will take about 10 days to get home."

Note 2 was blessed relief from great pain and torture:- "Field Gun 82 - 31 July 82
The Last Runs:-
Run 1 Pomp 025806/025806 1   Air   024701/024701 2
Run 2 Guzz 025206/025206 2   Pomp 025600/025600 1
Total runs:- Air 16, Guzz 16, Pompey 16.
Total Points:- Air 30, Guzz 24, Pompey 18.
Aggregate:- Air 450807, Guzz 464803, Pompey 470804.
Fastest:- Air 024309, Guzz 024501, Pompey 024905."

Note 3 read:- "Tombola tickets are now on sale. Get yours now. The hundred must go this week. The house was claimed by the MO on 55 the 61st number out for £29.50."

We now also had the 'Water usage' information at the top of Daily Orders. Today's read "Water - 15 tons in the last 24 hours".

TN - 2000   HMS BRECON alongside for fuel and victuals.

And still it goes on! OK! It's a new week and we're now going to think positive! However, the only positive thing so far was that nobody had shot at us or bombed us! The relief at that was probably the only thing keeping some of the troops going!

TUESDAY, 3 AUGUST 82 - DAY 72

0700* Call the hands
0730 Hands to breakfast
0745* Time check
0755* Out pipes
0800* Both watches muster on the Fore Deck
0800* Prepare for flying
0815 Mail closes
0815* Hands to Flying Stations
0830 Launch 373
1000* Stand easy
1015* Hands carry on with your work
1130 SRs/Watchkeepers to dinner
1145* Secure, JRs to dinner
1300* Hands carry on with your work
1315 Leg Stretch Party to shore (return on 1600 boat)
1600* Secure
1900* First Dog Watchmen clean messdecks and flats for Rounds
1925* Stand by for Rounds
2300* Pipe down

"CU - 1. For the two boys who mended the pipe.
      2. The Sports Representative for beating the Tombola sales record with
      £65.50 and for getting the combined total of house and snowball to £110.15.
KITC - To those who didn't buy a Tombola ticket."

"Programme - Fresh water consumption has been well within the limits over the past few days - well done! Because we are carefully conserving water we now have no need to leave this anchorage until Friday, AM. Thence to top up dieso and Avcat and anchor in Berkely Sound. Remember it may all change. Hot tip - The 1st Lieutenant is trying to do a little organising for Sunday lunchtime, SSSSSSHHHHHHH!!!!!!"

Note 1 read:- "Wednesday Evening:- a boat will go ashore to take members of the ship's company who are giving a Film and Slide Show, subject Ascension, St Helena Island and Falklands role in the sailing ship era, in the Junior School Hall. The boat will leave the ship at 1830 and return at 2230. Members of the ship's company may take this boat ashore. Names to the Ship's Office by 1200 on Wednesday. Those wishing to go ashore must first see their HODs."

Note 2 read:- "Tombola numbers drawn by the Sports Representative were:- 12, 2, 54, 44, 39, 60, 32, 83, 90, 24. Any claims for the line to the Ship's Office by 1200 today. The prizes for this week are:- Line £13.10, House £32.75, Snowball £77.40 (+ House = £110.15), Welfare £6.55."

"Water - 12 tons."

TN - 0815 HMS LEDBURY alongside

Not a lot of positive things to say, really!

WEDNESDAY, 4 AUGUST 82 - DAY 73

0700* Call the hands
0730   Hands to breakfast
0745* Time check
0755* Out pipes
0800* Both watches muster on the Fore Deck
0815   Mail closes
1000* Stand easy
1015* Hands carry on with your work
1030* Prepare for flying
1045* Hands to Flying Stations
1100   Launch 373
1130   SRs/Watchkeepers to dinner
1145* Secure, JRs to dinner
1300* Hands carry on with your work
1315   Leg Stretch Party to shore (Return on 1600 boat)
1600* Secure
1700* BFBS Videos start
1830   Boat to shore for Film/slides Party
1900* First Dog Watchmen clean messdecks and flats for Rounds
1925* Stand by for Rounds
2230   Special boat returns from shore
2300   Videos cease
2300* Pipe down

"CU - The Chief Stoker for being so pleasant and genteel to work with and for taking such loving care of his equipment.
KITC - The Sick Bay JR for wasting a whole film taking pictures of the Invisible Man."

Note 1 gave us the solution of the crossword in the second edition of "See-Dit", which had been won by an MN Officer. Again!

Note 2 read:- "Tombola numbers drawn by an RNP2100 JR were:- 14, 40, 69, 21, 48, 56, 5, 41, 71, 77. Any claims for the line to the Ship's Office by 1200 today."

"Water - 12 tons."

TN - 0600   HMS BRECON & HMS LEDBURY slipped and proceeded on task
       2030   HMS LEDBURY alongside, sonar stabilisation defect

Positive thoughts - nil points! We were now at a stage where it was difficult to talk to some of the troops for very long. They were too easily wound up by nothing! So if you said the wrong thing in jest, you could end up with an argument! There appeared to be a build up of 'pent up emotion', as they say in the best journals! All they wanted to know about was, when they were going home?

THURSDAY, 5 AUGUST 82 - DAY 74

0700* Call the hands
0730   Hands to breakfast
0745* Time check
0755* Out pipes
0800* Both watches muster on the Fore Deck
0815   Mail closes
1000* Stand easy
1015* Hands carry on with your work
1130   SRs/Watchkeepers to dinner
1145* Secure, JRs to dinner
1300* Hands carry on with your work
1315   Leg Stretch Party to shore (Return on 1600 boat)
1600* Secure
1700* BFBS Videos start
1900* First Dog Watchmen clean messdecks and flats for Rounds
1925* Stand by for Rounds
2300   Videos end
2300* Pipe down

Note 1 read:- "Tombola numbers drawn by one of the FSU SRs were:-
47, 85, 61, 62, 66, 3, 6, 88, 20, 52. Any claims for the line to the Ship's Office by
1200 today."

Note 2 was back to the war! - "Darken ship - When we sail from Stanley on Friday
we will once again be required to darken ship at night. Everyone is to ensure that
their cabin darken ship screens are available and are in place by sunset on Friday.
Presidents and Leading Hands of Messes are responsible for the darken ship screens
in their Messes."

Note 3 was the old favourite again:- "Securing for sea - ensure everything is stowed
correctly and secured for sea. No gash is to be left loafing."

"Water - 15 tons."

TN - AM   HMS LEDBURY slipped
       1645 HMS BRECON alongside
       2000 HMS LEDBURY alongside 1939 Sonar defect

You realise how bad things are when 'Tombola' is the first note! I bought an excellent pair of binoculars today from the Ship's Shop! It was the first money I had spent on anything for quite some time, it seemed strange! All our beer was on a mess bill, so we had got used to not carrying money around other than for tombola tickets. Weird! Anyway, the binoculars enabled me to look at the land and see all the wildlife, it opened up a whole new world of entertainment for me. A few others soon had the same idea, until the shop ran out of binoculars! At least somebody's doing all right out of all this and it isn't the bloody penguins!

Some strange rumours were surfacing! The buzz was that the MHSCs' task was nearing successful completion and their lordships were running out of excuses to keep us down here! It was also rumoured that the MN Officers and Crew wanted to visit St Helena Island on the way home to visit their families and do some crew changes that were now due. It was also being 'buzzed' that, if this wish was not granted, the St Helenian crew members would jump ship when we stopped at Ascension Island for fuel on the way home! It should be interesting watching the RPO sort that one out!

Thank God for the binoculars!

FRIDAY, 6 AUGUST 82 - DAY 75

0700* Call the hands
0715 Mail closes
0730 Hands to breakfast
0745* Time check
0755* Out pipes
0800* Prepare for flying
0800* Both watches muster on the Fore Deck
0815* Hands to Flying Stations
0830 Launch 373
0830 To SCOTTISH EAGLE to refuel Dieso and Avcat (weather permitting)
(Then to Ruggles Bay or Fox Bay at midnight) OR Direct to Ruggles Bay or
Fox Bay
1000* Stand easy
1015* Hands carry on with your work
1130 SRs/Watchkeepers to dinner
1145* Secure, JRs to dinner
1300* Hands carry on with your work
1600* Secure
1630* Darken ship
1900* First Dog Watchmen clean messdecks and flats for Rounds
1925* Stand by for Rounds
2300* Pipe down

"CU - Happy birthday to the Aircrewman on the Flight.
KITC - MO - See Note 1."

Note 1 read:- "Tombola numbers drawn by an FSU JR were:-
1, 9, 10, 25, 70, 34, 59, 55, 82, 53. Line claimed by the MO on 61 the 23rd number
out for £13.10. Any claims for the snowball/house to the Ship's Office by 1200
today."

"Water - 15 tons."

TN - 0300 SW gale force 7 - 8, MHSCs slipped and anchored independently

Thank God for the Tombola, or we wouldn't have anything to talk about! Never
mind, it's weekend!

SATURDAY, 7 AUGUST 82 - DAY 76

0700* Call the hands
0730 Hands to breakfast
0745* Time check
0755* Out pipes
0800* Both watches muster on the Fore Deck
0800* Prepare for flying
0815* Hands to Flying Stations
0830 Launch 373
0830 To SCOTTISH EAGLE to refuel Dieso and Avcat (weather permitting)
o/c   Slip and proceed to Ruggles Bay/Fox Bay
1000* Stand easy
1015* Hands carry on with your work
1130 SRs/Watchkeepers to dinner
1145* Secure, JRs to dinner
1630* Darken ship
1900* First Dog Watchmen clean messdecks and flats for Rounds
1925* Stand by for Rounds
2300* Pipe down

"CU - The FSU SR who organised 'Arrival Home' Sweep.
KITC - The weather."

Note 1 read:- "Tombola numbers drawn by an RNP2100 JR were:-
22, 68, 17, 11, 37, 45, 87, 35, 72, 28. Any claims for the snowball/house to the Ship's Office by 1200 today."

Note 2 read:- "'Arrival Home' Sweep - Total amount raised for the winner/winners of this sweep is £59. (There are no expenses, rake offs, wages, etc - as with all our other ventures). The winner/winners will be the one/ones closest to the date when we drop anchor or go alongside in a UK port. (That includes Scotland and Wales!)."

"Water - 14 tons."

TN - Passage to Ruggles Bay
       0800   Collect mail from MHSCs
       0845   Weigh anchor and proceed to Ruggles Bay
       2100   Anchored in Ruggles Bay

What a weekend, all this and now the weather's gone back to horrific as well! I feel sorry for the non-drinkers myself! They've got nothing, at least we can get pissed!

SUNDAY, 8 AUGUST 82 - DAY 77

0700*	Call the hands
0730	Hands to breakfast
0815*	Time check
0825*	Out pipes
0830*	Both watches muster on the Fore Deck
0830	FSU to Module cleaning stations
0830 - 0930	Fleetwork teach in on Bridge - All RN & MN Bridge Watchkeepers
0920	OIC FSU Walkround of Upper Deck/Tween Deck Modules
0930*	Secure
1045*	Church Service in Forward Lounge
1100*	Pipe down
1130	Hands to dinner
1630*	Darken ship
1900*	First Dog Watchmen clean messdecks and flats for Rounds
1925*	Stand by for Rounds

"CU - No qualifiers.
KITC - The JR who wastes good mayonnaise on his jelly!"

Note 1 read:- "Welfare Committee Meeting - 1400 Tues, 11/8/82, in the Wardroom. Reps are to hand items for the Agenda to the Secretary by 0800, Mon, 10/8/82."

Note 2 read:- "Tombola numbers drawn by a Flight SR were:-
80, 42, 76, 74, 8, 7, 86, 75, 43, 84, 27, 57, 89, 65, 49. Claims for the house to the Ship's Office by 1200 today."

(The water information stopped today!)

TN - Passage to Port San Carlos
      1300 Weigh anchor
      1730 Anchored Port San Carlos

We had a 'male bonding' day today! At lunchtime the 'iron curtain' was drawn back in the Forward Lounge and a Pub Lunch for the whole ship's company was held. All boys together plus two stewardesses! It was a good way for some of the troops to let off steam and for everybody to let their hair down a little! It was definitely needed! It was also a good chance to sell a lot of Grand Raffle tickets, especially when they'd had a few!

MONDAY, 9 AUGUST 82 - DAY 78

0700* Call the hands
0730   Hands to breakfast
0745* Time check
0755* Out pipes
0800* Both watches muster on the Fore Deck
1000   SRs' Mess Meeting
1000* Stand easy
1015* Hands carry on with your work
1130   SRs/Watchkeepers to dinner
1145* Secure, JRs to dinner
1300* Hands carry on with you work
1600* Secure
1630* Darken ship
1900* First Dog Watchmen clean messdecks and flats for Rounds
1925* Stand by for Rounds
2300* Pipe down

"CU - Caterers for the Sunday lunch session AND those buying Grand Draw tickets. KITC - All those who didn't."

"Programme - When we left Port Stanley our programme was intended to be:-

Date:	7 - 8/8/82	9 - 10/8/82	11 - 12/8/82	13 - 16/8/82
Place:-	Ruggles Bay	San Carlos	Stanley	Sail for UK????????
Task:-	Route Survey	Position STENNA INSPECTOR on HMS COVENTRY	Prepare for sailing	

Already, as you have seen, the programme has changed. This is as much as I know and of course it may all change. CINCFLEET has murmured that HMS BRECON should effect an Auxiliary Engine change before proceeding home to UK (???). I shall keep you informed - WATCH THIS SPACE."

Note 1 read:- "Grand Draw - no profits, no rake offs, etc. All takings will be ploughed back in as prizes. We now have £305 in takings. The more money we collect the more prizes we can buy and the more YOU win. So keep buying the tickets."

Note 2 read:- "Tombola tickets now on sale. House claimed by the LSTD on 49, the 65th number out, for £32.75."

TN - 1100   HMS LEDBURY alongside

Needed a gentle day today, to sort the hangovers out! However, the idea had worked, life onboard was less tense, now a few drips had been publicly aired! Also, the hint that we may have a date for going home had helped! The only problem there was, thinking back to our attempts to set off to war from the UK, if their lordships couldn't make a bloody decision then - what's changed?

TUESDAY, 10 AUGUST 82 - DAY 79

0700*	Call the hands
0715*	Prepare for flying
0730	Hands to breakfast
0730*	Hands to Flying Stations
0745*	Time check
0745	Launch 373
0755*	Out pipes
0800*	Both watches muster on the Fore Deck
1000*	Stand easy
1015*	Hands carry on with your work
1130	SRs/Watchkeepers to dinner
1145*	Secure, JRs to dinner
1300*	Hands carry on with your work
1400 - 1600	Pay queries in the Ship's Office (RN)
1600*	Secure
1630*	Darken ship
1900*	First Dog Watchmen clean messdecks and flats for Rounds
1925*	Stand by for Rounds
2300*	Pipe down

"CU - Sports Representative for AGAIN beating the Tombola sales record - £84. KITC - Those who didn't buy a ticket from him."

Note 1 read:- "'BUZZES' - Memo issued today, reference STUFT ships returning to UK, does not mean we have any more information on the date of return to UK. It is only so we can have all preparations well in hand and be one jump ahead."

Note 2 read:- "Welfare Meeting delayed 24 hours due to the 1st Lieutenant setting up the Artemis System with HMS BRECON/STENA INSPECTOR."

Note 3 read:- "Tombola drawn by a St Helenian crewman:- 54, 4, 73, 29, 65, 35, 72, 89, 84, 18. Claims for line to the Ship's Office by 1200. This weeks prizes are:- Line £16.80, House £42.00, Snowball(48) £94.20 (+ House = £136.20), Welfare £8.40."

Note 4 warned of the 'BIG SELL':- "Grand Draw - Yellow tickets now on sale."

TN -	0600	HMS LEDBURY slipped
	1500	RAS(L) from BRITISH TAY
	PM	Recovered Trisponders

Back to serious work after the hangover! One of my messmates had a fully-iced home made fruit cake, sent to him by his family. He mentioned this in passing, I told him how good fruit cake tasted with port and cheese. He had never heard of this and said if I supplied the port and cheese he would supply the cake! An offer I couldn't refuse! I recalled a few favours, port and Lancashire cheese were quickly obtained and that evening, hidden in my office, we finished the bottle of port and made a big hole in the cake and cheese. Pure luxury and delight, it nearly made you wish you had taken the exams for the Wardroom!

WEDNESDAY, 11 AUGUST 82 - DAY 80

0400	Weigh and proceed to Port Stanley
0700*	Call the hands
0730	Hands to breakfast
0745*	Time check
0755*	Out pipes
0800*	Both watches muster on the Flight Deck
1000*	Stand easy
1015*	Hands carry on with your work
1130 approx	Anchor Port Stanley SH5
1130	SRs/Watchkeepers to dinner
1145*	Secure, JRs to dinner
1300*	Hands carry on with your work
1400 approx	HMS LEDBURY & HMS BRECON alongside
1430	Welfare Committee Meeting in the Wardroom
1600*	Secure
1900*	First Dog Watchmen clean messdecks and flats for Rounds
1925*	Stand by for Rounds
2300*	Pipe down

"CU - One of the MN officers belated birthday wishes AND a Flight SR who was 21 today, yet again!
KITC - The Flight who insist on making so much noise when they have to turn to a few minutes earlier than usual in a morning."

Note 1 was a result of some of the work I had been involved with. The FSU because of their travels back home had a lot of outstanding paperwork problems. They had now been sorted, with the Awards and Restorations of outstanding Good Conduct Badges, outstanding Advancements and Confirmations in rank/rate, etc.

Note 2 read:- "Tombola numbers drawn by one of the FSU SRs were:-
12, 16, 3, 88, 48, 45, 13, 44, 7, 49. Any claims to the Ship's Office by 1200 today."

Note 3 read:- "Lost Property - One "Papermate" stainless steel pen. Please contact Ship's Office if found."

Note 4 was interesting:- "First Day Covers - A selection of 1st Day Covers from the South Atlantic Islands will be on sale in the Purser's Cabin between 0900 and 1000, today."

Note 5 was boring politics, even down here we couldn't escape! - "By-Election - Anyone who originates from Northfield, Birmingham and wishes to vote in the forthcoming By-Election contact the POWTR."
There was also a reminder that "YELLOW RAFFLE TICKETS" were now on sale.

TN - Passage to Port Stanley
- 0400 Weigh and proceed to Port Stanley
- 1030 Anchored in Berkely Sound, stored vegetables VERTREP with AVALONA STAR
- 1500 Proceed to Port Stanley
- 1800 Anchored Port Stanley SH5. HMS BRECON & HMS LEDBURY alongside

St HELLTEM 16/82 "Duty Free Goods on returning to UK" arrived today! Was this the sign we had all been desperately waiting for? This memorandum explained the rules for us when we got home! - "On return to UK and being drafted or given at least 7 days leave, you are entitled to land the following goods duty free:- Spirits - 0.5 litres OR Fortified Wine - 1 litre PLUS Table Wine - 2 litres, 2 fluid ounces of Perfume, 9 fluid ounces of Toilet Water, Other Goods to a total value of £6 and Tobacco as in Standing Orders." This was followed by a long list of prices of the above goods from the Purser Catering.

The second Welfare Meeting was held this afternoon and turned out to be a lengthy affair! It covered various subjects including:- Resignation of one of the JRs' representatives and acceptance of his relief; welcoming of the MO as the new Vice Chairman and the Purser as an observer; acceptance of the minutes of the last meeting; a vote of thanks to the editor of the "See-Dit" and also the Sports Representative for all their efforts; actions arising from the previous meeting (beer issue times increased for the JR Watchkeepers, Purser attending meetings as an observer and "Hot Racquets" would be screened at a convenient time); a financial statement from the Treasurer crediting the Welfare Fund with £132.96 and stressing to the Ship's Company that people running the Tombola and Grand Draw were NOT being paid for their efforts and all money made was being ploughed back in as prizes; a proposal to re-start the Inter-Mess games; a query about the laundering of Dining Hall table cloths; a query about 'water times'; BBC News broadcasts being recorded and played back to the ship's company; a query reference the final disposal of the Welfare Fund money and assets; future programme reference a visit to St Helena; a query about why we were still darkening ship when the war appeared to be over; a complaint about the length of time mail was taking to get to St Helena Island; duty free allowances at the end of this trip; the likelihood of more pub lunches; 'Crossing the Line' Certificates; ship's 'T' shirts and jumpers; arrival dates in UK; Flight Deck cinema shows; SODS Opera; gun practice and splicing the mainbrace. (It was good to see so much healthy interest, instead of the usual apathy!)

We were keeping busy and that appeared to be one of the secrets of survival down here! If your brain was occupied, you didn't dwell on all the other more sensible things you should be doing in the middle of August! Holidaying, sunbathing, going down the beach, going to the country, barbequing, spending time with the kids, etc.

Thank goodness we had the Ship's Magazine! Edition 3 had surfaced today! It was full of the usual moans and groans, insults, hairy dits, dirty jokes, etc, etc, along with tiny bits of intellectual stuff like the Crossword! It also contained the following:-

GOOD BUZZES

1.   We are returning to UK via South Georgia, Capetown, Durban, Mombasa, St Helena, Ascension, West Indies, USA, Gibraltar, Azores, Spain, Portugal, France, Channel Islands and the Isle of Wight. (That should cover further buzzes!)

2.   On arriving in UK we will visit Plymouth, Portland, Portsmouth, Chatham, Rosyth and Great Yarmouth, giving points out of ten for the 'Welcome Home' at each port.

3.   The RMS ST HELENA is then to continue in service with the RN as an oil rig supply vessel out of Aberdeen.

4.   The MN Crew are about to sign on for 22 years service. The MN Officers are about to cry.

5.   For the information of the JRs and MN Officers, the Chippy is a carpenter not a shop.

6.   Look at any greenie and you'll realise why people have trouble with the Electricity Board.

7.   SNOFI was so impressed with the Cocktail Party, he wants us to do his Christmas Party.

8.   RS Bridge isn't his real name.

9.   When the LSTD went flying recently they offered him some TWA coffee but he declined saying he would rather have some TWA tea!

10. The Sick Bay JR is not on drugs - he's just a rugby player.

11. The Sports Representative is taking the Aptitude Test for Clubswinger - (Joannas, Harbour Lights, Flaming Joes, 21 Club, Black Angus, etc, etc.).

12. The Flight Commander has been on drugs but they were for his cold.

13. The person who wins the Snowball will get filled in.

14. So will the one who wins the Video Machine.

15. Pay Queries in the Ship's Office will be from 0400 - 0415 every day of the week.

16. There will be no corrections to the clues for this week's "See-Dit" crossword.

17. The JRs have given up playing for the Challenge Trophy as they knew they still wouldn't be able to beat the SRs.

18. Universal Studios have bought the Film Rights for Daily Orders.

P.S. - Notice we never mentioned H2O this time, as promised - but wait until next time!

The "Hot Racquets" video saga continued today. Having made heavy arguments in favour of showing the video at the first Welfare Meeting, the mess representatives won the battle today at the second Welfare Meeting. It was going to be shown in its entirety at a convenient time! There had been a lot of grumbling throughout the ship about being treated like school children, this decision might help to calm things down, even if it was a little late coming and should never have been required in the first place!

Not another run ashore!

THURSDAY, 12 AUGUST 82 - DAY 81

0700* Call the hands
0730   Hands to breakfast
0745* Time check
0755* Out pipes
0800* Both watches muster on the Fore Deck
0800* Prepare for flying
0815* Hands to Flying stations
0830   Launch 373
1000* Stand easy
1015* Hands carry on with your work
1130   SRs/Watchkeepers to dinner
1145* Secure, JRs to dinner
1300* Hands carry on with your work
1600* Secure
1900* First Dog Watchmen clean messdecks and flats for Rounds
1925* Stand by for Rounds
2300* Pipe down

"CU - Ship's Company for hanging loose, keeping cool (literally), staying flexible whilst definite plans were <u>always</u> changing.
KITC - No qualifiers as it was such a nice day!!!!!!!!!!!!!!!!!!!!!!!!"

Note 1 read:- "Mail - There has been no mail, due to weather, for 48 hours. Hopefully it will arrive today. The Stanley Airport will close on the 14th for two weeks. The last mail will leave the Islands by Hercules on the 13th, so mail will close onboard at 0745 on 13 August 82. SO GET IT WRITTEN NOW. This is your last chance until Ascension in approximately two weeks time."

Note 2 read:- "Boat Routines - as per normal:-
From the ship:-   0900   1115   1315   1545
From the shore:-   0915   1130   1330   1600"

Note 3 read:- "Tombola numbers drawn by the Flight Aircrewman were:-
14, 17, 47, 57, 22, 82, 62, 40, 64, 53. Any claims for the line to the Ship's Office by 1200 today. From now the number for the snowball will be increased by 2 each week. (This week is still the 48th number out or less.)"

Note 4 read:- "Grand Draw - It is now imperative that you get your YELLOW TICKETS as soon as possible as they are going like hot racquets. Get your share now as there isn't long to go."

In the middle of the page was printed "YELLOW"!!

<u>TN</u> - Preparations for sailing to UK in all 3 ships

Today a letter was sent to thank WS Cowell Ltd of 8 Butter Market, Ipswich, for their generous donation of 12,000 Tombola Tickets. They were also sent a Ship's Crest, "as a token of our heartfelt appreciation, as Tombola had done much to keep morale high in this bleak outpost of the world". The SNO wasn't kidding either!

What a bombshell! Right out of the blue - we might be going home soon! However, we didn't start celebrating in case it was a rip off! Remember how long it took for them to make up their minds when we left UK! This news did, of course, lift spirits and made the mood onboard much happier, so that was a start! It was worth just a couple of pints!

Falkland Islands Coat of Arms

FRIDAY, 13 AUGUST 82 - DAY 82

0700*   Call the hands
0730   Hands to breakfast
0745   Mail closes for the LAST TIME
0745*   Time check
0755*   Out pipes
0800*   Prepare for flying
0800*   Both watches muster on the Fore Deck
0815*   Hands to Flying Stations
0830   VERTREP from SAXONIA
1000*   Stand easy
1015*   Hands carry on with your work
1130   SRs/Watchkeepers to dinner
1145*   Secure, JRs to dinner
1300*   Hands carry on with your work
1600*   Secure
1900*   First Dog Watchmen clean messdecks and flats for Rounds
1925*   Stand by for Rounds
2300*   Pipe down

"Programme:- 1200   14 Aug   Sail from Port Stanley
             1200   26 Aug   Arrive Jamestown, St Helena
             0700   28 Aug   Sail from St Helena
             1500   30 Aug   Arrive Ascension Island
             2300   30 Aug   Sail from Ascension Island
             1500   7 Sep   Arrive Gibraltar
             0800   9 Sep   Sail from Gibraltar
             0900   15 Sep   Arrive Rosyth"

Note 1 really was an old favourite this time:- "Securing for sea - We were lucky on our passage south, weatherwise, we may not be so lucky on the way north. Ensure that all workspaces, recreation spaces, etc, are properly secured for sea. If you need cordage for lashing objects down securely consult the Buffer or the Bosun. The First Officer, 1st Lieutenant and OIC FSU will be walking around the ship PM to ensure that all is properly secured for sea."

Note 2 read:- "Tombola numbers drawn by the RPO were:- 32, 51, 6, 87, 9, 34, 19, 59, 76, 56. Any claims for Snowball/House to Ship's Office by 1200 today. Line claimed by a St Helenian crew member for £16.80 on 82 the 26th number out."

The line of asterisks, which usually separated the sections on the Daily Orders, had been replaced with continuous "YELLOW" on one line and continuous "TICKETS" on the other, for some strange reason!

TN -   1600   MHSCs slip
       1730   Weigh and proceed to FORT TORONTO for 90 tons of fresh water
       2000   Slip and proceed

The tasks completed by our mini Task Force had included:- finding and diving on the wrecks of HMS COVENTRY and HMS ARDENT; finding MV ASTRONOMER anchor cable; sweeping two minefields; two exploratory operations; EOD clearance in San Carlos Water, Port San Carlos, Port Stanley, Fox Bay and Port Howard; Route Surveys; location of sunken Argentine ships for intelligence purposes and maintaining Trisponder chains operating on six days continuous cycle.

Who said Friday the thirteenth was unlucky! We all tearfully watched the Falkland Islands disappear into the distance and promised ourselves that we would definitely never see them again! I'm sure there must be worse places in the world but I've never seen them! We were extremely thankful that we had not been attacked by the Argentinians, because we would have had no chance whatsoever in this rust bucket! We were also extremely thankful and glad to be going home, because a lot didn't! Thank goodness we had come out of it unscathed. A lot of people said "thank goodness" a lot of times that night!

Thank goodness for Water Carrier SS Toronto!

PART FIVE

THE RUN HOME

or

I WILL NOT RETURN

SATURDAY, 14 AUGUST 82 - DAY 83

0700*   Call the hands
0730   Hands to breakfast
0745*   Time check
0755*   Out pipes
1000*   Stand easy
1015*   Carry on with your work
1130   SRs/Watchkeepers to dinner
1145*   Secure, JRs to dinner
1900*   First Dog Watchmen clean messdecks and flats for Rounds
1925*   Stand by for Rounds
2300*   Pipe down

"CU - For the JR for finding the recently advertised lost property and returning it to its owner.
KITC - No qualifiers."

Note 1 was a sign of normality returning:- "SRs' Mess Messman - A volunteer is required to act as Messman in the SRs' Mess, from Ascension Island to Rosyth (3 weeks maximum). Full training will be given. Permission must be gained from HOD. Names to the Mess Manager."

Note 2 was more fruits of my labour:- "Local Overseas Allowance (RN) - The daily rates of LOA from St Helena to Gibraltar will rise to:- Lt Cdr £5.50, Lt £5.14, FCPO £5.06, CPO £4.88, PO £4.76, LH £4.16, AB & below £4.16. This is not taxed."

Note 3 read:- "Tombola numbers drawn by a Flight SR were:-
79, 11, 66, 71, 81, 74, 5, 86, 38, 1. Any claims for the house/snowball to the Ship's Office by 1200 today."

Today, the lines of asterisks had been replaced by continuous "YELLOWTICKETS" lines!

TN - Passage to St Helena Island

That's it, we're away from it! We've survived! However, we're not out of the Exclusion Zone yet, so save the champagne! This was one weekend where we didn't mind being at sea. The more miles we covered the better, nautical or otherwise!

SUNDAY, 15 AUGUST 82 - DAY 84

0700* Call the hands
0730   Hands to breakfast
0815* Time check
0825* Out pipes
0830* Both watches muster on the Fore Deck
0930* Secure
1045* Church Service in the Forward Lounge
1100* Pipe down
1130   Hands to dinner
1645* Darken ship
1900* First Dog Watchmen clean messdecks and flats for Rounds
1925* Stand by for Rounds

Note 1 was a repeat! - "Securing for sea - I SAY AGAIN - We were lucky on our passage south, weather wise, etc, etc, (as yesterday)."

Note 2 read:- "Tombola numbers drawn by an FSU JR were:-
30, 25, 70, 60, 2, 31, 46, 42, 21, 8, 68, 26, 50, 23, 63. Claims for the house to the Ship's Office by 1200 today."

A separate note read "STILL YELLOW"!

We had a claim for the Snowball and House today! However, on checking his ticket I found that it was one of the boys trying it on! The claim that the ticket had been soaked and crumpled in his overalls didn't help hide the black biro marks on one of the figures! Because of the great feeling of joy and relief about the ship, I read his horoscope severely and sent him on his way! For all the crap that would have ensued it just wasn't worth the hassle of reporting it!

Otherwise, a very pleasant day! A lot of relaxing and unwinding was going on. Life had stopped being hard work for a while! Survival gear was laid aside but kept handy! There was a lot more idle chatter about and a lot more smiling! Life could only get better from here! A few prayers, other than the ones in the Church Service, were said that day by a lot of people who usually never bothered!

MONDAY, 16 AUGUST 82 - DAY 85

0700*   Call the hands
0730   Hands to breakfast
0745*   Time check
0755*   Out pipes
0800*   Both watches muster on the Fore Deck
0830*   Flying Brief
0845*   Prepare for flying
0900*   Hands to Flying Stations
0900   Standard RAS
0915   VERTREP
1000*   Stand easy
1015*   Hands carry on with your work
1130   SRs/Watchkeepers to dinner
1145*   Secure, JRs to dinner
1300*   Hands carry on with your work
1600*   Secure
1715*   Darken ship
1900*   First Dog Watchmen clean messdecks and flats for Rounds
1925*   Stand by for Rounds
2300*   Pipe down

"CU - ???? No qualifiers.
KITC - The MN Officer who claimed the House."

"Programme - It is intended there will be a RAS/VERTREP every third day, weather permitting. There will be a Crosspol on Saturday evening - names of volunteers to the RPO. Clocks will be advanced 1 hour at 2330 (local) tonight, Monday, Thursday, Sunday and Wednesday. We will arrive in St Helena on Thursday 26th."

Note 1 brought us back down to earth:- "Beards - Water rationing has ended, shaving is thus mandatory. The correct procedure must be followed to discontinue shaving, ie. Request Form to the RPO, who will keep a list of potential sets. Beards will be inspected, prior to Shore Leave in St Helena, by the 1st Lieutenant."

Note 2 did the same:- "Haircuts - Too many RN members require haircuts. Get one!"

Note 3 was good news:- "Combat Kit - 'Dress of the Day' is now No8s. Combat kit or any item of combat clothing is not to be worn."

Note 4 read:- "Tombola - House claimed by an MN Officer on number 60, 54th number out, for £42. 2 numbers will be added to the Snowball - so next week will be on 50 numbers or less. Tickets are now on sale. So are YELLOW raffle tickets!"

TN -   0900 - 1030   RAS MHSCs

Lots of 'warlike stuff' was now being discarded but not all! We still darkened ship and played games! Nobody has mentioned if the war is over or not! Who cares let the boys play! As long as we are sailing in the other direction, they can do what they like!

TUESDAY, 17 AUGUST 82 - DAY 86

0700* Call the hands
0730   Hands to breakfast
0745* Time check
0755* Out pipes
0800* Both watches muster on the Fore Deck
0815   Flying Brief
0830* Prepare for flying
0845* Hands to Flying Stations
0900   Launch 373
1000* Stand easy
1015* Hands carry on with your work
1050   SNO's Defaulters muster at the RPO's Office
1100   SNO's Defaulters
1130   SRs/Watchkeepers to dinner
1145* Secure, JRs to dinner
1300* Hands carry on with your work
1600* Secure
1715* Darken ship
1900* First Dog Watchmen clean messdecks and flats for Rounds
1925* Stand by for Rounds
2300* Pipe down

"CU - The Flight SR who equalled the Tombola sales record with another £84.
KITC - No qualifiers."

Note 1 was back to business:- "Loan Clothing Returns - 0830 to 0930 - MN Officers/ Crew return all items of loan clothing (except Lifejackets/sleeping bags/liners/Foul Weather gear). MN Crew lifejackets/sleeping bags/liners/Foul Weather gear will be returned to the Stores Office on Wed 25 August, before arrival in St Helena."

Note 2 was more:- "Naval Stores on Ship's Charge - Destoring from Ascension - Departments SR I/C are to ensure that all items under their custody are labelled clearly showing Class/Group, Patt No and Description. Note - all items on PLR to be returned using Form S1091. Departments are to return all items to the Stores Staff on the Jetty at Rosyth. Valuable and Attractive Items are to be returned to the Stores Office on 12 September. Note - all items on PLR to be returned using Form S1091. Air Stores Returns from Flight/FDO - all items to be returned to Stores Office by 9 September, clearly stating if items are serviceable/unserviceable."

Note 3 read:- "Found Property - A pen has been found in the vicinity of the SRs' Mess, any claimants to the RPO."

Note 4 was a BZ:- "The following CU has been received from CINCFLEET - "You have supported the MCM operations well and earned yourself considerable credit. Well done and a happy return to UK"."

Note 5 was another BZ:- "The following CU has been received from SNOFI - "I have been impressed by your teams 'CAN DO' attitude and your ability to get on with the job independently and with the minimum of fuss. Well done. Bon voyage and a safe homecoming"."

Note 6 read:- "Drafting on return to UK - A signal will be sent to HMS CENTURION before we arrive in UK giving AVDATES. We cannot work these out until the ship's programme on return to UK is known. The RPO has Drafting Preference Cards, but if you fill one in now and post it from Ascension it will probably reach Drafty after drafting action has been taken. We expect you will all be redrafted to your last establishment. Those who are due sea drafts will be drafted taking into account your last Drafting Preference Card."

Note 7 read:- "Radio Telephone Calls and Radio Telegrams - Now restrictions have been lifted, members of the ship's company and MN Crew wishing to make telephone calls/send telegrams are to contact the Radio Officer or RS. A cash basis will operate, ie. on completion of call/telegram payment should be made to the Radio Officer."

Note 8 read:- "Grand Draw - £425 mark has now been passed and we are on RED tickets. After our next mail at Ascension, it is hoped to produce an up to date list of prizes which will include the Video Machine, booze, sweaters, T shirts, cosmetics for men and women, various fancy goods and of course "Hot Racquets". So get your tickets now - the more you spend the more prizes we have. You could become the proud owner of handfuls of prizes."

Note 9 read:- "Tombola numbers drawn by the Chief Stoker were:- 87, 3, 76, 60, 31, 54, 25, 14, 7, 29. Claims for the line to the Ship's Office by 1200 today. Prizes for this week are:- Line £16.80, House £42.00, Snowball (50) £111, (Combined total = £153), Welfare £8.40."

A subtle note, in the middle of a blank part of Page 1, said "RED NOW" - Onward, ever onward!

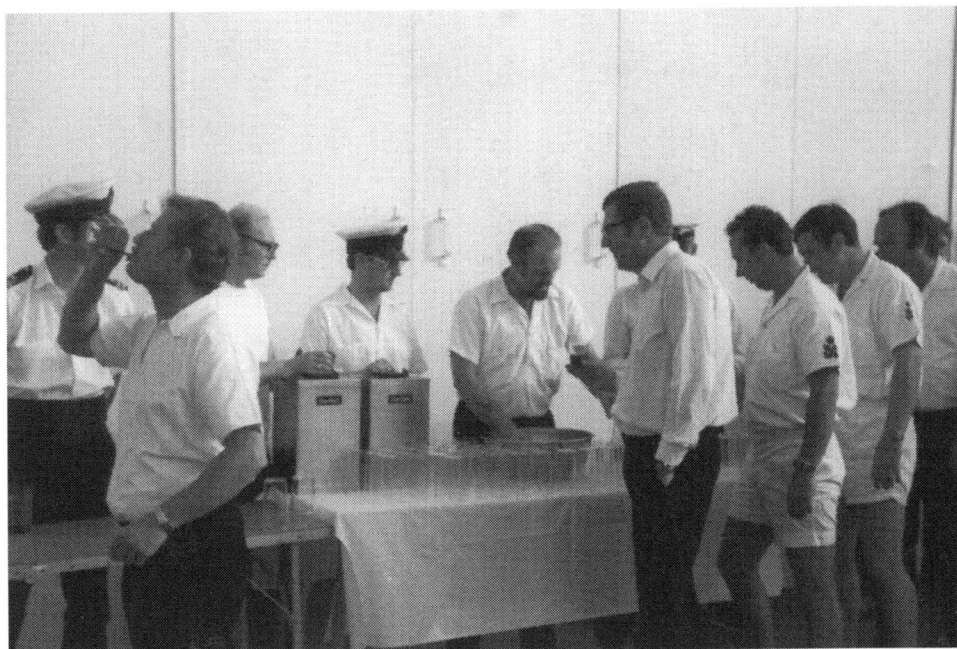

Splice the Mainbrace (with the gallon of rum supplied by RFA Fort Grange)

WEDNESDAY, 18 AUGUST 82 - DAY 87

0700*	Call the hands
0730	Hands to breakfast
0745*	Time check
0755*	Out pipes
0800*	Both watches muster on the Fore Deck
0900 - 1100	RN Officers and SRs return Loan Clothing (See Note 1)
1000*	Stand easy
1015*	Hands carry on with your work
1130	SRs/Watchkeepers to dinner
1145*	Secure, JRs to dinner
1300*	Hands carry on with your work
1600*	Secure
1715*	Darken ship
1900*	First Dog Watchmen clean messdecks and flats for Rounds
1925*	Stand by for Rounds
2300*	Pipe down

"CU - No qualifiers.
KITC - Those who eat the sandwiches on the Bridge when they aren't on duty there."

Note 1 was a repeat of yesterday's Note 1 about Loan Clothing.

Note 2 meant pure luxury - clean clothes again! - "Laundry - will be used by the Catering Staff today and tomorrow. From Friday it will be open from 0800 until 1900 daily for the general use of the ship's company."

Note 3 read:- "Tombola numbers drawn by a JR from the Radio Shack were:-
5, 38, 79, 43, 74, 12, 80, 8, 62, 13. Any claims for the line to the Ship's Office by 1200 today."

Two little added notes simply said "RED" "RED".

St HELLTEM 17/82, "Sport in St Helena and Gibraltar", read:-
1. Soccer - It is hoped to run a Knockout Competition in St Helena and a similar competition in Gibraltar, with teams representing HMS BRECON, HMS LEDBURY, RMS ST HELENA RN JRs and RMS ST HELENA 'The Rest'. In St Helena the KO competition will be followed by a representative match, with a 'Task Force Team' playing against the Island of St Helena Team. The 'Task Force Team' being selected during the KO competition.

Draw for St Helena:-	HMS BRECON	-v-	RMS RN JRs
	RMS 'The Rest'	-v-	HMS LEDBURY
	Two winners then play off in the final.		
Draw for Gibraltar:-	HMS BRECON	-v-	RMS 'The Rest'
	HMS LEDBURY	-v-	RMS RN JRs
	Two winners then play off in the final.		

2. Golf:- It is hoped to run the St Helena Open Golf Tournament (at a different time to the soccer), at the Golf Course at St Helena. The only problem being the shortage of clubs for hire. If you are interested inform the POWTR of the following:- Name,

handicap (max 24), own clubs with you?, minimum clubs you could play a round with? It is hoped to play golf in the afternoon (Stableford Competition), have tea and then have a PU or go to the soccer matches (and have a PU).

3.   Volleyball:- There will be opportunity for good standard games in Gibraltar -v- Police Force, Fire Brigade, etc. Any budding spikers or setters give names to POWTR. Volleyball is one of the most popular sports played in Gibraltar and they take it very seriously so get training now.

4.   Tennis:- Limited facilities for tennis will be available at St Helena. Those interested give names to POWTR.

5.   Other sports and equipment:- Any other ideas for sport etc, to MO, your very own Sports Officer. It would also be appreciated if HMS BRECON and HMS LEDBURY could consult our Sports Officer re strips and associated equipment.

Life was getting pleasanter every day!

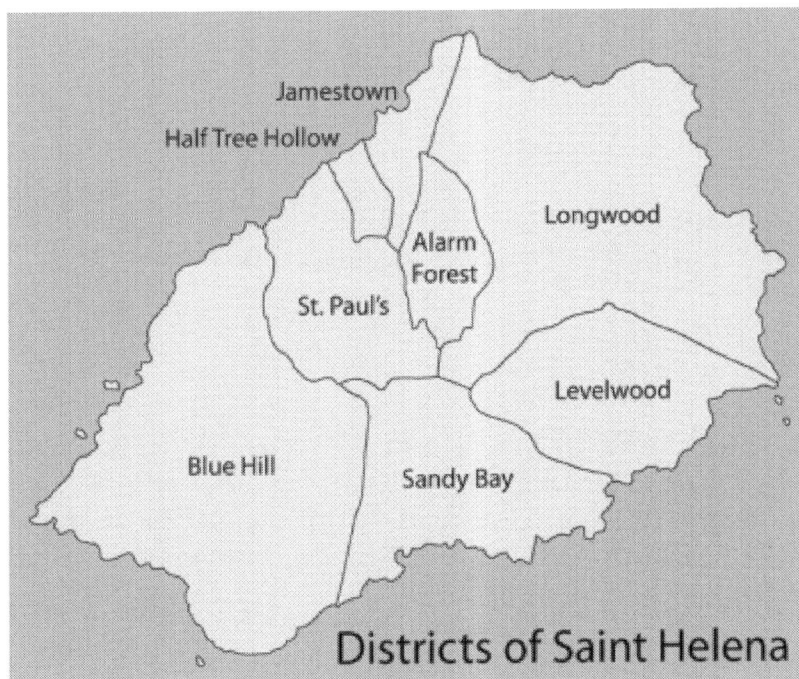

Districts of Saint Helena

A week away from our first major run ashore since goodness knows when!

THURSDAY, 19 AUGUST 82 - DAY 88

0700*	Call the hands
0730	Hands to breakfast
0745*	Time check
0755*	Out pipes
0800*	Both watches muster on the Fore Deck
0900	Standard RAS
0900 - 1100	JRs return loan clothing (See Note 1)
1000	Flying Brief
1000*	Stand easy
1015*	Hands carry on with your work
1015*	Prepare for flying
1030*	Hands to Flying Stations
1045	VERTREP
1045	Meeting in Wardroom to discuss St Helena visit - CO HMS BRECON, CO HMS LEDBURY, Master, SNO, 1st Lt, Purser.
1130	SRs/Watchkeepers to dinner
1145*	Secure, JRs to dinner
1300*	Hands carry on with your work
1330*	Hands to Flying Stations
1335	HDS
1600*	Secure
1700*	Darken ship
1900*	First Dog Watchmen clean messdecks and flats for Rounds
1925*	Stand by for Rounds
2330*	Pipe down
2330	Advance clocks 1 hour

Note 1 was another:- "Loan Clothing Return - JRs return all items of loan clothing between 0900 and 1100 at the Laundry Flat, except for lifejackets, sleeping bags, liners and foul weather clothing, these items will be returned the day before arrival at Rosyth. Flight ratings disembarking at Portland are to return items the day before arrival at Portland."

Note 2 dulled the joyfulness:- "SNO's Rounds - will take place on Saturday morning." (It was amazing, the effect these few simple words had on the ship's company - the RN ratings only, of course!).

Note 3 read:- "Tombola numbers drawn by one of the St Helenian crew members were:- 2, 47, 19, 58, 69, 50, 59, 41, 22, 32. Any claims for the line to the Ship's Office by 1200 today."

Two notes at the foot of the page stated:- "RED ALERT." "RED ALERT"!!!

Here we all were, bright and cheerful, happily working away and dreaming of home! Our first weekend on a relaxed war footing, a chance to unwind and clear a bit of stress. What do we get? Bloody SNO's Rounds! Give us a break! Never mind, it's character building isn't it?

FRIDAY, 20 AUGUST 82 - DAY 89

0700* Call the hands
0730   Hands to breakfast
0745* Time check
0755* Out pipes
0800* Both watches muster on the Fore Deck
0900   Standard RAS
1000   Flying Brief
1000* Stand easy
1015* Hands carry on with your work
1015* Prepare for flying
1030* Hands to Flying Stations
1045   VERTREP
1045   Meeting in the Wardroom to discuss St Helena visit - CO HMS BRECON,
         CO HMS LEDBURY, Master, SNO, 1st Lt, Purser.
1130   SRs/Watchkeepers to dinner
1145* Secure, JRs to dinner
1300* Hands carry on with your work
1330* Hands to Flying Stations
1600* Secure
1730* Darken ship
2300* Pipe down

Note 1 was a pay bonus! - "Hard Lying Money - has been approved from leaving
Ascension Island to 15 August 82. A total of 48 days at 55p will leave you, after tax,
with approximately £17." (The pure extravagance of it all is unbelievable!).

Note 2 read:- "Tombola numbers drawn by an RNP2100 JR were:-
36, 89, 75, 51, 68, 24, 49, 33, 16, 17. Claims for snowball/house to Ship's Office by
1200 today. Line claimed by LSTD on number 2, the 21st number out, for £16.80."

We had our 'location' back today:- "Position - 31 deg 30 min S, 29 deg 41 min W.
Nearest land - Cape Frio, Brazil - 840 miles NW." Also 'Dress of the Day' was
"No8s/10ARs" - which meant the sun was back too!

TN - 0855 - 1045 RAS MHSCs

Cleaning the bloody cabin again tonight for SNO's Rounds, mutter, grunt! Let's try
the positive thinking again! It's weekend, it's getting warmer and sunnier, we're going
home, our war is slowly diminishing, we've got a real 'Run Ashore' to look forward
to at St Helena and of course on top of all this we'll have a nice clean ship!

SATURDAY, 21 AUGUST 82 - DAY 90

0700* Call the hands
0730 Hands to breakfast
0745* Time check
0755* Out pipes
0800* Both watches muster on the Fore Deck
1000* Stand easy
1015* Hands carry on with your work
1055* Stand by for SNO's Messdeck Rounds
1100* SNO's Messdeck Rounds
1130 SRs/Watchkeepers to dinner
1145* Secure, JRs to dinner
1345 Flying Brief
1400* Prepare for flying
1415* Hands to Flying Stations
1430 CROSSPOL by 373 (HMS BRECON - 3 JRs, HMS LEDBURY - CO, 1 SR
         and 2 JRs)
1715* Darken ship
2300* Pipe down

"Revised Programme - we will detach from MHSCs on Sunday evening to proceed to St Helena, arriving there at 0800 on the 25th. The MHSCs will berth alongside us at midday on the 25th. We will then sail from St Helena at midday on 27th and arrive at Ascension Island at midday on 29th for bunkering, stores, mail and landing advance leave party only."

Note 1 sounded good:- "St Helena - We are at present investigating the possibility of having a Ship's Company Dance at St Helena on the evening of the 25th."

Note 2 didn't sound too bad either:- "Pub Lunch - Sunday, in the Forward Lounge from 1200 to 1315 - Rig - clean night clothing. Bring a lot of money with you - RED raffle tickets MIGHT be on sale."

Note 3 read:- "Tombola numbers drawn by a St Helenian crew member were:-
10, 65, 81, 21, 86, 11, 46, 26, 82, 48. Claims for snowball/house to Ship's Office by 1200 today."

"Position - 28 deg 4 min S, 24 deg 55 min W. Nearest land - Ilas de Trinidade, 502 miles NNW."

TN - 1300 -1530 Stopped, engine defect.

After Rounds, the weekend improved dramatically! Probably because we had a nice clean ship!

Well, tonight was the night! We've seen it! "Hot Raquets"! As stated earlier, it was only soft porn! So after about an hour, it got quite boring! What had all the fuss been about? Their lordships have some strange ideas about motivating the troops. They are very good at winding them up, but I'm not sure that's the same thing?!

SUNDAY, 22 AUGUST 82 - DAY 91

0700*	Call the hands
0730	Hands to breakfast
0815*	Time check
0815	Flying Brief
0825*	Out pipes
0830*	Both watches muster on the Fore Deck
0830*	Prepare for flying
0845*	Hands to Flying Stations
0900	RAS/VERTREP
0930*	Secure
1045	Church Service in Wardroom
1100*	Pipe down
1200 - 1315	Pub Lunch (RED Raffle Tickets AND maybe even GREEN)
PM	Detach from MHSCs
1900*	First Dog Watchmen clean messdecks and flats for Rounds
1925*	Stand by for Rounds
2330	Advance clocks 1 hour

Note 1 was an attempt at a BZ! - "Rounds - The standard of cleanliness for SNO's Rounds was very good overall. However, the following points should be noted before the next rounds:- gash bins scrubbed and disinfected then liner inserted, lamp shades cleaned internally and ventilator flaps cleaned."

Note 2 read:- "Tombola numbers drawn by an RNP2100 SR were:-
67, 20, 56, 85, 55, 15, 52, 72, 61, 70, 1, 40, 9, 39, 42. Claims for the house to the Ship's Office by 1200 today."

"Position - 25 deg 55 min S, 19 deg 30 min W. Nearest land - Ilas de Trinidade, 600 miles NW."

TN - 1300 - 1530 Stopped, engine valve defect.

The Pub Lunch was another extremely well organised affair, the MN showing their talent for entertaining at sea. This time the banter was not full of dripping and moaning and the whole atmosphere was a lot more relaxed. The food was excellent and the beer flowed steadily. This all helped to make it fairly easy to sell a lot more Grand Draw tickets! In the afternoon we even managed a spell of volleyball in the sun! Pure luxury!

MONDAY, 23 AUGUST 82 - DAY 92

0700* Call the hands
0730   Hands to breakfast
0745* Time check
0755* Out pipes
0800* Both watches muster on the Fore Deck
1000* Stand easy
1015* Hands carry on with your work
1130   SRs/Watchkeepers to dinner
1145* Secure, JRs to dinner
1300* Hands carry on with your work
1600* Secure
1900* First Dog Watchmen clean messdecks and flats for Rounds
1925* Stand by for Rounds
2300* Pipe down

"CU - From the passengers to the Chief Engineer for arranging for the ship not to go on Saturday and Sunday afternoons to facilitate more comfortable bronzie bronzie conditions.
KITC - The RS for cheating at volleyball!"

Note 1 was on its own:- "We are now on GREEN tickets. This is the last book, so hurry and get your tickets now before we run out."

"Nearest land - St Helena 700 miles NE."

The sun felt good, especially after the wonderful summer we had enjoyed so far this year! Sorry, too negative! As can be seen from the Daily Orders, life was now much more sedate. Relaxation was doing us all the world of good.

This evening we had a film/slide show all about St Helena Island and its history. It was the normal presentation given to the civilian passengers on the cruises, so it was all done very professionally by the Purser. It was extremely interesting and gave us a good insight into the place and people. It all added to the exciting prospect of our visit. It would be wonderful to be on dry land again and all the indications were pointing towards a memorable occasion.

TUESDAY, 24 AUGUST 82 - DAY 93

0700* Call the hands
0730 Hands to breakfast
0745* Time check
0755* Out pipes
0800* Both watches muster on the Fore Deck
1000* Stand easy
1015* Hands carry on with your work
1130 SRs/Watchkeepers to dinner
1145* Secure, JRs to dinner
1300* Hands carry on with your work
1600* Secure
1900* 1st Dog Watchmen clean messdecks and flats for Rounds
1925* Stand by for Rounds
2300* Pipe down

"CU - The FSU SR who equalled the Tombola sales record.
KITC - The MN Officer who has now won TWO houses."

Note 1 was important, even though it meant more work for me:- "Cash for St Helena - If you want cash for St Helena get your cheques in to the POWTR now."

Note 2 read:- "Grand Draw - We now have £560+ in the kitty. GREEN tickets are still available, but this is the last book and they are going fast."

Note 3 read:- "MN Loan Clothing - All outstanding loan clothing, held by MN Crew who are leaving the ship at St Helena, is to be returned to the Laundry at 0900 today."

Note 4 appeared to be the clue that might indicate that 'our war' was officially over? - "Wasp Jollies - Now that the situation of Active Service, and with it emergency regulations have been lifted, it is necessary to revert to normal rules, regulations and procedures. Unfortunately, it can no longer be operationally justified for the Wasp to carry out as frequent navigational/continuation training flights. All future flying by the Wasp will be of an operational nature only eg. VERTREP, CASEVAC, Aid to Civil Government authority etc. Sorry to all those readers who have missed the opportunity to be lifted by a paraffin parrot."

Note 5 read:- "Tombola numbers drawn by an RNP2100 JR were:-
22, 33, 68, 70, 41, 11, 29, 21, 90, 67, 23, 69, 53, 20, 7. The last house was claimed by an MN Officer (his second house!) on number 1, the 61st number out, for £42.00. Prizes for this week are:- Line £16.80, House £42.00, Snowball £127.80, Welfare £8.40. House/Snowball combined - £169.80. Claims for the line by 1200 today."

"Position:- 19 deg 12 min S, 10 deg 32 min W.
Nearest land - St Helena 340 miles NE."

A signal had been received today reference Annual Promotion Reports for Senior Rates (S264Cs). Nobody had bothered about this sort of thing in the rush to get to war! Luckily enough, the Scribes had ensured we had a supply of the relevant forms before we left Portsmouth, just in case we were away from home for longer than their lordships expected! It was also suggested that Divisional Reports (S264As), should also be raised for all the RN Party going on draft, in accordance with QR(RN). So a memorandum was issued and the POWTR was inundated with more typing! Shot in the foot again! Luckily, he had also remembered to get some forms that explained to the Divisional Officers how to fill these forms in (S264Ds)!

St HELLTEM 18/82 "Visit to St Helena" arrived today reading:- "RMS ST HELENA, in company with HMS BRECON and HMS LEDBURY, will make a routine visit to the island of St Helena. The ship will anchor in Jamestown Bay approximately half a mile from the shore. Estimated time of arrival 1200 hrs 25 August 82 and Estimated Time of Departure Friday, forenoon 29 August.
The Island lies 1000 miles from the West African Coast and was first discovered on 21 May 1502 by Juan de Nava Castella. The first person to live on the island was a Portuguese Army Officer, banished there in 1516. The first British settlers landed in 1659. The Island has a total area of 47 square miles, is 10 miles long and 6 miles wide and rises to a height of 2697 feet above sea level. Ascension Island lies 704 miles north of St Helena and Cape Town is 1700 miles to the south east. St Helena is the Main Island of the British Dependency which consists of St Helena, Ascension Island and Tristan da Cunha. The Island is most famous as the place to which Napoleon was finally exiled in 1815. Arriving on the Island on 15 Oct 1815 he lived for the first two months at the Briars, before being moved to Longwood House, where he died in 1821. His tomb is still on the island but his body was returned to France in 1840. Zulu Chief, Prince Dinuzulu, was also exiled there by Queen Victoria in 1890. There are several plants unique to the Island, most notably the male and female Cabbage Tree.
The Customs Shed is situated near the landing place and everyone has to clear customs each time they land.
Leave will be granted to non duty personnel from 1200 until 0730 JRs and 0745 SRs. A Boat Routine will be run by the local agents. They will run every hour. A large swell can run into the Bay making the landing place dangerous, so be careful and listen to the boatmen.

Dress will be plain clothes for Libertymen. A Shore Patrol will be landed at 1800 each day to the local Police Station. It will consist of 1 Leading Hand (RMS) and 2 Able Rates (HMS BRECON & HMS LEDBURY). Rig half blues.
Official entertainment:- Wed 25th - 1830 to 2000 CTP in HMS BRECON.
2030 to 0100 Public Dance at Civic Centre, admission free, Bar & Food available on cash basis.
Thurs 26th - 1830 Reception for 35 Officers and Senior Ratings at Plantation House. There are 3 bars on the Island, all in Jamestown, the Consulate Hotel, the Standard and the White Horse Inn. Licensing Laws are strict. Opening times are 1030 - 1400 and 1730 - 2200 with a 10 minute drinking up time that is enforced by the police. Drinking in the streets is forbidden.

Tours of the Island by taxi are recommended and are inexpensive. Taxis are unmarked but will have an RMS ST HELENA baggage label in the windscreen. A tour should cost about £5 per head. Always agree a price before departure. If the taxi waits for you there is a charge of £1.25 approximately per hour or part of an hour.

Suggested spots to visit are:- Napoleon's Tomb, Longwood House, The Briars, Jacob's Ladder (699 steps), Jamestown Museum.

Any mail posted on the Island will be taken by us to Ascension Island and then sent home. Cost of letters and postcards to UK are 11p each.

The Football Pitch is available on Thursday afternoon. Other sports which may be available are golf, swimming and tennis. You are reminded that swimming in the sea is dangerous due to the large swell and underflows. If you want to swim there is an Olympic size pool in Jamestown, near the Jetty.

Have a good visit and enjoy yourselves."

The St Helenian crew members were extremely happy - home tomorrow! Some were even happier than the rest - they were being relieved by new crew members! The rest of us were just happy!

St. Helena Coat of Arms

FINAL Lest we forget - RMS ST HELENA arrives home in St. Helena!?
(This is the official version). Their lordships couldn't even get this right!

WEDNESDAY, 25 AUGUST 82 - DAY 94

0001	Clocks advanced one hour (Z)
0700*	Call the hands
0730	Hands to breakfast
0745*	Time check
0755*	Out pipes
0800*	Both watches muster on the Fore Deck
1000*	Stand easy
1015*	Hands carry on with your work
1100*	Hands to dinner
1145*	Hands fall in for Entering Harbour (Dress No10s)
1200	Anchor Jamestown, St Helena
1830 - 2000	CTP in HMS BRECON
1900*	First Dog Watchmen clean messdecks and flats for Rounds
1925*	Stand by for Rounds
2030 - 0100	Public Dance in Community Hall
2300*	Pipe down

"Routine - Saturday Sea/Harbour". "Dress of the Day - No10ARs, (Libertymen - plain clothes)." "Leave as piped to 0730/0745". Wonderful additions to Daily Orders, these few words were. However, let's not forget "The ship is under sailing orders"!

"CU - A Comms staff JR on his birthday.
KITC - RS for dropping him in it."

Note 1 reminded us of life back in Pompey Dockyard:- "Evening Meals - Wednesday and Thursday evening meals will be from 1730 - 1830 for ALL."

Note 2 read:- "Laundry will be closed for painting during the stay in St Helena."

Note 3 read:- "Tombola numbers drawn by an FSU JR were:- 89, 14, 38, 65, 43, 83, 46, 25, 47, 55, 85, 13, 12, 62, 45. Claims by 1200 today."

"Programme -	Wed	25 Aug	1200	Arrive St Helena
	Fri	27 Aug	1200	Depart St Helena
	Sun	29 Aug	1200	Arrive Ascension berth ALVEGA (Fuel)
	Sun	29 Aug	2000	Depart Ascension

Further information regarding Gibraltar/Rosyth will be published when confirmed."

TN -	1200	Anchored off Jamestown
	1400	Call on Governor
	1830 - 2000	CTP in HMS BRECON
	2030 - 0100	Ship's Company Dance in Community Hall given by Islanders.

When we anchored it was expected that the Jetty would be crowded with cheering people! The MN Officers had told us that when the ship anchored normally, the whole island turned up to watch, cheer and welcome back family and friends. The rest of the day would then be a holiday! It was the middle of the day and the Jetty was deserted!? (In certain written works covering this event, this occurrence has been whitewashed and it is stated that "they received a rapturous welcome from the Islanders".) Where were all the people, they knew we were coming, where was the great welcome back from the war? We were informed later that they were protesting publicly about the British Government taking their ship and only lifeline away. (Funnily enough, the British Government has a long history of leaving the St Helenians to look after themselves! In fact for decades they have done very little for the island at all and many articles and books have confirmed this fact! So what had happened - absolutely nothing as usual! So the sudden loss of their ship without warning had been the final straw!) They had been left stranded and intended everyone to know about it! After half an hour, the scene changed and they all appeared from out of the houses, etc. Then we had the rapturous welcome'!

The trip ashore was, as had been promised, a little hairy! The swell was horrendous and getting off the boat on to the shore was very hazardous. It would be interesting when we went back the other way, with the state of some of the boys! Most of us were slightly land sick when we got ashore! We could still feel the motion of the sea, having been onboard for so long with little break. However, the local beer soon shifted that! What a wonderful place, it was like going back in time! The cars were all ancient British cars which the locals were expert at keeping going. Life was slow and the people were happy - what a difference to what we were used to back home!

A group of us went sightseeing in a taxi. What a trip. Jamestown was the only part of the island at sea level, so we had to go up! About 2,000 feet on a road dug out of the side of the rock with only a tiny wall, no crash barrier or other means of protection from the sheer drop. There was hardly room for two vehicles to pass and it was twisting and turning whilst climbing straight up! And the speed the locals drove at in these near 'vintage' nearly clapped out cars was absolutely frightening. When we got to the top, however, it was like another world, all jungle and mountain tops. There were scattered homesteads and lots of greenery, it was lovely to see after all that sea and desolate Falkland Island scenery. That evening, along with the inspection of the local bars, we had the dance. Again it was like going back in time, it was an old style entertainment with all the family attending, kids everywhere, everyone dancing and generally enjoying themselves. It was a revelation and a good time was had by all!

Jamestown, St. Helena from our anchorage

THURSDAY, 26 AUGUST 82 - DAY 95

0700* Call the hands
0730   Hands to breakfast
0745* Time check
0755* Out pipes
0800* Both watches muster on the Fore Deck
0900   Watchkeepers leave
1000* Stand easy
1015* Hands carry on with your work
1130   SRs/Watchkeepers to dinner
1145* Secure, JRs to dinner
1800   Officers and SRs for Governor's Reception to muster
1900* First Dog Watchmen clean messdecks and flats for Rounds
1925* Stand by for Rounds
2300* Pipe down

Note 1 read:- "Tombola numbers drawn by an FSU SR were:-
87, 76, 6, 72, 84, 77, 32, 73, 59, 79, 31, 3, 51, 30, 71. Claims for snowball/house to
Ship's Office by 1100 today. Line claimed by an MN Officer on 85, the 26th number
out, for £16.80."

The 'Routine' was 'Saturday Harbour' again - so it was a case of nursing the
hangover through the morning and then have lunch and a couple of pints to recover
before setting off to enjoy the rest of the visit! It was the soccer tournament today so
that would help to sweat some of the badness out, especially in this heat and at
altitude! On our way to the soccer tournament we had a little bit of a scare in the
minibus that I was in! At the top of the cliff, where the road had left the cliff edge to
go inland, we were about twenty yards along the road leaving the cliff edge when the
minibus, which had been struggling all the way, suddenly ran out of gears to drop
down into! It started going backwards towards the 2,000 foot drop! We all
clambered out, which helped slow it down a little, and pushed! I decided there and
then, that I would be going down on one of the other minibuses! All the islanders had
turned out to see the soccer and to see their team perform, so there were picnics and a
real party atmosphere to the whole event. The football pitch had been hacked out of
the rock by the Royal Engineers and was the only piece of flat land on the whole
island. Today it hosted an extremely large crowd of enthusiastic revellers who fully
intended enjoying themselves - and they did!

FRIDAY, 27 AUGUST 82 - DAY 96

0630* Call the hands
0645   Single up HMS BRECON & HMS LEDBURY
0700   Embark passengers/Slip HMS BRECON & HMS LEDBURY
0715   Hands to breakfast
0730* Time check
0745* Out pipes, commence shortening in
0750* Fall in for Leaving Harbour (No10s)
0800   Weigh and proceed to Ascension Island
1000* Stand easy
1015* Hands carry on with your work
1130   SRs/Watchkeepers to dinner
1145* Secure, JRs to dinner
1300* Hands carry on with your work
1900* First Dog Watchmen clean messdecks and flats for Rounds
1925* Stand by for Rounds
2300* Pipe down

Note 1 read:- "Tombola numbers drawn by an RNP2100 JR were:- 58, 54, 86, 16, 35, 52, 27, 57, 34, 56, 36, 75, 49, 15, 64, 78, 17, 61, 82, 39. Claims for snowball/house to Ship's Office by 1200 today."

TN - 0730   MHSCs slipped
      0800   Weigh and proceed

We sent off the letter ordering the Video Recorder for the Grand Draw. A company in Bournemouth had promised to deliver it to the gangway when we arrived back in UK.

A very quiet day was had by most today! Much Alka-Seltzer and Aspirin were required! We all tearfully watched St Helena disappear in the distance - BUT we meant it this time! A 'magic' place and a wonderful run ashore. Thank you to all on the island for looking after us so well. It was a rare treat!

Jamestown from top of Jacob's ladder – a 602 ft ladder – silly!

SATURDAY, 28 AUGUST 82 - DAY 97

0700* Call the hands
0730   Hands to breakfast
0745* Time check
0755* Out pipes
0800* Both watches muster on the Fore Deck
1000* Stand easy
1015* Hands carry on with your work
o/c   FSU01 Photograph on the Flight Deck (Dress No10s)
1130   SRs/Watchkeepers to dinner
1145* Secure, JRs to dinner
1900* First Dog Watchmen clean messdecks and flats for Rounds
1925* Stand by for Rounds
2300* Pipe down

"CU - St Helena Island for a pleasant stop along the way.
KITC - The MO for spoiling everybody's fun - see Note 3."

Note 1- more work for me:- "Extensions of Service – Personnel who had applied or wish to apply for the October Continuance in Service Board, contact the POWTR."

Note 2 was of great interest to the investors/collectors among us:- "Commemorative First Day Covers - For RMS ST HELENA's first day as a Post Office. This is a limited issue of 500 , a definite collectors item."

Note 3 heralded the end of a way of life! - "Tombola - snowball/house claimed by the MO (money to money!) on 16, the 49th number out, for £169.00. He would like to thank all you mug punters for giving all your hard earned savings to him, he is now going to purchase large amounts of GREEN raffle tickets hoping his luck can hold out. So get yours now before he buys the lot" (How will I fill Daily Orders now?!).

Weekend again! Time flies when you're enjoying yourself!

The Royal Mail pennant flies on the RMS St. Helena for the first time

SUNDAY, 29 AUGUST 82 - DAY 98

0700   Mail closes
0700* Call the hands
0715   Hands to breakfast
0745* Hands to Flying Stations
0800* VERTREP Advance Leave Party, Mail and Stores
AM   Alongside ALVEGA refuelling (Approx 8 hours). Sail for Gibraltar o/c.
0815* Time check
0825* Out pipes
0830* Both watches muster on the Fore Deck
0930* Secure
1045   Church Service in the Wardroom
1100* Pipe down
1900* First Dog Watchmen clean messdecks and flats for Rounds
1925* Stand by for Rounds

"CU - The MO for getting the beer in and one of the St Helenian crew members on the birth of his son.
KITC - To all the holidaymakers - Enjoy yourselves and don't do anything we wouldn't do."

Note 1 was an addition to yesterday's Note 2:- "First Day Covers - to add authentic realism to your new 1st Day Covers the Master's signature could be added. For this purpose the Master will be seated at a card table on the Ironing Board Flat from 0900 to 1000 this morning."

Note 2 was sporty:- "Jacob's Ladder - During their visit last week HMS LOWESTOFT 'cracked' Jacob's Ladder (699 steps and 602 feet). One member of their team took 5 mins 20 secs, 6 man aggregate 35 mins 29 secs, team average time 5 mins 55 secs. All names for the Gibraltar 'Rock Run' to the Sick Bay JR." (Appropriate!).

TN - 0800   Alongside ALVEGA for fuelling
                 Advance Leave Party to Wideawake.

There were a lot of very happy faces leaving the ship for the airfield today - the Advance Leave Party. Some, however, were a little disappointed they would miss the run ashore in Gibraltar but you can't win them all! Anyway, it meant they would also miss the trip across the Bay of Biscay, so they definitely couldn't complain! We all stood and stared at Ascension Island, as we weren't allowed ashore, but we didn't care, we were going home!

MONDAY, 30 AUGUST 82 - DAY 99

0700* Call the hands
0730   Hands to breakfast
0745* Time check
0755* Out pipes
0800* Both watches muster on the Fore Deck
0930   SNO's Defaulters
1000* Stand easy
1015* Hands carry on with your work
1200* Secure, Hands to 'Make and Mend'
1900* Clean up messdecks and flats for Rounds
1925* Stand by for Rounds
2300* Pipe down

"Programme - Arrive Gibraltar 1200 7 Sep - Sail 0800 9 Sep 82. The ship will then go first to Rosyth, arriving 1000 on 15 Sep to land FSU01 and destore MHSCs' spares. On completion (approx 22 Sep) we will sail to Portsmouth arriving 24 Sep to complete destoring/restoring for the Ship's next voyage. Leave and draft details will be promulgated when known. Remember it may still all change."

The only Note was about:- "Green Raffle Tickets - Our video recorder has now been ordered and we are about to start putting together the list of other prizes. The last few green tickets are now on sale so get yours now."

TN - 0200 Slip and proceed.

What about today then?! A general 'Make and Mend'! On a Monday afternoon? The RN's all heart isn't it! So what's the catch? It's all very puzzling! We all went back to work anyway, because we had to get everything ready for tomorrow's 'SODS Opera'! So they hadn't really gone soft, it was more of a 'con job'!

A stowaway found on board today!
(It's Napoleon really – an old reluctant St. Helenian!)

TUESDAY, 31 AUGUST 82 - DAY 100

0700* Call the hands
0730   Hands to breakfast
0745* Time check
0755* Out pipes
0800* Both watches muster on the Fore Deck
1000* Stand easy
1015* Hands carry on with your work
1100   Distribution of 'Crossing the Line' Certs/Scripts from Ship's Office
1130   SRs/Watchkeepers to dinner
1145* Secure, JRs to dinner
1300* Hands carry on with your work
1400   Rehearsal for SODS Opera
1900* Clean messdecks and flats for Rounds
1925* Stand by for Rounds
2015   SODS Opera
2300* Pipe down

Note 1 was boring:- "1982 Pension Code - The increased Pensions and Gratuities rates from 1 April 82 are now available in the Ship's Office for those interested."

Note 2 was the award of the First Good Conduct Badge to the JR in the Sick Bay.

Note 3 read:- "Welfare Committee Meeting - Items for the Agenda to the Secretary by 1600 today. Meeting will be at 1030 Wednesday."

Note 4 read:- "SODS Opera - This mammoth spectacular will take place in the Forward Lounge at 2030. A cash bar will open at 2015. Entry via the Wardroom Door only. Officers are requested to have finished their evening meal by 1930. There will be a final rehearsal for all involved at 1400 in the Forward Lounge."

"Position - 01 degs 6 mins N, 15 degs 48 mins W. Nearest land - Monrovia, Liberia, 430 miles NE."

As ever, a good night was had by all! The professionalism of the Purser again being highlighted in his capacity as Ship's Entertainments Officer! Of course, on this one he didn't have to hold back and keep it clean! So they didn't! An excellent evening's entertainment rendered and received in good spirit!

WEDNESDAY, 1 SEPTEMBER 82 - DAY 101

0700* Call the hands
0730   Hands to breakfast
0745* Time check
0755* Out pipes
0800* Both watches muster on the Fore Deck
0830   Flying Brief
0845* Prepare for flying
0900* Hands to Flying Stations
0915   VERTREP
1000* Stand easy
1015* Hands carry on with your work
1030   Welfare Committee Meeting - Wardroom
1130   SRs/Watchkeepers to dinner
1145* Secure, JRs to dinner
1300* Hands carry on with your work
1900* Clean messdecks and flats for Rounds
1925* Stand by for rounds
2300* Pipe down

Note 1 stated bluntly:- "There are no notes today."

"CU - Aircrewman for inscribing the pretty bit on 'Crossing the Line' Certificates. KITC - Nil."

"Position - 6 degs 11 mins N, 16 degs 37 mins W. Nearest land - Freetown, Sierra Leone. 250 miles ENE."

The rest of the victims for the 'Crossing the Line' Ceremony were ducked and certified today. What a disgusting ceremony it is - RN style that is! The only way to get rid of the taste of the seawater was by having a couple of cans of beer!

The third Welfare Meeting was held this morning. It covered a range of subjects including:- actions arising from the previous meeting (latest update on Inter-Mess games, disposal of Welfare money and assets, thank you letters for Tombola ticket printers, St Helena Island mail, more pub lunches, 'Crossing the Line' Certificates, Flight Deck film shows and gun practice); acceptance of minutes of last meeting; Treasurer's Financial Report; forwarding of mail on disbandment of RNP2100; leave in Rosyth; volunteers for the next trip down south on RMS St HELENA; thanks for the collection for Ladyfield Home on St Helena Island; next meeting to be after Gibraltar and finally disposal of Welfare Fund money and assets as follows:-

Welfare Fund money: 1. £50 for prizes in Grand Draw
2. 4 crates of beer for next pub lunch
3. Augmentation of bottles of spirits donated so 1 bottle goes to each man.
4. Remainder to South Atlantic Fund

Welfare Fund assets: 1. FSU01 - volleyball gear and dartboard
2. RMS St HELENA - Board Games
3. Video tapes to winner of Video Recorder in Grand Draw
4. St Helenian Crew Mess - dartboard
5. Remainder to HMS NELSON for re-distribution.

I had the duty! Another quiet day of recovery after all the recent excesses. Also, of course, a chance to recharge the batteries ready for the run ashore in Gib!

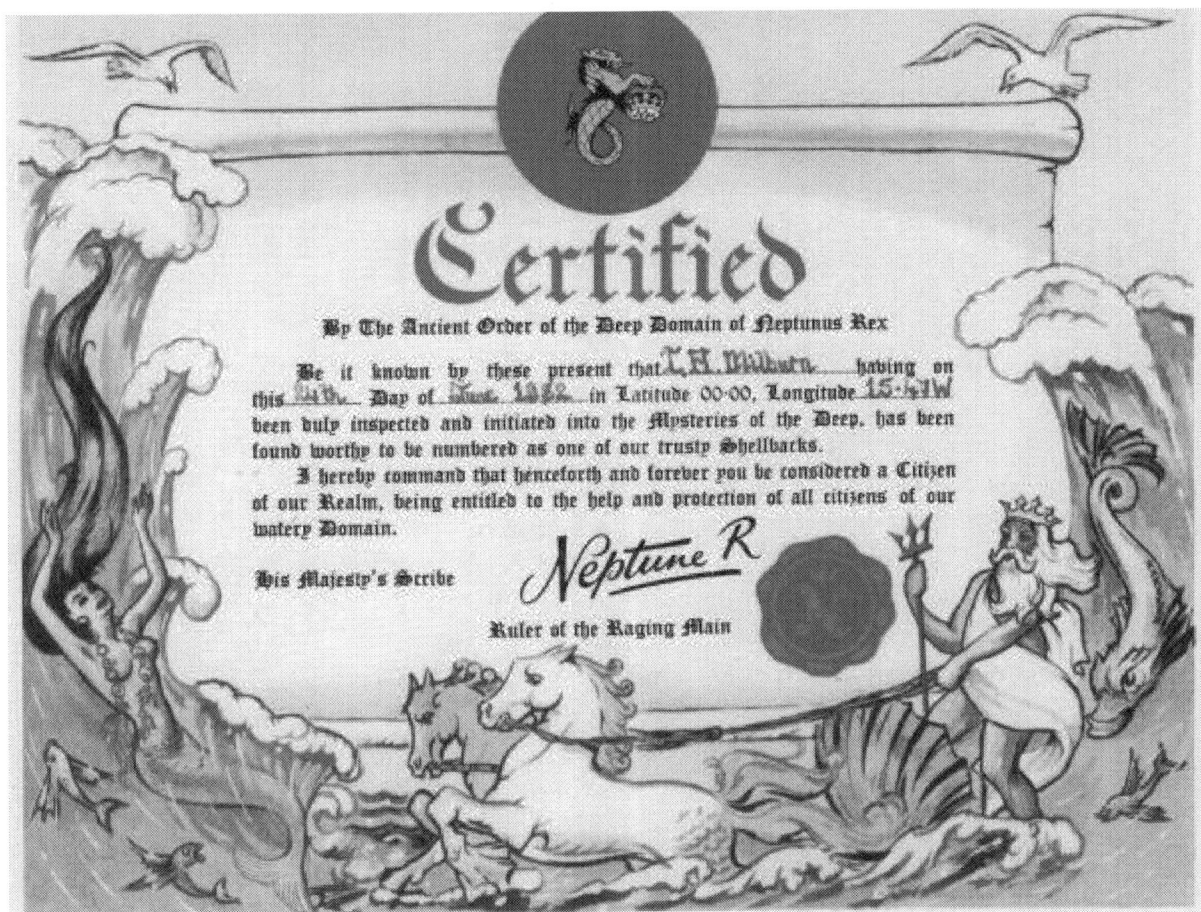

'Crossing the Line' certificate

THURSDAY, 2 SEPTEMBER 82 - DAY 102

0700* Pipe down
0730   Hands to breakfast
0745* Time check
0755* Out pipes
0800* Both watches muster on the Fore Deck
0815   Flying Brief
0830* Prepare for flying
0845* Hands to Flying Stations
0900   VERTREP
1000* Stand easy
1015* Hands carry on with your work
1130   SRs/Watchkeepers to dinner
1145* Secure, JRs to dinner
1200* Hands to 'Make and Mend'
1900* Clean messdecks and flats for Rounds
1925* Stand by for Rounds
2300* Pipe down

"CU - The Purser, The Doc and all the other performers.
KITC - The weather."

"Programme - ETA Gibraltar 0800 8 Sep 82
                    ETD Gibraltar 1600 9 Sep 82
The ship is now due to arrive at Rosyth at 1330 on 15 September"

"Position - 11 degs 19 mins N, 17 degs 26 mins W. Nearest land - The Lost Horizon as far as the MN can guess!"

TN - 1330 VERTREP MHSCs

Dear Mum, weather's a bit dodgy but otherwise it's a nice cruise - NOW!!
(Helped enormously by the second 'Make and Mend'!? Why are they being so nice?
I'll bet they're going to send us back again!)

FRIDAY, 3 SEPTEMBER 82 - DAY 103

0700* Call the hands
0730   Hands to breakfast
0745* Time check
0755* Out pipes
0800* Both watches muster on the Fore Deck
0900* STANDARD RAS
1000* Stand easy
1015* Hands carry on with your work
1130   SRs/Watchkeepers to dinner
1145* Secure, JRs to dinner
1200* 'Make and Mend'
2300* Pipe down
2330   Advance clocks 1 hour to 'BST'

"Position - 16 degs 50 mins N, 17 degs 42 mins W. Nearest land - St Louis, Senegal, 100 miles ESE. (We will pass Dakar at 0200)."

TN - 0900 - 1130 RAS MHSCs

This morning I had a very innocent visitor in my office! The youngest member of the ship's company arrived to 'pay his electricity bill' for the trip so far! This was an ancient and cruel RN custom played on the young and innocent crew members! Obviously, the boys were bored and had come up with this old chestnut! A piece of paper was set up to look like an official ship's document and was presented to the victim as his electricity bill for the trip so far. It was explained to him, by someone in authority over him, that he was paying for the electricity he had 'personally' used on his bunk light, radio, razor, etc. He was then told to walk this bill round the ship, to various workshops and offices, for verification and payment! Members of his section then ensured that the relevant people knew he was coming! Eventually, totally convinced by now after a full tour of the ship, he ended up at the Ship's Office, cheque book in hand, ready to pay the bill! I took his cheque and 'officially' stamped his bit of paper and informed him that he would have to see the SNO, as his bill was a bit over the top. So in accordance with Ship's Standing Orders he had to explain his excesses to the SNO! The SNO gently let him down and explained it all to him! He got a good cheer that night when he walked into the dining hall. He blushed a bit but survived the ribbing and later in the mess gained a few extra cans for his bravery!

On Day 22 we shut and secured the 'window' in the office (big square porthole!). Today, we opened it up again. How pleasant, we had a wonderful view of the blue seas, sun and the two MHSCs steaming along beside us. Not many RN Ship's Offices with a 'window', eh? Luxury, pure luxury!

No Notes again, but what is worrying is all this time off! Three 'Make and Mends' in one week! Only the Weapons Electrical Branch could ever contemplate or understand such goings on! Something _was_ obviously going on, but what? The buzz mongers were beginning to stir. However, they were being baffled by all the time off they were getting, which was allowing them to thoroughly contemplate the situation!? Complicated, eh? A bit of a vicious circle! Waiter, bring me another cocktail! Thank goodness we've got Rounds tomorrow, the cleaning will give us something to do later!

Requestmen

SATURDAY, 4 SEPTEMBER 82 - DAY 104

0700* Call the hands
0730   Hands to breakfast
0745* Time check
0755* Out pipes
0800* Both watches muster on the Fore Deck
1000* Stand easy
1015* Hands carry on with your work
1055* Stand by for Master's Rounds
1100* Master's Rounds
1130   SRs/Watchkeepers to dinner
1145* Secure, JRs to dinner
1600   Clay pigeon shoot
1930   Barbeque and Beer Bar
2300* Pipe down
2330   Advance clocks one hour

Note 1 was important:- "RNP2100 (Exempt FSU01 and Flight) - Are reminded to request to the RPO for Railway Warrants for the proposed Extended Long Weekend 22 Sep to 27 Sep from Rosyth."

Note 2 was work for me:- "Cash for Gib - Get your cheques cashed for Gib NOW."

Note 3 was a blow:- "All videos have now been shown. Any requests for a particular repeat to the POMA by 1600 today."

Note 4 was more work:- "Sweatshirts, 'T' shirts, Jumpers, Ties - Money will be taken at the Ship's Office today. All monies are to be paid by arrival in Gibraltar."

Note 5 was for the big homecoming:- "Fleet Form 3s - Anyone intending to meet the ship in Rosyth (wife, girlfriend, mistress, etc.) WILL need a Fleet Form 3 to get in the Dockyard. You must, therefore, send this form to the person concerned when you are in Gibraltar. Obtainable from the RPO."

Note 6 was an added bonus:- "Gizzits - The ship received Duty Free gifts in Ascension Island, everyone onboard will receive 400 cigarettes and 2 small bottles of whisky. There is a limited amount of Brandy, anyone who would prefer Brandy to whisky names to the RPO. A draw will take place if necessary."

"Position - 21 degs 43 mins N, 15 degs 51 mins W. Nearest land - Cap Blanc, Spanish Sahara, 60 miles SSE."

Homecoming was now growing on the agenda! The excitement was rising! It was weekend again! More time off than the average admiral's bunk light! Let's have another look at the cocktail list, waiter!

SUNDAY, 5 SEPTEMBER 82 - DAY 105

0700* Call the hands
0730   Hands to breakfast
0815* Time check
0825* Out pipes
0830* Both watches muster on the Fore Deck
0930* Secure
1045   Church Service in the Wardroom
1100* Pipe down
1900* Clean messdecks and flats for Rounds
1925* Stand by for Rounds

Note 1 was nearly a BZ again:- "Master's Rounds - were very good. However, the majority of showers require attention and some overheads spoiled what would have otherwise been a very good effort in cabins. Best cabin - B8 wins the box of biscuits."

Note 2 read:- Jumpers/Sweat Tops/'T' Shirts/Ties - Some jumpers have been sent via BFPO Ships Air Mail and MAY, therefore, be awaiting us in Gib. The rest of the order will be awaiting our arrival in Rosyth."

"Position - 25 degs 55 mins N, 15 degs 5 mins W. Nearest land - Cabo Bojador, Spanish Sahara, 35 miles ENE."

Life in the office was hectic now with the prospect of mail, etc, in Gibraltar. I was also trying to sort out the 'STUFT Report' that had to be forwarded. Each department having to make its own report, then the whole lot had to be collated for onward transmission. Very boring! Never mind, it's still weekend and it's still sunny. Now, where had we got to on that cocktail list?

MONDAY, 6 SEPTEMBER 82 - DAY 106

0700*	Call the hands
0730	Hands to breakfast
0745*	Time check
0755*	Out pipes
0800*	Both watches muster on the Fore Deck
0845	Flying Brief
0900*	Prepare for flying
0900 - 0930	Heaving Line transfers
0915*	Hands to Flying Stations
0930	VERTREP
1000*	Stand easy
1015*	Hands carry on with your work
1100	SRs' Mess Meeting
1130	SRs/Watchkeepers to dinner
1145*	Secure, JRs to dinner
1200	'Make and Mend'
1500 - 1530	Hands to bathe
1600 - 1730	OOW manoeuvres
1900*	Clean messdecks and flats for Rounds
1925*	Stand by for Rounds
1945 - 2045	Tombola in the Stern Gallery
2030 - 2130	Relative Velocity Exercise
2300*	Pipe down

Note 1 read:- "Gizzits - Brandy winners names are on the Notice Board outside the Ship's Office."

"CU - 1. Catering Staff for another excellent 'do'.
    2. RPO/Buffer for cash collected from the shooting sessions for the Raffle.
KITC - Nil."

"Position - 30 degs 0 mins N, 12 degs 10 mins W. Nearest land - Lanzarote, Canaries. 80 miles SW."

This afternoon we engaged in the quaint old RN custom of 'hands to bathe'. The MN were highly intrigued by the idea, whilst the swimming freaks amongst us got quite excited at the prospect! As the sea here was shark infested, armed sentries were posted along the sides of the ship to deter any unwelcome visitors! Eventually, the hour arrived, the ship's engines stopped and the pipe for 'hands to bathe' was made. All the idiots, sorry swimmers, dived or jumped off the side of the ship into the water below. There was much shouting, screaming and general joyfulness! However, within seconds this joy had turned to panic and fear? The OOW had stopped the engines and then made the pipe, BUT he had not realised that the ship would need a little time to actually stop in the water! So the swimmers were slowly disappearing into the distance in the wash of the ship but out of the range of the armed sentries! The spectators of this fiasco were throwing lifebelts and lifejackets into the water hoping that our aquatic victims would be able to get to them. Boats were hurriedly being launched and HMS BRECON and HMS LEDBURY, who were enjoying the same exercise, were alerted! Eventually our intrepid swimmers were all returned onboard by one means or another! There were some very lucky people about! The poor sharks never got a thing! Lucky really, as most of the things they would have caught would have been very gristly and extremely salty!

After the excitement of the afternoon's spectacular events, in the evening we had a 'bingo' night RN style! Rude, but a chance for everybody to get together, have a laugh and enjoy a few beers. The entertainment value was enhanced by the drunken 'swimmers' who were on shock, or was it shark, therapy!

Some wonderful dits will be told around the RN Dockyards after today's events!

'Hands to bathe'

TUESDAY, 7 SEPTEMBER 82 - DAY 107

0700*	Call the hands
0730	Hands to breakfast
0745*	Time check
0755*	Out pipes
0800*	Both watches muster on the Fore Deck
0900	SRs' Mess Meeting
0900 - 0930	RAS Apps
1000*	Stand easy
1015*	Hands carry on with your work
1130	SRs/Watchkeepers to dinner
1145*	Secure, JRs to dinner
1200	'Make and Mend'
1830 - 1900	Man overboard drills
1900*	Clean messdecks and flats for Rounds
1925*	Stand by for Rounds
2030 - 2130	Relative Velocity Exercise
2300*	Pipe down

"CU - Task Group Commander for allowing hands to bathe and to the fortitude of the marathon swimmers and lifejacket/lifebelt hurlers - well done!
KITC - To whom it may concern."

Note 1 was back to RN Law:- "No8 Shirts - As from 1/9/82 ratings with shoulder flaps on these shirts are to wear shoulder rate badges on them. All other ratings are to be in possession of these shirts by December 1983. DCI(RN) 357/82 refers."

Note 2 was boring:- "Clothing returns - all outstanding items of loan clothing, eg. foul weather gear, combat gear, etc, are to be returned to the Naval Stores Office 0900 - 1000 today. (Foul weather gear can be re-drawn on a temporary basis if needed)."

Note 3 was about our next visit:- "Organised sport in Gib - volleyball we hoped to arrange has been cancelled due to the short stay. The only organised sport, IT IS HOPED, is the soccer on the Fleet pitches opposite HMS ROOKE, on Wed 8 Sept 82.
1600 HMS BRECON   -v-   RMS ST HELENA 'The Rest'
1640 HMS LEDBURY   -v-   RMS ST HELENA JRs
1720 The Final between the two winners.
SUPPORTERs - don't forget the Fleet Pavilion is next to the grandstand, a short walk from the Dockyard Gate, so come and support your team AS WELL!!"

"Position - 33 degs 57 mins N, 8 degs 17 mins W. Nearest land - Casablanca, Morocco. 37 miles SE."

St HELLTEM 19/82 about "Customs Clearance" arrived today. It informed us about the following:- completion of Customs Forms, what must be declared, prohibited and restricted items, duty free allowances, attractive and expensive articles, helpful hints, documents required and finally our routine for clearing customs.

A quiet day, after yesterday's excitement! Another 'Make and Mend'! The prospect of another good run ashore tomorrow! The sun was still shining! It was all too much for most of us - we needed a rest!

HMS Rooke crest - HM Naval Base, Gibraltar

Rock of Gibraltar from the airport

WEDNESDAY, 8 SEPTEMBER 82 - DAY 108

(We had all the extra bits again today, about 'Daily Harbour' routine, "Dress for leave - Plain clothes, leave times, etc, etc. All those wonderful words we used to have in the real Navy! We still had to have "The ship is under sailing orders", though!).

0700* Call the hands
0730   Hands to breakfast
0745* Time check
0745* Mail closes
0755* Out pipes
0800* Both watches muster on the Fore Deck
0810   All RN personnel clear off the Upper Deck - Procedure Charlie
0830   Arrive Gibraltar (Berth 43)
1000* Stand easy
1015* Hands carry on with your work
1030* Clear Lower Deck of all FSU ratings in the Stern Gallery
1130   SRs/Watchkeepers to dinner
1145   Secure, JRs to dinner
1310* Out pipes
1315* Hands carry on with your work
1600* Secure
1800* Hands clean into night clothing
1900* Clean messdecks and flats for Rounds
1925* Stand by for Rounds
2300* Pipe down

"CU - The two SRs who ran the very enjoyable Tombola session.
KITC - Nil."

Note 1 was back to the old favourite:- "Securing for sea - during this last leg north we could well encounter rough weather, so make sure everything is stowed correctly and secured for sea. No gash is to be left loafing. The Buffer is available for any assistance required!?"

Note 2 was a sneaky bit from the policeman:- "JR Cabins - Rounds were carried out AM Tuesday. The general standard of tidiness was abysmal. In future daily rounds will be carried out at 0900. All JRs' cabins must be up to the required standard by this time."

Note 3 was bad news:- "Shop - 'Final opening day' will be on Sunday 12 Sept 82 at the evening session. Due to stocktaking/bond it will NOT open again, so stock up on nutty, toiletries, sweat shirts, etc, now."

Note 4 read:- "Grand Draw - will take place during the Pub Lunch on Sunday, 12 Sept 82."

TN - 0800 Alongside Gibraltar

A letter was despatched today to the 'Manpower People' in HMS CENTURION in Gosport. They had asked us to respond to a letter of theirs querying the Scheme of Complement for the RNP2100. They had 'guesstimated' our personnel requirement quite well but "next time" this type of ship would benefit from 2 extra JRs, according to the SNO, 1 Communicator and 1 Writer! Which officially proved that I was overworked as well as underpaid!

It was good to see the Rock again! A lot of us had spent a bit of time in Gib on previous ships and I had nearly been drafted here once! So it was with great expectations that we made our way ashore through the dockyard. It was a warm and sunny evening, ideal for a stroll! We walked to HMS ROOKE where we decided to visit the SRs' Mess for a quick pint before the football. Thinking we would get a wonderful welcome after our last few months of 'doing our bit for Queen and Country', in we trotted, about a dozen of us! Wrong! Some of our group were dressed in jeans! No jeans allowed - mess rules! We attempted to explain our predicament, that we had been at war and these were the only civvy clothes we had been allowed to take with us! No matter! Mess Rules! Standards! You cannot come in! To add to this the bar was empty, except for some people rigging up the mess for that evening's entertainment, who funnily enough, were dressed in jeans! This was irrelevant, THEY were working! By this time, our blinkered official was close to a heart attack and was becoming quite rude and aggressive! With his petty attitude, he had managed to wind up some of the group and the situation was beginning to look dangerous. We decided to take our custom elsewhere and take up this matter officially, at a later date, with the President of the Mess. Our Mess later sent their Mess a letter saying how totally unimpressed we had been with their treatment of us. We heard nothing in reply, strangely enough! Ignorance is bliss!

As usual, the rest of our stay was brief but excellent. The football tournament was a great success and the Fleet Pavilion profits soared! So did the profits of quite a few of the local bars!

THURSDAY, 9 SEPTEMBER 82 - DAY 109

0700* Call the hands
0730   Hands to breakfast
0745* Time check
0755* Out pipes
0800* Both watches muster on the Fore Deck
1000* Stand easy
1015* Hands carry on with your work
1130   SRs/Watchkeepers to dinner
1145* Secure, JRs to dinner
1300* Hands carry on with your work
1330   All leave expires
1600* Secure
1600   Sail for home
1900* Clean messdecks and flats for Rounds
1925* Stand by for Rounds
2300* Pipe down

"CU - To yet another new dad in the ship's company.
KITC - Nil."

Note 1 was a legal job:- "Customs - Any Duty Free Drinks purchased ashore in Gib
must be declared to the OOD on returning onboard and placed in bond."

TN - Slip and proceed to Rosyth.

Well, that's it, we're off on the homeward stretch to 'Bonny' Scotland. We'd made it
in one piece! They hadn't made us go back, when we thought we were safe! We'd
had a couple of good runs ashore to make up for the normal life we had missed.
Small recompense, I know, but it was better than nothing! It was still sunny, so we
had to make the most of what small amount of summer we had left! When we get to
Rosyth we can guarantee it will be raining, so "Let the wind blow high, let the wind
blow low, etc." Another wee dram, please Jimmy!

FRIDAY, 10 SEPTEMBER 82 - DAY 110

0700* Call the hands
0730   Hands to breakfast
0745* Time check
0755* Out pipes
0800* Both watches muster on the Fore Deck
1000* Stand easy
1015* Hands carry on with your work
1130   SRs/Watchkeepers to dinner
1145* Secure, JRs to dinner
1300* Hands carry on with your work
1600* Secure
2300* Pipe down

Note 1 was bad news and good news all at once:- "Rounds tomorrow - will be the last Saturday Rounds before we turn the ship back to the MN. Ensure all overheads are cleaned and paintwork washed. All woodwork, doors, etc, to be polished. Shower curtains to be taken down and washed in a disinfectant solution (See POMA), etc."

Note 2 read:- "Weekend Request Forms are now available from the RPO. (For RNP from 22/9/82 to 27/9/82 - hopefully)."

"Sports Reports:-
1.   Soccer - a very enjoyable game was had by all. RNP2100 drew with FSU01, 10 - 10. (A fair result). Some startling performances were witnessed. The JRs involved could only stand back in awe of their elders who were displaying their wizardry. Outstanding amongst this elite were the Flight SR who scored 4 goals, the RS, and of course the POWTR who was superb.
2.   Volleyball (played after all) - Result - RMS ST HELENA 2 -v- HMS ROOKE 1. The HMS ROOKE team was thoroughly outclassed by our team, who had been in special training the night before. Everyone played above themselves and the POWTR was superb, AGAIN."

"Nearest land - Cabo Espichel, Portugal. 28 miles NE."

St HELLTEM 20/82, was the last St Helltem and was titled "Programme 11/9/82 - 1/10/82". It gave us brief details of the proposed programme for the end of the trip but of course was likely to change! (Guaranteed, more like!).

Again it was time to rest after the delights of Gibraltar! However, that dream was soon shattered with the promise of Rounds! Thank goodness it was the last time! This ship will be going back to Curnows cleaner than it's ever been, they won't recognise it!

SATURDAY, 11 SEPTEMBER 82 - DAY 111

0001 Clocks retarded 1 hour
0700* Call the hands
0730 Hands to breakfast
0745* Time check
0755* Out pipes
0800* Both watches muster on the Fore Deck
0900 Sale of First Day Covers - Purser's Cabin
1000* Stand easy
1015* Hands carry on with your work
1055* Stand by for SNO's Rounds
1100* SNO's Rounds
1130 SRs/Watchkeepers to dinner
1145* Secure, JRs to dinner
2300* Pipe down

"Programme - Due to HMS BRECON's engine defects, it looks likely that our arrival in Rosyth will be delayed 24 hours making our new ETA 16/9/82. This will be confirmed when we know more. In the event of this, Next of Kin will be informed by the Navy."

Note 1 was a real warning:- "Shop - shuts tomorrow and will not re-open. Make sure you stock up now - this is your last chance. (Note - there is a lot of new gear on sale)."

Note 2 read:- "Personal Insurance - Any person (in FSU01) who is insured by and has recently written to the Australian Mutual Provident Society, contact the POWTR."

Note 3 was war stuff:- "Geneva Convention ID Cards - are to be returned to the RPO by 1600 today."

Note 4 was work:- "Valuable and Attractive Stores - Custodians of Permanent Loan Records are to return all V & A items to the Naval Stores Office today. Form S1091 is to be completed."

Note 5 was the Purser not wanting to waste the opportunity to sell, sell, sell:- "First Day Covers - There will be a last quick sale of the First Day Covers from the Purser's Cabin at 0900 today. This is your last chance before stocktaking."

"Nearest land - Cape Silleiro, Spain. 33 miles E."

Considering it was weekend, life was hectic! We'd had Rounds and now everybody was sorting out for home! Cabins were being sorted and gear packed, offices were being cleared, etc, etc. Hopefully, we would not have to spend many more weekends on here! So we'd better think positive and enjoy it whilst we can! Another pint please, landlord!

SUNDAY, 12 SEPTEMBER 82 - DAY 112

0700*   Call the hands
0730   Hands to breakfast
0815   Flying Brief
0815*   Time check
0825*   Out pipes
0830*   Both watches muster on the Fore Deck
0830*   Prepare for flying
0845*   Hands to Flying Stations
0845*   Clear lower deck of all FSU ratings in Stern Gallery
0900   HDS
0900*   Clear lower deck of all RN & MN personnel
0930*   Secure
1045   Church Service in the Wardroom
1100*   Pipe down
1200   Pub Lunch/Grand Draw
PM   Last opening of the shop
1900*   Clean messdecks and flats for Rounds
1925*   Stand by for Rounds

"CU - Flight JRs and RS for helping to fold the Raffle tickets.
KITC - No volunteers."

"Programme - The ship's ETA at Rosyth is now 0800 on Thursday, 16 September
82. See St Helltem 20/82 for further details."

Note 1 signalled the beginning of the end:- "Games, sports gear, fishing tackle, etc,
belonging to the Welfare, is to be returned to the Sick Bay by 1200 today."

Note 2 simply stated:- "The shop closes today."

Note 3, even on the very last one, was still only nearly a BZ!! - "SNO's Rounds -
The standard of cleanliness of cabins was very good. However, overheads still
require attention."

Note 4 read:- "Free whisky - The bottles of whisky given to us in Ascension contain
18.75cl each, making a combined total of 37.50cl, which is just under 0.5 litres,
keeping you just inside your duty free allowance."

"Nearest land - Pta Candelaria, Spain. 125 miles S."

'Dress of the Day' was "No10ARs/No8s" - this meant a choice of tropical gear or normal UK gear! The sun was getting cooler and lower and the winds were getting chillier. That was our mini-summer gone already!

This afternoon saw the Audit of my mess. As Treasurer, I had to sort out the books and cash ready for inspection. I was also the Welfare Fund Treasurer. As I possessed the only available safe onboard, situated in the Ship's Office, because of my RN Cash Account, I was the perfect 'volunteer' for these tasks! As with all RN funds, the safe was checked every fortnight. This meant that everything had to be well recorded and up to date. The audit was completed without problems.

It was the big day, today! The Grand Draw - all that effort by lots of different people! A good lunch was put on, as usual, 'Pub Style', for all the ship's company in the Forward Lounge. The first ticket out was put in an envelope and sealed - that was the winner of the Video Recorder! All the other prizes had been numbered and were drawn for in numerical order. There were a lot of prizes - 90 in all! Most people won something, some had a field day! In general, everybody seemed well pleased with the outcome! At the end there were two tickets still to be revealed. They had been hidden in envelopes and displayed where all could see them, so there was no fiddling! One was for the Video Recorder the other for our now infamous 'Blue Movie' - "Hot Racquets"! The winner of the Video Recorder was identified first - The RPO! The ship's company was devastated! The fates had played a dirty trick on us! What could we say? Then the identity of the winner of the "Hot Racquets" video was revealed - the 1st Lt!! The very person who had stopped it being shown in the first place! The Gods had evened things out! The result was not fixed, but I think the 1st Lt thought that it had been! He wasn't impressed and refused to accept his prize! He wasn't a happy person! However, the ship's company had been appeased - a balance had been struck! Overall, we had a good session, lots of good food, good conversation, plenty to drink and lots of prizes well spread throughout the ship's company. What more could we want? To re-draw the first prize, maybe?!

PART SIX

BY JINGO - WHAT A GLORIOUS HOMECOMING

or

YET ANOTHER BLOODY WINTER

MONDAY, 13 SEPTEMBER 82 - DAY 113

0700*   Call the hands
0730   Hands to breakfast
0745*   Time check
0755*   Out pipes
0800*   Both watches muster on the Fore Deck
0800   All requests for Leave Warrants to RPO (Inc. FSU)
0830   Flight return sleeping bags/liners, etc.
AM   Prepare stores for landing
1000   Mail closes
1000*   Stand easy
1015*   Hands carry on with your work
1015   Flying Brief
1030*   Prepare for flying
1045*   Hands to Flying Stations
1100   Disembark Flight - 2 lifts
1100   OIC FSU Rounds of FSU Modules (inc holds)
1130   SRs/Watchkeepers to dinner
1145*   Secure, JRs to dinner
1300*   Hands carry on with your work
PM   Prepare stores for landing
1600*   Secure
1900*   Clean messdecks and flats for Rounds
1925*   Stand by for Rounds
2300*   Pipe down

"CU - Goodbye Flight - nice meeting you, see you on the way back down!
KITC - The RPO for obvious reasons."

Note 1 was a boring repeat:- "Loan Clothing Returns - Any items of clothing still outstanding on loan are to be returned to the Naval Stores Office between 0900 - 1000 today. Any items not returned will be covered by C126 action."

Note 2 was a warning:- "Customs - Quantities of Argentinian Firearms and Military Equipment have been found in several ships returning home from the Falkland Islands. The Customs at Rosyth could, therefore, give us a thorough search. Make sure you declare everything and make sure you have no contraband. Advice on what to declare can be obtained from the RPO. All customs declaration forms to be handed in to the RPO by 1200 today."

TN - 1100 Disembark 033 Wasp Flight to Royal Naval Air Station, Portland.

Life was hectic now. We could actually see the 'homeland' in the distance, so going home had now got serious! The topics of conversation now included de-storing, de-ammunitioning, leave, weekends off, returning gear and clothing, going on draft, etc, etc. Outside it was grey and drizzly but what more could you expect in England in autumn! In fact, with the positive thinking, who bloody cared! It was 'Home sweet bloody home', thank goodness!

TUESDAY, 14 SEPTEMBER 82 - DAY 114

0700* Call the hands
0730   Hands to breakfast
0745* Time check
0755* Out pipes
0800* Both watches muster on the Fore Deck
0800   Commence stripping aerial runs
AM   Prepare stores for landing
1000* Stand easy
1015* Hands carry on with your work
1130   SRs/Watchkeepers to dinner
1145* Secure, JRs to dinner
1300* Hands carry on with your work
PM   Prepare stores for landing
1600* Secure
1900* Clean messdecks and flats for rounds
1925* Stand by for Rounds
2300* Pipe down

Note 1 read:- "Landing of duty free allowance - (RN Personnel) - Anyone wishing to land his duty free allowance on Thursday, in accordance with DCI 191/80 . Names to the RPO by secure today."

Note 2 read:- "SNO/Master's Walkround - an informal walkround of SRs' cabins at 1400 on Wednesday, to check for defects, etc."

Note 3 read:- "MN Personnel - are to return all outstanding RN clothing/bedding, etc, to the Wardroom at 0900."

"Nearest land - Ramsgate, 8 miles NW."

Up to my neck in paperwork and I get the Audit of the Welfare Fund this afternoon. They also checked the cash in my safe as well. Everything was in order and all the necessary signatures were obtained. Hard work though when you're busy anyway!

Busy, busy, busy! Not long to go now! The excitement is rising!

WEDNESDAY, 15 SEPTEMBER 82 - DAY 115

0700* Call the hands
0730 Hands to breakfast
0745* Time check
0755* Out pipes
0800* Both watches muster on the Fore Deck
1000* Stand easy
1015* Hands carry on with your work
1030 Farewell Steam Past
1130 SRs/Watchkeepers to dinner
1145* Secure, JRs to dinner
1300* Hands carry on with your work
1400 SNO's walkround SRs' Cabins
1600* Secure
1900* Clean messdecks and flats for Rounds
1925* Stand by for Rounds
2100 Approximately - Anchor Dalgety Bay. (Unless detached earlier).
2300* Pipe down

Note 1 was back to the paperwork:- "Cheque cashing - get your cheques cashed NOW for your Customs Charges and before we get in."

Note 2 was another:- "Pay Queries - All queries to the POWTR AM today, so they can be sorted with HMS CENTURION as soon as we have got the telephones installed onboard."

Note 3 read:- "Ladyfield School Collection raised £41.12."

Note 4 read:- "Honda Generators - Anyone knowing the whereabouts of 2 x 24 volt Honda Generators (Serial No 1008241/1008254), contact the 1st Lt."

"Nearest land - South Shields 28 miles W."

Today saw the last literary masterpiece come 'hot off the press'! The final "See-Dit", containing the usual insults and libel, was actually sent by mail to our members who had departed early, eg Flight, St Helenian Crew Members in St Helena, etc, etc. It was the usual feast of poetry, odes, dits and brain teasing and even had a dit from the SNO at the front, which read:-

"SNO's Lament:- "See-Dit" has given us all the opportunity to extract the Michael from more or less anybody we want without fear of retribution - almost! Many of the inevitable characters onboard have spent boundless energy trying to prove that their jokes are the 'in' ones and that they deserve the penguin's beak for duty above and beyond the call of duty! Incidentally, one rockhopper penguin produces one pint of oil and penguins really do make good hurricane lamps. We, in RMS St HELENA, have battled with the air conditioning, hot water, fresh water and endless free gifts of cigarettes, booze and instant curries in a pot, to prove that we are the toughest and best that Britain can produce. We have protected our bodies from the onslaught of the sun's heat by the best lotions that Curnow's Shop can provide (duty free) and we have emerged triumphant and fully browned off to present our shrivelled frames to our adoring families. Daily at 1300 we have managed to survive the onslaught of Hitler Youth Propaganda over the public address system and we have avoided (almost) the trap laid by the Kamikazi Radio Officer to join the queue for Raid-eee-ooo Tele-fone-in-calls at fiff-tee-foweurer pence a minute. The booby trap of Pub Lunches and Darts Matches were defused and all in all we have emerged unscathed despite the chef's efforts. To be serious for a brief paragraph, may I thank you all for getting down to it and making a bloody good job of the task in hand. It is my hope that everybody will remember this adventure. Once again may I thank all of you for your help during the past four months."

It also produced the last crop of "Good Buzzes":-

1. FSU is to be re-named "Falklands Support Unit", but we don't know why!

2. After this trip the Purser has been booked to tour the Fleet doing SODS Operas.

3. The LSTD has been appointed as Marketing Manager to the Water Biscuit Company.

4. Anyone knowing the whereabouts of the Buffer, tell the Bridge. (Tower Bridge?).

5. The 1st Lt is now the agent to "PRIVATE" publications.

6. The Chef is about to open a second hand shop stocked with raffle prizes.

7. Purser Catering is retiring to South Fork, a 'small' residence near Dallas in Texas.

8. Curnow Shipping will make a 'modest' little profit this year.

9. Falkland Island ducks/geese taste bloody awful.

10. Would the matelot who nicked the grand piano from out of the Forward Lounge - please put it back.

11. The MN Officer who won the Tombola house several times has not got golden bollocks - we checked at the soccer match in St Helena.

12. The MO and RPO have.

13. The Messman is asking for a branch change to the Army Catering Corps.

14. Appendix 3 to Annex X of the 4th copy of the enclosure to the second amendment to the 3rd change to the Ship's Programme was correct. (I think).

15. It isn't sweat stains on the chairs in the Stern Gallery - it's penguin shit (or maybe even bullshit).

16. RNP have a good leave, as we have to get back to Stanley to do SNOFI's Xmas CTP.

17. On the way back to Stanley the SRs have got a special invitation back to the SRs' Mess in HMS ROOKE, to show those who missed them their dog tags. (Dress - jeans and flip flops.)

18. The POWTR has been offered terms with Manchester United.

19. We didn't mention the water again, did we?

20. Many thanks for reading this little column over the past issues, good luck to you all. One final thought to you all - GET STUFT.

At last! Here we were, home sweet home! Even though it was slightly north! The Forth Bridges towering above us, the smell of the rich Scottish land - wonderful! It's amazing how good the land smells after being at sea for so long! There was a big banner on the Road Bridge saying "Welcome Home" to the three ships! There was also a big homecoming dance at the Dockyard Club that night! However, due to the engine problems with HMS BRECON we were late getting back here and nobody had thought to mention it to those concerned! So we sat at anchor, awaiting Customs Clearance the following morning, whilst our 'homecoming celebration' was held without us! Wonderful! Organisation - nil! To say there were a lot of very unhappy people onboard that night, would be a vast understatement! The dilemma was not helped by the fact that we had been faithfully promised that if our ETA was changed the RN would inform all those concerned! Needless to say, a lot of mess beer and spirit allowances were broken that evening!

So near yet so far!

THURSDAY, 16 SEPTEMBER 82 - DAY 116

"Routine – Daily Harbour". Thank goodness for that!

0700* Call the hands
0730   Hands to breakfast
0745* Time check
0755* Out pipes
0800* Both watches muster on the Fore Deck
AM   Clear Customs (See St Helltem 19/82)
o/c   Return all sleeping bags and liners to the Stores Office
1000* Stand easy
1015* Hands carry on with your work
1015   Approximately. Weigh and proceed to North Wall (MHSCs to P1)
       Procedure Alpha - Dress No2s for entering Rosyth
1030   Hands fall in for entering harbour
1100   Alongside, families embark, lunch onboard
PM   As piped, families depart. Night Leave commences to non-duty personnel
1900* Clean messdecks and flats for Rounds
1925* Stand by for Rounds
2300* Pipe down

"CU - Nil.
KITC - Buffer, RS & POWTR for winning a Mars Bar each for the best cabin on Master's Rounds."

Note 1 brought life back down to earth:- "Meal times during destore:- Breakfast - 0730 to 0830, Lunch - 1130 to 1230, Tea - 1600 to 1615, Supper - 1730 to 1830, Snack - 2345 to 0015."

TN - Commence disembarking FSU01 stores.

It was a very emotional day. We had spent the previous evening looking blankly at the shore and wondering what the hell we had to do to get ashore! This morning, the same people who had made us sit in Dalgety Bay all night like a shower of idiots, the Customs men, were actually late arriving onboard! The absolute neck of it all! When they eventually deemed to turn up, feelings onboard towards them and officialdom in general were not good! This was really taking the piss, as they say!

Eventually they left and we went into the Dockyard to let all the families onboard! It had seemed at times that it was never going to happen, but it did! A lot of happy families came onboard from all over the country and a lot of tears were shed! Relief from stress can be a strange thing! Seeing grown men crying all over the place can also be a little spooky! Of course, there were a few of us from the South Coast still stuck onboard and not able to see our families yet, so it was a bit of a weird situation to be in. The only answer for us was a run ashore in Dunfermline, with a few pints of heavy and a few wee drams!

FRIDAY, 17 SEPTEMBER 82 - DAY 117

0700* Call the hands
0730   Hands to breakfast
0745* Time check
0755* Out pipes
0800   Commence disembarking stores - Both watches
1200   B Watch secure
1600   A Watch secure, B Watch turn to
       Then 8 hours about until completion of task. (Approximately Tues, 21/9/82)
       See St Helltem 20/82 for further details.

Note 1 was a final BZ:- "The following was received from the Commander of the Task Group:-
1. Very many thanks for your excellent support and cooperation which enabled us to voyage to the Falklands and return and to accomplish our tasks in the Falkland Islands.
2. I doubt that any other 'STUFT' has had such total involvement with the RN and you have ably shown what can be done.
3. Good luck and best wishes for the future."

Life was now similar to when we left Portsmouth, but in reverse! Everything was now being taken off and got rid of! What a funny old world we live in!

SATURDAY, 18 SEPTEMBER 82 - DAY 118

0700*   Call the hands
0730   Hands to breakfast
0745*   Time check
0800   Watch change
1130 - 1230 Hands to dinner
1600   Watch change
Midnight   Watch change

Note 1 read:- "Destoring - A very good start has been made to the destoring, well done to all concerned."

Note 2 read:- "Sweaters, etc. - Swaps/sales, etc:-" - gave us the details of various swaps and sales onboard (unwanted raffle prizes, etc.)

What a way to spend a weekend! Haven't we said that before, somewhere?

SUNDAY, 19 SEPTEMBER 82 - DAY 119

0700*	Call the hands
0730	Hands to breakfast
0745*	Time check
0800	Watch change
1130	Hands to dinner
1600	Watch change
Midnight	Watch change

Note 1 marked the end of an era:- "Welfare Fund - A cheque for £54.31 has been sent to the South Atlantic Fund, which was the cash left in the Welfare Fund after all outstanding bills had been paid. The Fund is now closed."

Note 2 read:- "Lost Property - The following articles of Lost Property have still not been claimed:- Pen knife, pen, calculator. You have 24 hours before they are given to the finder."

Note 3 was more 'Sweater Swaps'!

Note 4 was another clue about the war finishing! - "Anti Gas Respirators on Loan - are to be returned to the Buffer in Cabin 29 at 1200 today."

Note 5 was notifying the troops that a late order for sweaters, etc, was just about to be sent off.

We had a 'Bad News - Good News' day in the SRs' Mess today. The bar was dismantled, being the bad news! The good news, however, was that we had to get rid of the remaining stock and profits! This meant we had to shift a fair amount of free beer! It's amazing how quickly you can do that, even at duty free prices!

Destoring continues with a vengeance! Jack wants to go on leave and proves he can therefore work very hard when 'he' wants to! It's also amazing how they fitted all this gear in such a small space, not forgetting the stuff we got rid of down south! (The loo rolls had all gone, by the way).

MONDAY, 20 SEPTEMBER 82 - DAY 120

0700*	Call the hands
0730	Hands to breakfast
0745*	Time check
0755*	Out pipes
0800*	Prepare for de-ammunitioning
0800	FSU01 return loan clothing, etc.
1000*	Stand easy
1015	Hands carry on with your work
1130*	Hands to dinner and Secure for FSU01 for leave
1230 approx	Shift berth to Crombie RNAD
o/c	On arrival commence de-ammunitioning
o/c	Return to Rosyth

"CU - FSU01, well done on destoring. Cheerio and have a good leave.
KITC - No takers."

Note 1 read:- "Loan clothing, bedding, etc, - All FSU01 ratings to return all sleeping bags, liners, etc, to Naval Stores Office between 0800 - 0830. (Chisels will be available to remove the sleeping bags from the occupants and the MA will be in attendance with pain killers.)" (This was not a joke!)

Note 2 read:- "New orders for sweaters, etc, to be in by 1600 today!"

The FSU01 boys had all disappeared back to their base in Rosyth Dockyard. That left the rest of us at the mercy of 'Drafty'! Most of the boys were being sent back to the jobs they had left so suddenly a few months ago but, yet again, I was the lucky one! I'd been drafted to HMS NELSON in Portsmouth to await the rest of my sea time! The fact that I lived in Gosport and was therefore going to add to the local traffic chaos mattered not! Neither did the fact that I'd just spent three years being trained as a Computer Programmer in the RN's Pay, Pensions and Drafting Computer Centre at HMS CENTURION in Gosport! Also at this time HMS CENTURION was upgrading the whole of the computer system and was crying out for experienced programmers! Pusser at his very best, 3 years extremely expensive training thrown down the drain - but after the money wasted on this war, that was a mere drop in the ocean, as they say!

So now, it was just the original RNP2100 RN types left with the MN Officers and Crew! It was getting quieter! The ammunition was gone, the technicians were gone, did this mean we weren't a 'warship' anymore? If it did - it meant we were a 'Cruise Ship' again!

TUESDAY, 21 SEPTEMBER 82 - DAY 121

0700* Call the hands
0730   Hands to breakfast
0745* Time check
0755* Out pipes
0800* Hands turn to
1000* Stand easy
1015* Hands carry on with your work
1130   Hands to dinner
1315* Hands carry on with your work
1600* Secure

"CU - All who helped to de-ammunition.
KITC - The weather."

Note 1 was a BZ:- "De-storing/de-ammunitioning - has now been completed. Well done all concerned, the work has been achieved faster than we had hoped."

Note 2 was the reward for the effort at Note 1:- "Leave - it is hoped Extended Long Weekend will be piped to RN personnel today."

This meant that the RN personnel left the ship 'en masse' that afternoon! Most were catching trains south. The train from Edinburgh to London had quite a party in the bar that afternoon! Several hours later, I had to ring my wife to let her know the train arrival time at Portsmouth Harbour Station, so my children could do their own 'Welcome Home' thing as I got off the Gosport Ferry! Cute, eh! Very embarrassing and very touching!

So the MN were on their own again to sail the ship to Portsmouth. They were probably extremely glad to get back to the old ways! So today was the last Daily Orders. The end of an era!

WEDNESDAY, 22 SEPTEMBER 82 - DAY 122

ELWE

THURSDAY, 23 SEPTEMBER 82 - DAY 123

0800   Sail to Portsmouth

ELWE

FRIDAY, 24 SEPTEMBER 82 - DAY 124

PM   Arrive Portsmouth Dockyard

ELWE

SATURDAY, 25 SEPTEMBER 82 - DAY 125

ELWE

SUNDAY, 26 SEPTEMBER 82 - DAY 126

ELWE

MONDAY, 27 SEPTEMBER 82 - DAY 127

We returned from ELWE at Portsmouth Dockyard as ordered, only to find the ship wasn't there! It had been sent to Southampton Docks for some strange reason we never did find out about! However, this was a novelty for most of us who were left, as it was a new place to work from and made a change from Pompey Dockyard!

When we got back onboard, it all seemed very strange! People were milling about and nobody appeared to know what was going on. It appeared the ship was going back down south to ferry personnel and stores around the islands. We had plenty of volunteers to stay on from the RN boys but it was only the MN who were going! This meant it was time for me to clear my office, as the rest of the ship was beginning to look like a cruise ship again!

TUESDAY, 28 SEPTEMBER 82 - DAY 128

I'd spent all the previous day packing up the files, etc, in the Ship's Office. So today I had to find out where I was to dispose of all this paperwork. As I mentioned at the beginning of the trip, ships leaving from Plymouth had been highly organised and dealt with very efficiently by HMS DEFIANCE, the shore base in Devonport. They also sorted them out when they returned! (A certain notorious Submariner Coxswain sorted things). After the help I got on leaving Portsmouth and as I wasn't even in Portsmouth Dockyard now, I didn't expect a lot of assistance! Sure enough I didn't get it! Consistent, if nothing else! I made a few telephone calls from onboard when I could get near the solitary telephone available! Nothing, not a hope, nobody had any idea! I then went to HMS WESSEX, the Solent Royal Naval Reserve Depot based in Southampton Docks, to see if anybody there could help me – nothing! Little did I know but this was to become yet another epic example of Pusser's lack of organisation! To keep the story short, I contacted the following offices to find out how I was to dispose of all of our paperwork:-

a. Flag Officer Portsmouth's Office - "No idea, never had to deal with it before, no facilities, use your initiative, you set it up, you get rid of it."!
b. Flag Officer Plymouth's Office - "As you didn't start or finish here we can't deal with you! We only have enough facilities for our own 'STUFT' ships! We've had enough trouble with what we've already got."!
c. HMS WESSEX - "No sorry, we don't have the staff here to cover that sort of thing, we wouldn't know where to start."!
d. HMS NELSON (Commodore's Office) - "Pass - ships have nothing to do with us."!
e. HMS CENTURION (Historical Records) - No, sorry, our historical records are all to do with pay, pensions and drafting. Yours are a different thing altogether."!
f. Ministry of Defence, London - After being sent from one department to another, where nobody knew or cared, eventually the RN Historical Branch was suggested!
g. RN Historical Branch - "No thanks, we're up to our necks in it and we don't have any room for any more."!
h. Submarine Museum, Gosport - (as a last resort) - sorry, we only have limited space and we deal mainly with submarine material."!

At this point, I nearly followed the many suggestions to bin it all over the side! Then I thought about it and decided that one day someone might actually be interested in the history of all this! So I didn't! I put it all in the boot of my car and took it home until I could get rid of it officially. There it has stayed until this day, stored in boxes and hidden away in cupboards. Hopefully, I will now be able to pass it on to someone who cares or even to the RN Historical Branch who might have room for it by now!

WED 29 SEPTEMBER 82 - DAY 129/THURS 30 SEPTEMBER 82 - DAY 130

These two days were then spent clearing the RN presence from the ship with me also still vainly trying to get rid of my paperwork. Unsuccessfully, of course! As the boys finished working on their part of ship, they were sent off early on leave and draft, as there was nothing left onboard that they could do. I was one of the last to go. Having said my goodbyes, I went on leave early with the bleak prospect of winter in HMS NELSON from the 1st November! Roll on the rest of my sea time! (Funnily enough, Drafty was to get me again! After a wonderful winter in Pompey, he drafted me to HMS FEARLESS to complete my sea time! That ship was called away at short notice for 6 months at the Lebanon War! Wasn't I the lucky one?!).

DAYS 131 TO 138 - These were the days of extra leave given, leading up to the official date of our leave and draft. Day 138 was the official completion date for RNP2100, it was THE END. (Except for a few more drips and moans!).

My next new house, HMS Fearless, going to the Lebanon War

Our next door neighbour - USS New Jersey

EPILOGUE - 2012

Lest we forget – 255 people died in this War and that was only on our side!

For what exactly?

In 1770, the author Dr Samuel Johnson, wrote a pamphlet, on behalf of the government at the time, during the first Falklands crisis, called "Thoughts on the Late Transactions Respecting Falklands Islands". He wondered why we would want to fight for the islands and said:- "Beyond this, what have we acquired? – What but a bleak and gloomy island thrown aside from human solitude, stormy in winter, and barren in summer, an island which not the southern savages have dignified with habitation?"

So it wasn't just me then! What more can you say? - The Scottish Isles are much safer, nicer and handier in case of emergencies!

The final insult to the members of this Task Group, who completed their highly dangerous task in record time, was their 'non-qualification' for a Falklands Campaign Medal (South Atlantic Medal)! Two types of the Medal were awarded. One was for being in the Exclusion Zone at any time within the two dates decreed by a Civil Servant in an office in Whitehall, (see below)! The other was for actually supporting the war effort in some way, eg. RAF personnel at Ascension Island. (We will come back to this bit later!)

The two dates, when the war took place according to Whitehall, were not decided until later after the event! If they had decided sooner when they were going to decree these dates, it could have saved us quite a lot of wasted money, time and effort. We need not have sailed half way around the world and back in total panic, had air raid warnings, gone to defence watches and action stations, worn war gear for weeks on end, darkened ship, fitted guns to the ship, had three winters one after another, etc, etc, etc, etc! We could have had a nice cruise instead! However, here are a few relevant dates:-

1.	Warlike activities by the Argentines started	-	19 Mch 82
2.	Warlike activities by us started	-	20 Mch 82
3.	The day when WE were told war started	-	28 Mch 82
4.	Civil Service decreed war started	-	2 Apl 82
5.	Argentine surrender at Port Stanley	-	14 Jun 82
6.	Civil Service decreed war ended (74 days in all)	-	14 Jun 82
7.	Argentine surrender at Goose Green	-	15 Jun 82
8.	Argentine surrender at Southern Thule	-	20 Jun82
9.	British Government formally declare end of hostilities	-	20 Jun 82
10.	Official signal told US to stay in war mode!	-	29 Jun 82
11.	Confirmatory signal for US to stay in war mode!!	-	3 Jul 82
10.	PM Thatcher starts enquiry into causes of war	-	6 Jul 82
11.	WE go into Defence Watches within TEZ	-	6 Jul 82
12.	Argentines release ONLY acknowledged POWs	-	8 Jul 82
13.	WE arrived at Port Stanley (Day 48!)	-	10 Jul 82
14.	Argentines still had NOT formally		

surrendered BUT our government decided they did not need to, but they had to give us back the rest of our POWs!	- 11 Jul 82
15. Last day of 30 to qualify for South Atlantic Medal	- 12 Jul 82
16. I was in an 'Air Raid Warning Red' today! (Dressed in FULL War Gear and Survival Suit)!	- 14 Jul 82
17. British Government lifts TEZ	- 22 Jul 82
18. The day WE were told war ended	- 14 Aug 82
19. The day WE were allowed to stop playing war games	- 24 Aug 82
20. The day WE handed in our AGRs, etc	- 19 Sep 82
21. Argentine formal surrender of FIs	- Still we wait!

Let's take a closer look at number 6 – On the day the Civil Service decreed it was all over, 14 June, in fact it was only the day that the Argentines in Port Stanley surrendered, as we can see above! It was still a WAR ZONE and nobody had told us otherwise!! There were minefields at sea, land mines all over the place, unused ordnance, booby traps, explosive devices of all kinds, unexploded bombs and missiles from both sides and bloody Argie fighter planes ! When was this lot declared safe?

The case was taken up by a Member of Parliament several months later after complaints had been made about our not qualifying for the Medal. However, he was told that we did not qualify because we were not there on the decreed dates! Since then a regular series of Parliamentary Questions and requests for a rethink have been made from various sources, all with the same bland civil service reply! Now they have also added the new rule that we should have done all this within 5 years of the war!!! So we definitely can't have them!!

Funnily enough, however, in all our other various conflicts, the troops carrying out the same minesweeping, etc, task, all appear to have been awarded General Service Medals for their efforts! (Probably a different 'Budget', eh?).

So, the civil servants in the Ministry of Defence, the Royal British Legion, the Veterans Agency, etc, have shown little or no interest in sorting out this injustice! As ever, loyalty only goes one way, and it's still UP! Never mind, at least we all got our 50p war pay every day!

I think we must have missed this one on the way in!! Of course it may only recently have been put up due to the tourism boom! Anyway, the Yorkie boys will sort them out and they'll get lots of cracking scampi now!!

TN:-   Finally let's look at the manpower, ships and logistics of our little Task Group!
        (Not that I have the qualifications for this!)

RN Officers:- A mix - some semi-retired, some very young and inexperienced!

RN Ratings:- A mix - mostly young and inexperienced with some very ancient SRs!

(Normal requirements for war meant bigger RN ship's companies, plus the need to
supply personnel for STUFT ships, plus the previous drastic cutting of service
personnel numbers. All this meant there was not much left to choose from, especially
experienced ones! Now 30 years on, their lordships are still slashing away at these
numbers!?)

MN Officers:- A mix of senior and junior officers all totally inexperienced for war
Games and just not built for it. No idea about service discipline!

MN Crew:- St Helenian crewmen – keen, but totally out of their depth in a warship!

Wasp Helicopter - not exactly the latest thing, so they must have run out of Lynx.
(But I'm not sure they could have got one of those on our flight deck?)

2 x MHSCs:- <u>COASTAL</u> mine hunters/sweepers! Not Atlantic! (They were used to
heading for the nearest port every night!)

RMS St Helena:- Cute, but a rust bucket all the same! Not designed for this sort of
thing! One stray bullet in an AVCAT drum on the promenade deck and that would
have been that!!! They would have had trouble finding any remains!
Certainly NOT a warship!

STUFT:- Their future in the defence of our country – PREPOSTEROUS!
Will the budgeteers and their lordships ever learn from their previous mistakes?
No they'll blame it all on another government and we'll go through it all again!
NEXT TIME THEY WILL NOT GET AWAY WITH IT!

NOMINAL LIST – RNP 2100 – 1982

RN = Royal Navy
MN = Merchant Navy
SHC = St Helenian Crewman

ADAIR AL	PO(AH)	RN
ADAMSON G	AB(M)	RN
ATKINSON D	PURSER CATERING OFFICER	MN
BAILEY PA	RO1(G)	RN
BAINBRIDGE TF	MEM(M)1	RN
BALL RJ	LT	RN
BARON CE	SURGEON LT	RN
BEARD G	SG2	SHC
BENDALL R	2/ENG	MN
BETHELL SJL	MA	RN
BEVERIDGE JT	AB(M)	RN
BLANCHARD A	RO1(G)	RN
BOUY DT	PO(R)	RN
BOWERS D	SG1	SHC
BOX MA	MEM(L)1	RN
BRADLEY PM	MEM(M)1	RN
BUCKLE DS	AEA/APP(M)	RN
BURCHFIELD IJ	LCK	RN
BURGESS ID	AB(M)	RN
BUTLER PA	AB(MW)	RN
BUTT JD	CMEM(M)	RN
BUTTLE JS	RO1(G)	RN
CARRINGTON PA	ALWEM(O)	RN
CHAPPELL P	AEMN(M)1	RN
CHESSUM I	2/OFF	MN
COLE SJ	AEMN(L)1	RN
COLLIER-WOODS CM	WEM(R)2	RN
COLLINS T	LSA	RN
COLLINS TA	POAEM(R)	RN
CROSTON W	3/ENG	MN
CROYSDALE RA	CWEM(O)	RN
CURNOCK GG	AEM(M)1	RN
EARWICKER P	LSA	RN
ELLICK P	CK/ASS	SHC
FARMER JJ	POWEM(R)	RN
FRANCIS G	STEWARDESS	SHC
FRANCIS P	SG1A	SHC
FRASER NC	MEM(M)1	RN
FREEMANTLE MG	MEA1(P)	RN
GAFFNEY JJ	WEMN2	RN
GARRATT JP	AB(M)	RN
GREEN F	STD	SHC
GEORGE W	SG1A	MN

HAMILTON CA	MEM(M)1	RN
HAMMERTON KG	LT CDR	RN
HAYDEN RC	MEMN1(P)	RN
HEATHCOTE J	WEM(O)1	RN
HEELAS DN	LT CDR	RN
HENNY MWC	AB(MW)	RN
HINDMARSH G	LRO	RN
HOWIESON J	FCPO(EW)	RN
HUBBARD RL	LACWEA	RN
HUGHES C	CH/OFF	MN
HUTCHINSON L	LMEM(M)	RN
ISTED RB	ARPO	RN
JOHNSON R	CPO DECK	MN
JONAS M	STEWARDESS	SHC
LAFFORD-SMITH GP	SA	RN
LAIGHT H	CHEF	MN
LAWRENCE C	MG1	SHC
LINETON GG	WEMN1	RN
MCMINN J	CH/ENG	MN
MCNIE DA	WEM(O)1	RN
MERCURY P	SG2	SHC
MILBURN IH	POWTR	RN
MITTENS E	2/COOK	SHC
MORTON D	MEM(M)1	RN
NEWLANDS JE	LT	RN
OLIVER PP	AEM(L)1	RN
PASCOE ST	LSTD	RN
PRICE SC	ALWEM(O)	RN
PROUD G	SA	RN
QUINN S	3/OFF	MN
ROBSON MGT	AB(MW)	RN
RUSSELL WA	WEMN1	RN
RUSSELL WS	MEA1(L)	RN
SAUNDERS WA	POSA	RN
SHALLCROSS P	PURSER	MN
SHEIBER CR	WEMN1	RN
SIM A	LS(MW)	RN
SIM P	PO DECK	SHC
SMITH MLM	MASTER	MN
STEVENSON ME	MEA1(M)	RN
STOVES EJ	RO1(G)	RN
STRANNIX WF	RS	RN
TANDY GN	WEM(O)1	RN
TAYLOR JG	POACMN	RN
THOMAS F	STEWARD	MN
THOMAS GS	AB(MW)	RN
THOMAS I	MG1	SHC
THOMAS P	MG1	SHC
THOMAS RD	ALWEM(R)	RN
THOMAS W	2/CK	SHC

VEITCH FJ	POAEM(L)	RN
WARD T	LACPO(MW)	RN
WEBSTER D	ELEC/OFF	MN
WHITELEY NJ	POMA	RN
WILLIAMS B	STEWARDESS	SHC
WILLIAMS L	PO MOTOR	SHC
WILLIAMS P	SG2	SHC
WILLIAMSON NS	MEM(M)1	RN
WILLIS PJ	FCMEA(P)	RN
WILSON R	R/OFF	MN
WOOD P	4/ENG	MN
WRIGHT SK	ALMEM(L)	RN
WRIGHT-JONES JN	PO(M)	RN

The new version and our RMS St.Helena

ANNEX A – Ship's paperwork

(As dumped on the POWTR, in Southampton Docks, on completion of the commission)!

1. QM's log
2. Senior Rate on Watch (SROW) Rounds log
3. Ashore on duty books x 2
4. Radio Operator's log
5. Rounds Report book
6. Copies of Standing Orders x 5 (including Master copy with distribution)
7. Fleet Temporary Memoranda (FTMs) – with Sport FTMs
8. HELLTEMS (RMS St. Helena Temporary Memoranda)
9. Daily Orders – Creation Book!!
10. Unclassified Signals
11. RMS St. Helena – blank foolscap
12. Folders containing spare copies of pages of Standing Orders, Daily Orders, Memoranda etc.
13. SNO's Memoranda
14. South Atlantic Fund folder
15. Ship's Correspondence Register
16. Classified Signals Register
17. Marisat Log
18. Armament Stores Notes folder
19. Nominal Lists folder
20. Ship's Office Royal Navy Pack System:-

    100/2 – General Pay Information
    100/3 – Canteen Stores
    100/4 – Service Documents and Service Writing
    100/5 – Wills and Next of Kin
    100/6 – Officers Appointment Lists (OALs)
    100/7 – Court Martial
    200/1 – Operation Orders
    200/2 – After Action – 6/82 to 7/82 and 8/82 to 9/82
    200/3 – Reverse Osmosis Plant
    200/4 – Port Stanley – Information
    200/5 – STUFT Report
    200/6 – Redeployment and Mobilisation
    200/7 – Portland Weekly Practice Programmes
    300/1 – Welfare Committee Treasurer's Reports
    300/2 – Senior Rates Mess Treasurer's Reports
    300/3 – Holiday Bookings Reimbursements
    300/4 – Grand Draw/Tombola
    300/5 – First Day Covers/Stamps, etc
    300/6 – Enquiries and Miscellaneous (Including FSU01)
    300/7 – Navy News
    317/1 – RN Film Corporation

ANNEX B – 1982 Pop Music

In a previous attempt to publish this book, this is all the lady in charge was interested in, so I had to send her this!!

1.   There wasn't any decent stuff. It had hit the bottom of the barrel at that time, especially for 60s people and rock-and-rollers! It improved slightly at the end of 1982.

2.   "C'mon Eileen" by Dexy's Midnight Runners is the only one in the charts at the time that I recognise!

3.   The only music on board was the boys' own personal tapes in their lockers.

4.   There was no radio reception except foreign, and no TV reception.

5.   Videos had only just been invented – hence the major raffle prize was a video recorder. Films were shown on an old-style projector! (Another good dit!)

6.   Officers and SRs messes were only separated by a curtain, so pop music was not an option! The JRs were at the other end of the ship, so I don't know.

7.   One memory I have is of a "Pub Night" one lunchtime for all the crew on the way home. The music that kept being put on was Don Williams Greatest Hits – everybody could have a sing and there was a lot of melancholy stuff to keep the homesick happy!

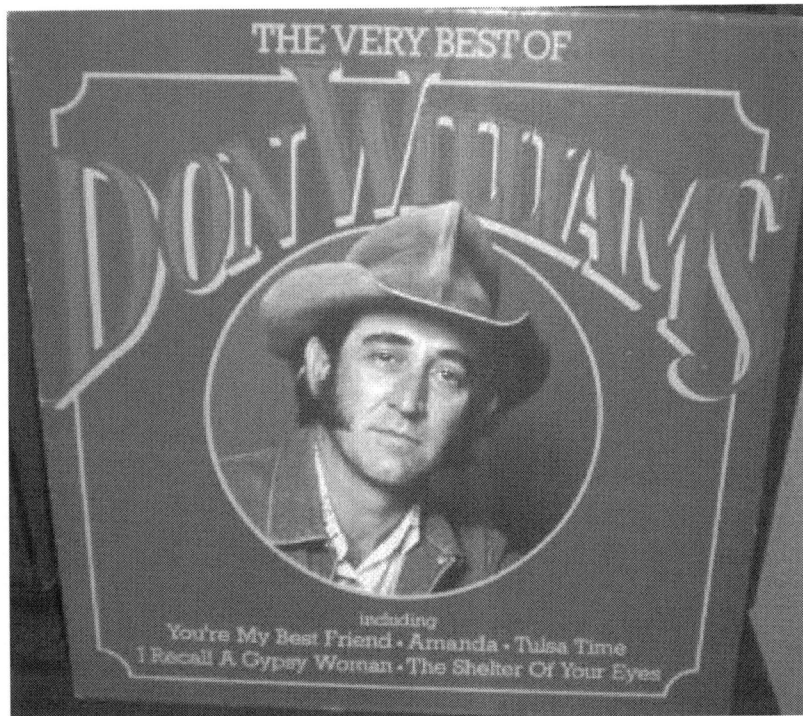

THE VERY BEST OF DON WILLIAMS

including
You're My Best Friend · Amanda · Tulsa Time
I Recall A Gypsy Woman · The Shelter Of Your Eyes

Thanks Don, for entertaining the troops!

ANNEX C

ALTERNATIVE TITLES

1. 2100 and all that!

2. MOD Pot Mess!

3. Leopoldo Galtieri - my part in his downfall!

4. Get STUFT!!!

5. Life in a blue suit – A Falklands Tale!

6. Life on the ocean wave – one variation!

7. Not another Falklands War book!

8. So near, yet so far away!

9. One good moan deserves another!

10. Voyage 26 (RN Charter)!

11. A new twist on war comics!

12. What a way to run a war!

13. A different sort of war story!

OR as the Curnow Shipping Co. had already named it – "Cruise into History 1982" – little did they know (see picture of shirt).

PSEUDONYMS

1. E.X. Andrew (Andrew – old name for RN)

2. (It was all as simple as) A.B. Sea

3. C.N.E. Nough

4. Jacques Thelad (Jack the Lad!)

5. Billy Biro (Mess deck name for Writers ie Scribes or Billy Biro)

St Helena's sterling work

THANK you for publishing a very informative guide on the Falklands conflict.

But there was no mention of the work carried out shortly after the war by the MCMVs HMS Ledbury and HMS Brecon along with the civilian support ship RMS Helena, which was partially manned by the Forward Support Unit (FSUO1) with a civilian crew mainly from the island of St Helena in the South Atlantic.

The civilian crew took us to their home port on the island before arriving at the Falklands, this was partly to allow the delivery of the post and goods that were part of the ship's normal delivery schedule.

I was on the St Helena and enjoyed their hospitality whilst on board and ashore on their home island.

The three ships did a large amount of work in checking for and clearing mines and diving on sunken aeroplanes in and around the waters of the Falklands.

After all, it was a long way to go in a balloon on water for the ships' companies of the minesweepers. It was even harder for the civilians on the St Helena to carry out RASes with little or no training.

● The minesweeper support ship St Helena – deserving of a mention – replenishing HMS Ledbury and HMS Brecon after the Falklands conflict

But everything always seemed to go to plan, even in rough seas.

I felt a little sorry for the civilians, as I believe they should have been given some sort of recognition for their hard work, but because we were not far enough south prior to June 14 1982, none of us got anything except maybe a thanks for a job well done from our CO.

– Allan Blanchard, former RO(G) on FSUO1, 1980-1982, Warwick

NAVY NEWS   AUGUST 2007

On 24 April 2007, the St Helenian crewmen received Certificates and Badges of Honour from their Government. (25th anniversary).

THE END

2673990R00132

Printed in Great Britain
by Amazon.co.uk, Ltd.,
Marston Gate.